DATE DUE

RECKLESS DISREGARD

RENATA ADLER

RECKLESS DISREGARD

Westmoreland v. CBS et al.;

Sharon v. Time

ALFRED A. KNOPF   New York   1986

THIS IS A BORZOI BOOK
PUBLISHED BY ALFRED A. KNOPF, INC.

Most of this work originally appeared in *The New Yorker.*

Library of Congress Cataloging-in-Publication Data
Adler, Renata.
Reckless disregard.
Includes index.
1. Westmoreland, William C. , 1914 –
2. CBS Television Network—Trials, litigation, etc.
3. Sharon, Ariel—Trials, litigation, etc.
4. Time, inc.—Trials, litigation, etc.
5. Trials (Libel)—New York (N.Y.)
I. Title.
KF228.W42A35   1986   345.73'0256   86–45513
ISBN 0–394–52751–8   347.305256

Manufactured in the United States of America
First Edition

To *Erna Strauss Adler*

RECKLESS DISREGARD

"One moment, please," Judge Pierre N. Leval said on January 17, 1985, to the twelve jurors and six alternates in Room 318 of the United States Courthouse, on Foley Square, in Manhattan. It was late Thursday afternoon. Judge Leval had already adjourned the case till Monday, wished the jurors a pleasant weekend and, after his customary admonition to them not to discuss the case with anyone or to permit themselves to be influenced by the press in any way, even said, "The jury is excused," before introducing an apparent afterthought. "The point that I want to raise," he said, "is that many of you are probably aware, or all of you may well be aware, that there is another case in the courthouse, in this courthouse, as to which parallels or comparisons have been drawn from time to time. . . . As I understand it, from what I have seen in the press, in that case the jury is now deliberating, and sometime in the future, today, tomorrow, I don't know when, the jury may come up with a decision in that case. I haven't the slightest idea what kind of decision the jury is going to reach in that case. I don't know a thing about that case. But the point that I want to make to you is that that case is that case and this case is this case. . . . It is absolutely and totally different. If you take two automobile accidents, they have nothing to do with each other, one is one, the other is the other." The judge added that he was calling the jurors' attention to the differences between the cases *before* the other jury reached its verdict so that they should not even draw the inference that "I am suggesting you should decide differently, or I don't know what." On January 24, 1985, the following Thursday, Judge Leval again alluded to the case in Room 110, two floors below, which seemed to be reaching another stage of its dénouement: "Remember, as I told you previously, that this case is this case, and any other case that is being tried has nothing to do with this one. You are not to be influenced in any way as a result of any other cases, or what anybody may say in the press about any other cases or this case. Have a pleasant weekend. You are excused."

"I am going to send the jury out on everything, virtually everything," Judge Abraham D. Sofaer had said earlier that month in the robing room, to the attorneys in "the other case," "no matter what they find. I am going to have the jury make all the findings now that we need *to put this case to rest forever."*

"That is an ambitious undertaking," counsel for the defense said; then, apparently warming to the thought, "I think that is a great idea. I think it is ambitious, but I think it is a great idea. If we can get away with it."

"Let's say, for example, they find—" Judge Sofaer began.

"I think you are right," defense counsel interrupted. "I think to the extent we can preclude the future by decisions, I think we ought to."

The trial, at this point, was far from over. The plaintiff had not yet completed his case, and the defense had not, technically, begun its presentation. Certain evidence, which had been sought for months by Judge Sofaer, with the complete agreement of counsel for both parties, had not yet been received and might never be received. But the judge, as is the custom in modern jurisprudence, was carefully working out, with the assistance of both parties, the charge he would ultimately make to the jury, and even the details of the verdict form. On the procedure by which the judge intended to "put this case to rest forever," plaintiff's counsel agreed enthusiastically with defendant's counsel. At only one other moment in the course of this particularly embittered litigation were opposing counsel so completely in accord that they worked virtually in tandem. On the morning of January 10, 1985, both attorneys went to yet another courtroom, on yet another floor of the federal courthouse, to argue before three appellate judges against an attempt to overturn an order by which Judge Sofaer had barred from his courtroom, for less than twenty minutes, during which certain testimony and documents temporarily under seal were presented to the jury, all spectators, including the entity mentioned so obliquely and yet insistently by Judge Leval: the press. For almost a day, then (until the judge lifted his own order, the matters temporarily under seal became public, and the appellate proceeding became moot), the courthouse contained yet one more anomalous lawsuit. Judge Sofaer himself became, however briefly, the defendant, assisted by both attorneys in the case before him, in *Washington Post, New York Times, Newsweek, Philadelphia Inquirer, CBS, NBC, Associated Press, Newsday, et al.* v. *Abraham D. Sofaer.*

O n the night of Saturday, January 23, 1982, CBS broadcast a ninety-minute documentary entitled "The Uncounted Enemy: A Vietnam Deception." The program, which consisted largely of interviews conducted by Mike Wallace, and which was produced within the CBS News department by George Crile, purported to describe, for the first time, certain events in 1967, which, according to the program's opening statement, reflected "a conspiracy at the highest levels of American military intelligence" —specifically, within the command and upon the orders of General William C. Westmoreland—"to suppress and alter critical intelligence on the enemy," and to deceive the American people, Congress, the Joint Chiefs and the President of the United States about the strength, in numbers, of the North Vietnamese Army and the Vietcong. The phrase "CBS Reports has learned" recurred at several dramatic moments in the program, and the deception CBS claimed to have discovered seemed to consist of understating enemy troop strength in two ways: by deliberate reduction of intelligence estimates of the rate of infiltration by North Vietnamese soldiers into South Vietnam in each of the five months before the Tet offensive, of January 30, 1968; and by deleting, in 1967, from what is known in the military as the Order of Battle, intelligence estimates of the number of civilians, in villages or hamlets, who actively, though irregularly and in no official capacity, supported enemy troops. The purpose of the deception, according to the broadcast, was to lead the people, Congress, the Joint Chiefs and the President to believe we were winning a war, which in fact we were losing. And among its results were a complete unpreparedness, in the White House and on the battlefield, for the size of the Tet offensive; an incalculable and unnecessary loss of American soldiers; and, by clear implication, the ultimate loss of the war.

The program was not just enthusiastically endorsed; it was, perhaps more implausibly, *believed*, without reservation, by almost the entire American press. On Sunday, January 24, 1982, the morning after the broadcast, in an editorial entitled "War, Intelligence and Truth," the *Times* called the report "more than a matter of history," for having "showed" that President Lyndon B. Johnson "was victimized by mendacious intelligence." On January 26, 1982, General Westmoreland, together with five former officials who were in a position to rebut the program in rather considerable detail, held an indignant press conference; there were also detailed protests from other officials, in letters columns. But even William F. Buckley, Jr., in his column of February 2, 1982, called the program a "truly extraordinary documentary," which established its substance "absolutely"; and, from *The Nation* to the *Wall Street Journal*, throughout the country and across the political spectrum, no serious journalist or publication called any element of the ninety-minute program into question. Editorials simply treated the broadcast as true and proceeded to draw various lessons from it.

On May 29, 1982, however, four months after the broadcast, two reporters, Don Kowet and Sally Bedell, published, in *TV Guide*, an analysis of "The Uncounted Enemy: A Vietnam Deception," in terms not of historical substance but of journalistic ethics and procedure. Their article, a cover story called "Anatomy of a

Smear," found errors and abuses ranging from arguably trivial violations of CBS network guidelines to distortions and misrepresentations of the most serious kind. CBS, to its great credit, undertook an internal investigation under the direction of a respected journalist, Burton Benjamin, which led to a document that has since become known as the Benjamin Report. Both the article "Anatomy of a Smear" and the Benjamin Report, which was not published, generated a small flurry of attention; but both the article and the report (and a book, *A Matter of Honor,* which was published almost two years later by Don Kowet) were also treated, in almost every subsequent discussion by the press, not as legitimate reporting—or as instances of precisely the kind of vigorous dispute that was contemplated by the founding fathers in creating the press protections of the First Amendment—but as instances of unworthy and unprofessional betrayal. Well before September of 1982, when General Westmoreland brought suit against CBS for libel, serious journalists regarded CBS, Mike Wallace and George Crile as victims, and the authors of the Benjamin Report as dupes of the American right, Sally Bedell, Don Kowet and *TV Guide.* In April of 1983 (fifteen months after the broadcast) Hodding Carter, on public television, raised certain questions about the program's accuracy and fairness. Then, regardless of what the story implied at that point about the press, the war, the law, or even what is meant by "conspiracy," "documentary," "military intelligence," the matter of what "CBS Reports has learned" receded for almost two years from the press and from public consciousness.

In its issue of February 21, 1983, *Time* published a cover story, "Verdict on the Massacre," based on the findings, in Israel, of the Kahan Commission, which, after four months of investigation, had just published its Final Report concerning responsibility for the massacre of several hundred civilians in the Palestinian refugee camps (actually, as the report pointed out, not camps at all but villages, composed of solid structures, with basements) at Sabra and Shatila, in Lebanon. Under a second heading, "Cover Stories: The Verdict Is Guilty," *Time* ran a long article that contained the following paragraph:

> One section of the report, known as Appendix B, was not published at all, mainly for security reasons. That section contains the names of several intelligence agents referred to elsewhere in the report. TIME has learned that it also contains further details about Sharon's visit to the Gemayel family on the day after Bashir Gemayel's assassination. Sharon reportedly told the Gemayels that the Israeli army would be moving into West Beirut and that he expected the Christian forces to go into the Palestinian refugee camps. Sharon also reportedly discussed with the Gemayels the need for the Phalangists to take revenge for the assassination of Bashir, but the details of the conversation are not known.

The story was picked up, within days, by newspapers throughout the world, and featured on the front page of every newspaper in Israel. Most, though not all, publications attributed to *Time* the information that a secret portion of the Kahan Report, Appendix B, contained details of a conversation in which, on the morning after the assassination of Bashir Gemayel (and on the eve of the Sabra and Shatila massacres), Ariel Sharon, the Defense Minister of Israel, had discussed with the Gemayels, at their family home in Bikfaya, "the need for the Phalangists to take revenge." There was no speculation as to whose was "the need" in question—or as to why "revenge" should be taken upon the Palestinians of Sabra and Shatila when, according to the Kahan Report itself, the group responsible for the assassination was not Palestinian at all but Lebanese, and supported by the Syrian government: the Mourabitoun. The Kahan Report, as published, had in fact mentioned Sharon's visit to the Gemayels at Bikfaya, characterizing it as a "condolence call" and seeming to attach no importance to it—in particular, attaching to it no footnote (as to accounts of every other secret meeting of significance to Sabra and Shatila the report did attach a footnote) to Appendix B. No publication mentioned this apparent discrepancy. Most simply accepted and even paraphrased *Time*'s story, to the effect that Sharon had actually urged the Phalangists to avenge Gemayel's death by the massacre that occurred the following day, and that the proof of this was contained in that secret part of the Kahan Commission's findings: Appendix B. Prime Minister Menachem Begin and Sharon immediately denounced *Time*'s story as a vile and utter fabrication and demanded an apology. Harry Kelly, *Time*'s Jerusalem bureau chief, promptly cabled the New York office, "We must really have struck a nerve. Cheers."

Some evenings later, at a dinner party in Jerusalem, Kelly met Ehud Olmert, a member of the Israeli parliament, who told Kelly that *Time* was mistaken, and that Appendix B contained no mention whatever of the discussion *Time* described. Olmert, a member of the Knesset Defense and Foreign Relations Committee, which had access to all documents of the Kahan Commission, offered to check again; the next morning, he called Kelly at *Time*'s Jerusalem bureau to report that he had reread Appendix B, and that the story was indeed completely wrong. Whether Kelly passed this information on to his editors, or to anyone, is a matter of some dispute. In a sworn deposition of September 19, 1984, Kelly says that he tried to reach Richard Duncan, *Time*'s chief of correspondents, in New York, "as soon as I could," following Olmert's phone call, but cannot recall the date (whether it was the day of Olmert's call, a Monday, or the weekend after) or whether he told Duncan what Olmert had said ("It follows logically I would have, but I can't recall the conversation"), or what, if anything, he said to Duncan or to anyone else about the matter, if in fact he mentioned it. In any event, asked at the same deposition whether he considered what Olmert told him "to be news," Kelly, the bureau chief, says "No, not really"; certainly he sent no telex to New York about it, and made no effort to check or confirm it in any way. To most other questions about the episode, Kelly says, "I don't recall." Months later, in his testimony about whether or not he told Duncan what Olmert had said, Kelly sounds both more definite and less clear: "I am positive—I am not positive that I told him. It was the reason I was going to call him. I can't believe that I didn't. . . . Now I am certain. I did tell him." He also says that a primary reason for not checking Olmert's information was that he had been "suspicious" of Olmert for in effect violating Israeli law by confiding "to me what is essentially a state secret"—namely, the contents (or, for that matter, the non-contents) of Appendix B.

O n September 13, 1982, William C. Westmoreland brought suit in South Carolina against CBS for libel, on the basis of its ninety-minute broadcast. On February 28, 1983, Ariel Sharon brought suit in an Israeli court against *Time*, on the basis of its paragraph. On November 18, 1982, General Westmoreland's suit was transferred to New York from South Carolina. On June 22, 1983, Sharon also filed suit against *Time* in New York. Both suits were ultimately tried in the federal courthouse on Foley Square in Manhattan, in the Southern District of New York. And although, as Judge Leval so many months later put it in *Westmoreland v. CBS et al.*—along with the network, Westmoreland had named as defendants Mike Wallace, George Crile, and a paid consultant for the program, Samuel A. Adams—"that case is that case and this case is this case," and, like "two automobile accidents, they have nothing to do with each other," there were unmistakable similarities. Both plaintiffs were former generals. Both defendants, CBS and *Time,* were press. The spectators in both courtrooms were mostly press. And most of what the outside world would ever hear of either case would come, inevitably, from the press. Both defendants, as it happened, were also represented by the same large and powerful New York law firm, Cravath, Swaine & Moore. And for many months, until almost the moment of jury selection, there was every reason to believe that neither case would ever come to trial. Westmoreland and, later, Sharon had both consulted lawyers (different lawyers, sympathetic to their respective cases) who had advised them in the strongest terms not to bring suit. As a matter of libel law, neither case, it seemed, could raise any issue of the slightest interest or importance. Each plaintiff, like any other "public official" since the strange and historic Supreme Court decision, in 1964, of *New York Times* v. *Sullivan*, would have the burden of proving, in an American court, that the allegedly libellous statements were of and concerning himself, that they were defamatory, and that they were false; also, that they were made with actual malice, and that he was damaged by them in some way. These burdens on libel plaintiffs are by far the heaviest imposed by any judicial system in the world. In England, for example, as in every other Western European country, the burden falls on the publishing defendant to prove the truth of the alleged libel, rather than upon the plaintiff to prove falsehood; and even the truth itself is sometimes held not to excuse but actually to aggravate a defamation. In this country, truth is an absolute defense.

Certainly as an intellectual, and even as a legal, matter, *Times* v. *Sullivan* had unintended consequences (mainly, vast sums awarded in bizarre jury verdicts, overturned upon appeal) and left problems that, after more than twenty years of litigation, were no more clearly articulated or resolved. Common-law "actual malice," for example, had been redefined in recent law to mean not what is conventionally understood by "malice," actual or other, but "knowledge of falsity" of a defaming statement, or "reckless disregard" as to whether it was false or not; and "reckless disregard" as to whether a given statement was false had, in turn, been redefined to include "serious doubt" as to whether it was true. Upon a moment's reflection, and quite apart from any effect this redefinition might have upon the interests of plaintiffs or defendants (both claim it works to their detriment), this runs counter not only to reason, coherence and common sense but also to any conceivable purpose the law is meant to serve. To begin with, a "serious doubt" is, obviously, a form or a sign not of "reckless disregard" but of its opposite. They are almost incompatible: "seriousness" in this sense with "recklessness"; and the concern that "doubt" implies with "disregard." It seems equally clear that any journalist, scholar or citizen of any other kind brings to much, perhaps most, of what he says or writes a "serious doubt," and then publishes what he has, on balance, honest reason to believe. The "doubt," moreover, is normally an expression not of bad but of good faith. In public discourse, false statements will inevitably occur; and, in the criticism, debate and polemic that democracy requires, some of these statements are bound to be defamatory; but it simply cannot be that the only false, defamatory statements that the law protects are those made with absolute, implacable certainty. And it cannot have been the intention of the framers to discourage good (or, for that matter, bad) faith doubt, or in the First Amendment actually to protect the polemical writings only of monomaniacs, the incurious, adherents of dogmas and other persons whose intellectual capacity precludes them, for whatever reason, from having about something they may say or write a serious doubt. While courts sometimes require the sort of declension that leads from common-law "actual malice" to *Sullivan*'s "knowledge of falsity" or "reckless disregard" (in itself a rather considerable "or"), when they arrive at a virtually unintelligible formulation ("serious doubt" as a form of "actual malice"), something is seriously amiss; and it is no wonder that juries are confused.

This problem, of an imprecisely articulated and ultimately unintelligible standard, creates instability in the law from time to time—particularly when, as in *New York Times* v. *Sullivan*, a fair, well-intentioned, timely, rightly decided, but not very carefully reasoned case makes a radical change in centuries of law. But neither Westmoreland's case nor Sharon's, it seemed, could raise even a minor issue under *Sullivan*. Generals, military men, live by rules other than those which govern civilians. In the conduct of war, they can, in fact as a matter of duty must, send men to die, and authorize the killing of other men; and it is often part of their professional obligation, for purposes of morale and propaganda, to deceive—particularly in the matter of enemy troop strength. It is true that if either Westmoreland or Sharon had engaged in the specific conduct that the alleged libels implied, he would have been in violation even of military law. Still, there was something unseemly in the notion of a military man's bringing this sort of civil action in a civilian court. The main legal point, however, was this: that in the unlikely event that either of them should prevail before a jury the decision would almost certainly be reversed upon appeal. The higher courts would simply find that within the category "public official" there exists a smaller category, "high military officer," which must meet an even more formidable burden of proof, or perhaps be precluded from suing for libel at all.

But in the summer of 1982, Dan M. Burt, a thirty-nine-year-old attorney who had never tried a jury case before, found his way to General Westmoreland and offered, as president of the Capital Legal Foundation (a conservative group concerned chiefly with warding off federal regulation of private enterprise), to bring the suit at no cost to General Westmoreland. In mid-1983, Ariel Sharon found his way to Milton S. Gould, a highly experienced lawyer in his mid-seventies and a partner in the respected law firm of Shea & Gould, who, after some discussion, decided to bring the suit at his own expense. Even after the suits were filed, however, it seemed unlikely that they would go forward. Cravath, Swaine & Moore has been known (particularly since the I.B.M. anti-trust cases, which lasted nearly fifteen years and ended, in 1982, with the absolute victory, in all cases, of Cravath's client, I.B.M.) as an unusually thorough and aggressive law firm. Thomas D. Barr, the Cravath partner who had been in charge of I.B.M.'s defense against the government's anti-trust case, was in charge of *Time*'s defense against Sharon. David Boies, the Cravath partner who had been in charge of I.B.M.'s defense against major suits by private companies, represented CBS against Westmoreland. Cravath proceeded, characteristically, on all fronts—including motions, supported by memorandums of three hundred and seventy-eight and a hundred and ninety-two pages, respectively, for summary judgment on behalf of CBS and *Time*. Motions for summary judgment are not at all unusual. Since the whole purpose of such a motion, however, is to prove that there exists "no genuine issue of material fact" to be decided between the parties, they are normally simple, and short. On September 24, 1984, Judge Leval denied CBS's motion; on November 12, 1984, Judge Sofaer denied the motion made by *Time*. In each case, there had already been months and volumes of discovery—the process by which, under American law, each side is entitled to receive from the other all evidence that is "relevant to the subject matter" of the trial. It is this process that means that, theoretically and in most cases, there can be no "surprises" of the sort that occurred in Perry Mason courtrooms; each side knows fairly specifically and in advance what the other side is going to say. The resources of Cravath and its media clients, however, so far exceeded the resources of their opponents it seemed possible that, simply by making the broadest possible discovery (blanket subpoenas for documents, deposition of witnesses all over the world), CBS and *Time* might (as richer litigants often do) exhaust the plaintiffs' finances on discovery alone.

Nonetheless, on October 11, 1984, at 10 a.m., with the words "I am advised that we are short one juror," Judge Leval opened the trial of *Westmoreland* v. *CBS et al*. On October 31, 1984, at 9:20 a.m., Judge Sofaer began selecting the jury for *Sharon* v. *Time*. The process of jury selection occupies sixty-eight pages of transcript in the Sharon case; the actual trial began on November 13, 1984. The Westmoreland transcript begins only with the actual trial. Twelve jurors and six alternates were empanelled in *Westmoreland*. Judge Leval encouraged them to take notes, on yellow legal pads. Six jurors and five alternates were empanelled in *Sharon*. Judge Sofaer did not permit them to take notes. The Westmoreland case lasted more than four months, the Sharon case slightly more than ten weeks. Both cases became, against all odds and in entirely unanticipated ways, historic. Westmoreland was suing for well over a hundred million dollars, Sharon for fifty million, but there was never any question, in anybody's mind, that both sums were arbitrary and preposterous—or, for that matter, that neither general had brought his suit for money. "If I may say," Sharon said on September 5, 1984, the second full day of his deposition, "I believe that my lawyers were the ones that fixed the figure . . . in order that people will take it seriously." Westmoreland had promised to donate any money he received to charity. Whatever their other motives may have been (pride, anger, honor, politics at home), the plaintiffs were clearly suing on *principle*, and that principle, in each general's mind, at least, was truth: not justice but plain, factual truth. General Westmoreland's claim that he did *not* order a false ceiling on estimates of enemy troop strength and thereby deceive, among other military and civilian superiors, his Commander-in-Chief, and Sharon's that he did *not* discuss revenge at any meeting with the Gemayels, and thereby encourage the deliberate massacre of noncombatants, including children, in the camps, were both pursued, in the courts, on an oddly journalistic basis: difficult as it might be to prove a negative, and whatever else either man might have felt he had to answer for, they decided to establish, for their contemporaries and for history, that in these particular instances the media, maliciously, and perhaps typically, got it wrong. As it happens, American courts are not designed, or even, under the Constitution, permitted, abstractly to resolve issues of this sort, to decide for history what is true and false. They exist not as ministries of truth but to resolve concretely whether this plaintiff has been injured by this defendant, and, if so, what amends the defendant should be required to make. CBS and *Time* were proceeding, too, on principle—a conception, for instance, of the First Amendment that required them, at vast expense and on behalf of *all* the press, to resist "chilling effect" and defend "breathing space," with a broad policy of not settling libel suits and of "standing by our story" whenever they felt themselves attacked.

So the generals came, in a sense, to establish a journalistic proposition; and the press defendants came to uphold what they thought of as a principle of Constitutional law. As for the lawyers, they came, of course, to win; and it was they, after all, who ran the cases. This is true, obviously, of most litigation: the clients, not trained in the law, are in the lawyers' hands. But the affinity between the attorneys from Cravath, for instance, and their media clients was exceptional, in that they often seemed actually to have exchanged roles—the lawyers undertaking, from the first moment of discovery, all the interviewing, checking and investigation that are normally the province of reporters; and the press witnesses crossing over so far into advocacy that the judges had frequently to remind them that they were in court to answer questions, not to lecture or debate. Both trials seemed to have, for various constituencies, broad political, and even moral, implications. The Westmoreland case, especially, became for ideologues of the left and the right what it could as a legal, intellectual, or factual matter never be: a trial of the American involvement in the war in Vietnam; or, for the other side, a trial of the press's involvement in that war. But, whatever else they were (and they were, under two remarkably fair, intelligent and articulate judges, strictly and preëminently trials), these cases also brought together, in an almost astrological configuration, four immense and powerful constellations within the American system: the courts; the military; the lawyers; and the press. And, from almost the moment the first depositions were taken, through all the months of testimony, until the cases ended, both trials called into question certain fundamental assumptions about these institutions—and resolved, almost in passing, at least two matters peripheral to the law but until now, it seemed, critical to press, and even military, understanding of modern life. *Westmoreland* v. *CBS* marked the end, for instance, for any thinking person, of whatever specious factuality was ever associated with "intelligence estimate." *Sharon* v. *Time* marked, at last, the reductio ad absurdum of the "confidential source."

When a European picks up his newspaper (and, for that matter, when a founding father did), he expects reporting based on political views very like his own. A reader of, for example, *L'Humanité* or *Le Figaro* believes that what he reads there is "true," but only in the sense that it accords in most respects with what he already believes in other ways. And that very slant, or party line, may sometimes uncover a truth that papers loyal to other party lines deny, obscure or will simply not pursue. The framers, to an even greater extent, expected the widest, fiercest diversity among publications: newspapers, essayists, pamphleteers debating and vilifying not only one another but public figures with whom they disagreed. It was this diversity among contending voices, with readers free to choose, that the founding fathers understood by "press," and intended, in the First Amendment, to protect against abridgment by the government: "Congress shall make no law . . . abridging the freedom of speech, or of the press." And the publications were, of course, within the rhetorical conventions, and on a scale of distribution, commensurate with the time. The Constitution can hardly have envisioned, on the part of the press, a power, a scale and, above all, a unity, which is in part, but by no means entirely, a result of technological advance.

With few and small exceptions—*The Nation,* say, or the *National Review*—an American no longer expects from his source of news a political viewpoint that comports with his own. His expectation, as in no other country and at no other time in history, is rather this: that, *given* the technology of news gathering and dissemination, given also the scale, the news is going to be, honestly and within human limits, factual. Whether it is a tabloid reporting a sensational murder or a network reporting a political coup somewhere, there is a trust that what is being reported (with the aura of authenticity not just of the printed word but of tape recordings and photographs) is factually true. And the contemporary American journalist aspires, in theory and as a professional matter, to meet that honorable, essentially moral expectation. The difficulty is that most facts, at least those with which journalism is concerned, are what they are; and, in spite of bromides to the effect that there is no such thing as objectivity in journalism, statements of fact are either true or not. Their implications, political and other, are, of course, another matter; but the "truth" of the facts in question tends to be unitary—tends, in an almost religious sense, to be one. No one disputes this with respect to those subjects on which so much of reporting, at all times, depends: the Yankees won on a certain day or they did not, and by a certain score; the people whose deaths are reported in the obituary section held certain positions and are dead, or not. Stock closing prices, earthquakes, invasions, election returns. It is only with stories of another kind that the unitary standard seems to waver and meditations about objectivity begin. The reporter, meanwhile, not only wants to find out and report the facts; as a competitor, he wants to report them before anybody else. And the difficulty with that form of competition is that once a journalist has been the first to publish certain "facts" amounting to a "story" all other journalists tend to go after the *same* story, wanting only to tell more of it, sooner. At the same time, there has arisen in the profession an almost unimaginable solidarity; it is exceptionally rare for a story in one publication to contradict, or even to take the mildest exception to, a story published in another. Whether by temperament, or for whatever other reason, whatever rivalry exists, however intense it may be, is the rivalry of a pack going essentially in one direction. There is simply no notion, for instance, among journalists of a counter-scoop—and journalists are notoriously vindictive when the work of any of their number is criticized in print.

For all these reasons, the press has become, over the years and

without anyone's express intention, in at least three ways monolithic. At the same time technology has made it possible to gather
and disseminate news on a scale and with a technical accuracy that
the framers can never have contemplated, the public expectation
is that the news will be politically unbiased, factually true and, in
that sense, one. As a competitive matter, each journalist considers
it his obligation either to be the first on any given story or, failing
that, to go after essentially the same story, only, as he would put
it, in greater depth. And professional solidarity, which extends
from "standing by our story" to refusing to contradict, or even
question, anybody else's, has virtually eliminated the very diversity that it was the purpose of the framers, in the First Amendment, to protect. Before long, however—and particularly with the
modern proliferation of bureaucracies, and their disaffected members—it began to seem that the best way to get a story first was
to get it in secret, from a secret source. There has always been
more than a superficial kinship between one sort of American spy,
for the C.I.A., say, or the military, and a certain kind of reporter:
it lies in their preoccupation with "secrets," and the notion that
what is obtained in secret is somehow most surely true.

Here, then, was *Time*'s predicament in the Sharon case. The
paragraph at issue in the lawsuit appeared in a long article with
the following byline: "By William E. Smith. Reported by Harry
Kelly and Robert Slater/Jerusalem." The paragraph had indeed
been written, in New York, by William Smith, and was based on
reporting, in a telex, by Harry Kelly, *Time*'s Jerusalem bureau
chief. But the information in the telex—the subject of "revenge"
in a discussion between Sharon and the Gemayels and the purported inclusion of details of such a discussion in Appendix B; in
short, the entirety of the alleged libel—came, it was revealed in the
initial phases of discovery, from a correspondent not mentioned
in the byline: David Halevy. And Halevy himself claimed to have
received the information (actually, he made several widely different claims at his deposition and in his trial testimony) from what,
no matter which of these claims one believed (or all, or any),
amounted, under New York law and in modern journalistic practice, to a "confidential source." Under the New York Shield Law,
reporters cannot normally be compelled to disclose the identity of

such sources (or, at least, be held in contempt for refusing to disclose them); and the federal courts, ever since the great decision, in 1938, of *Erie* v. *Tompkins,* have been required, except in matters of procedure, to apply the law of the states in which they sit. A shield law for journalists, in the states where it does exist, can serve sound purposes. To report, for instance, on corruption in government or on the activities of organized crime, the press must be able to hear from people whose names, if disclosed, might cause them to lose their jobs, or even their lives. Any legal shield, however—and, otherwise known as "privileges," there are many "shields" in the law: the privilege against self-incrimination, for example, embodied in the Fifth Amendment; or the ancient privileged nature of communications between husband and wife—is ordinarily limited, as lawyers and the courts like to say, to use "as a shield, and not as a sword." A witness who takes the Fifth Amendment, for example, is not permitted to give any related testimony that would help his case; he must remain silent or he has waived the privilege. For journalists, this means that once they have invoked the shield, and refused to name a source, they are not normally permitted to say anything more, affirmatively, about him: in particular, nothing about how reliable he is, how well qualified, honorable or highly placed. Since this nameless person will not be produced for cross-examination, or even for the jury to see and appraise him or, for that matter, to confirm that he did say what the journalist who purports to quote him says he said, he cannot be used for any affirmative evidentiary purpose. The jury is not even obliged to believe that he exists. In the peculiar circumstances of the Sharon case, however, so many shields of various kinds were invoked by both sides—the attorney-client privilege, which protects the confidentiality of communications between a client and his counsel; the work-product privilege, which protects work done by counsel in the preparation of his case; diplomatic immunity; Israeli secrecy law; and, of course, the journalistic shield—that Judge Sofaer simply treated all shields and privileges as though they balanced, and gave Halevy great, in fact unprecedented, latitude in what he was allowed to say about the competence, status, and reliability of each nameless source.

On December 6, 1982, Halevy had sent, by telex, for inclusion in that week's "Worldwide Memo"—an internal publication of facts, gossip and rumor, which *Time* distributes to its journalists and bureaus—what is known within *Time* as a Memo Item, which read:

GREEN LIGHT FOR REVENGE?

(Halevy-Jerusalem) The most crucial findings of the State Inquiry Commission investigating the Sabra and Shatila massacre might turn out to be the newly discovered notes which were taken during a conversation between Israel's Minister of Defense Arik Sharon and leaders of the Gemayel clan. Sharon came to the Gemayels' home village, Bikfaya, the morning after Bashir Gemayel was assassinated. He came actually to convey his and the Begin government's condolences. When Sharon landed at Bikfaya, he had with him only one senior intelligence officer, who went with Sharon to the meeting and took notes during the private session.

According to a highly reliable source who told us about that meeting, present were not only Pierre and Amin Gemayel, but also Fadi Frem, the Phalange Chief of Staff who is married to Bashir's sister. Sharon indicated in advance to the Gemayels that the Israeli army was moving into West Beirut, and that he expected them, the Force Lebanese, to go into all the Palestinian refugee camps. He also gave them the feeling, after the Gemayels' questioning, that he understood their need to take revenge for the assassination of Bashir and assured them that the Israeli army would neither hinder them nor try to stop them.

These minutes will not be published at all, in any form whatsoever, as they indicate a direct involvement and advanced planning by the Gemayel family, including Lebanon's president, Amin Gemayel.

Two days later, on December 8, 1982, *Time*'s New York office requested "clearance" for the Memo Item—that is, assurance from the correspondent or the bureau that the information in the telex was sufficiently reliable to be published in the magazine. Halevy, without, as it turned out, checking or making any further effort to confirm it, cleared it. There are indications that *Time* planned to use the item, in some form, in a piece about Israel that closed on December 10, 1982, and appeared the following week.

For whatever reason, *Time* did not use the item in December. On January 12, 1983, Halevy left Jerusalem for an assignment in Central America. On February 8th, the Kahan Commission published its report. That afternoon, Halevy returned to Jerusalem to help with *Time*'s cover story on the commission's findings. When Harry Kelly asked whether there was some way to find out the contents of the secret part of the report, Appendix B, Halevy replied that one thing it certainly contained was the information in Halevy's Memo Item of December 6, 1982. On February 10th, Kelly filed his story, including, in what became known as Take Nine of his telex, three paragraphs purporting to describe Appendix B. "And some of it, we understand," Kelly wrote, "was published in *Time*'s Worldwide Memo, an item by Halevy, Dec. 6, for which we gave clearance." Kelly added an inference: that "part of the Commission's case against Sharon is between the lines, presumably in the secret portion" (Appendix B). The Memo Item thus became the basis of Take Nine, and Take Nine, in turn, became the basis of the paragraph upon which Sharon brought suit.

Nearly every element of this account was at some point, on deposition or at trial, contested. Halevy, for example, throughout the five days of his deposition, insisted under oath that the words "for Revenge," in the headline of his Memo Item, "Green Light for Revenge?," were added by someone else to his own headline, which read simply "Green Light?" (On the witness stand, at trial, he abandoned this position, and added that he now considered the question of who wrote those two words "trivial" and "totally irrelevant.") Halevy also said, several times, in answer to questions at his deposition, that he left Israel for Central America on "December 12," and in "mid-December"—to explain that in the rush of his departure, between December 6th, when he filed the Memo Item, December 9th, when he cleared it for publication, and December 12th, when he left for his new assignment, there would have been no time to check. There is an uncharacteristic hesitancy in Halevy's deposition testimony about this; but there are so many anomalies about Halevy's entire deposition (and about every other deposition in the case) that opposing counsel does not seem to catch it. And Judge Sofaer himself, in his Opinion and Order denying *Time*'s motion to dismiss and for summary judgment, cites the date of Halevy's departure from Israel as "around December 12." At trial, however, Halevy reveals that according to his passport he left not on December 12th but on January 12th—which would have left him not six days but five weeks to check. Counsel somehow doesn't seem to catch this discrepancy, either.

Time, when it published the paragraph at issue in the case, did not, of course, have the benefit of Halevy's (or any other witness's) testimony under oath; nor could it possibly have anticipated the countless, inexplicable contradictions between any witness's sworn testimony at his deposition and at trial. And every publication, no matter how exacting its standards for the accuracy of what it prints, must have some degree of trust in its reporters. It may even be that most of what are called, in contemporary journalism, "investigative reporters," with their confidential sources, meeting in mythical garages (Deep Throat was mentioned, repeatedly and approvingly, by the defense), are inevitably a kind of rascal: the same capacity for ingratiation that works, on the occasions when it does work, on people who, for whatever reason, want to speak anonymously but for publication works equally on the editor who must gamble on the rascal, sometimes with valuable results. In contrast, for instance, with I. F. Stone, who worked from actual documents, and with a tradition extending back at least to Henry Adams and Charles Francis Adams, Jr. (whose "Chapters of Erie" remains one of the most systematic, courageous, and devastating pieces of investigative journalism ever written), the contemporary investigative reporter, with all his techniques of personal mystification, must often present an editor with a sort of quandary when he turns a story in. Still, from the moment the last deposition ended and the trial itself began, the situation was essentially this: that a serious news magazine, *Time,* and an enormous corporate edifice, Time Inc., was poised, like an improbable ballerina, on a single toe, David Halevy. And not even on Halevy himself but on these "sources" (the "highly reliable source," of the original Memo Item, became, within the very first day of Halevy's deposition, "between eight and fifteen" sources; "I will say many"; "I'll say less than fifteen and more than eight";

"yes, two prime sources. I don't recall if there were any more"; "but to be exact with you, I will say there were three prime sources"), whom no one else at *Time* claimed even to know. And the position was more precarious still. Because, in a professional development that seems, in retrospect, inevitable, Halevy had gone one further step. He claimed to have derived his information ultimately from official, forever secret documents: first, in the Memo Item of December 6, 1982, from the "newly discovered notes," or "minutes," of the meeting at Bikfaya; two months later, when the Kahan Report appeared, from its secret section, Appendix B. In other words, Halevy claimed for his account, or his sources' account, of the conversation between Sharon and the Gemayels the authority (in some ways exceeding the research of an I. F. Stone, a Charles Francis Adams) first of an exact stenographic record and then of the judicial finding of a court. Neither document, however, would ever become public. So the entire edifice of *Time* in this case was poised upon a single reporter claiming to have access to unnamed sources, who in turn had access to official documents, which would remain forever secret, and which supported *Time*'s paragraph—or else did not.

From a legal point of view, this odd position was entirely to *Time*'s advantage. The unavailability of these documents, no matter what they might have showed, certainly increased for Sharon the burden of proving, by "clear and convincing evidence," both that the conversation *Time* described did not occur and that the documents, particularly the one to which *Time* explicitly referred, Appendix B, contained no record of it. There was something, however, about this state of affairs, this pattern, that was reminiscent of a period long before "investigative reporting," in its present sense, came into fashion. Because it has by no means always been the case that, in its most clearly monolithic mode, the press has been antagonistic either to government or to power in any form. The press, rather, characteristically moves toward winners, turns on losers, and is particularly subject to the blandishments of men in power who claim both to rely upon agents or informants and to find the evidence for their subsequent accusations in a secret document. The comparison of Senator Joseph McCarthy is often called upon too easily and inappropriately. Without the press, however, solid, loath to contradict, the Senator could not have perpetrated, or even set in motion, that seemingly endless series of libels—based in significant part upon a "secret" document of sorts, the empty list of names. As the trial went on, and there were developments, including jury verdicts, unfavorable to *Time*, the press, however, turned, briefly and mildly but undeniably, as one, against *Time*, and even questioned some of its procedures; the magazine, and in an informal press conference its lawyers, seemed sincerely aghast, even hurt, at what was merely a characteristic gravitating toward winners and turning upon losers, and a temporary change in the direction of the phalanx (minus, in this instance, *Time*) that is the press.

From a journalistic point of view, if the secret documents *did* support *Time*'s paragraph, and particularly the attribution of what "*Time* has learned" to Appendix B, the magazine's position would be vindicated—and the case, of course, would be absolutely and beyond question won. If, on the other hand, the documents supported not *Time* but Sharon, the Israeli government was clearly in no hurry to release them. There was not only the problem of providing access to state secrets in what was, after all, private litigation; there was also the tendency of all nations to protect themselves against litigation of any kind, within the ancient doctrine of sovereign immunity. Moreover, the Israeli government currently in power had no incentive to advance the political or other fortunes of Ariel Sharon—whom many considered dangerous for reasons having nothing to do with the specific issues of the trial, and who was also a potential rival of both occupants, in the current coalition, of the office of Prime Minister. Shimon Peres in particular, it emerged at trial, over heavy objections and in direct contradiction to testimony on deposition, even had cause to feel loyal to Halevy. In any event, from the outset of the trial there seemed every reason for all sides to pursue, or, at least, *appear* to pursue, any prospect of obtaining from the Israeli government such evidence relevant to the disputed issues as existed in the secret documents: Cravath because it believed either that the documents supported *Time* or, more likely, that the Israeli government was not going to permit access to them; Gould because he believed Sharon, who had read Appendix B, and who said he knew no official "notes" could record events that never happened; and, most important, Judge Sofaer, who not only sought the "best evidence" as a legal obligation but who also exercised an ingenuity almost unprecedented in American jurisprudence in drafting letters (with the express consent of both parties) that requested from the Israeli government access to that evidence, in a form admissible in an American court. From the moment Judge Sofaer sent his first letter, through diplomatic channels, to the Attorney General of Israel—in August of 1984, three months before he denied Time's motion for summary judgment and the trial itself began—a quiet, gradual, almost imperceptible thriller was under way. Would the Israeli government give access to whatever documents were relevant to the issues of the trial; what effect, if any, would events in the courtroom have on Israel's decision, either way; and if access was provided would this evidence support Time's case or Sharon's?

The reason this suspense was an undercurrent rather than the central drama of the trial is partly that the testimony and demeanor of living witnesses, and the courtroom manner and strategy of lawyers, are inevitably more riveting than an apparently dry exchange of letters between an American federal judge and officials of a foreign government. (Diplomatic channels, with the concurrence of the State Department, were almost immediately abandoned; the judge and counsel for both sides were communicating with Israeli officials, direct.) Most journalists with any interest in the question had known, moreover, to a virtual certainty, within days of Time's publication of the disputed paragraph, that the magazine was completely wrong about Appendix B; but no reporter, after all, had actually *seen* the appendix, and (in an example of precisely that professional solidarity never contemplated in the First Amendment) none would have seen fit, even before the filing of the lawsuit, to rely on his own "sources," in flat contradiction to a colleague's, and to set the record straight.

Whatever it was journalistically, a mistake about Appendix B would not, in any event, lose the case for Time. The "notes," or "minutes," to which Halevy referred, or any other source or document that revealed that Sharon had discussed with the Gemayels, at Bikfaya, *or elsewhere,* or with *any other* Phalangists, *anywhere,* "the need . . . to take revenge," would have been, for *Time*'s case, sufficient. The libel itself, if libel it was, lay in reporting as fact the occurrence of the discussion. Attributing evidence of the report to Appendix B, a document not only secret but official, might aggravate the libel; but if the report itself, or something very like it, was true the location of evidence for it was incidental. Truth, regardless of an error about its source, or any insubstantial imprecision, was still an absolute defense. Thus, though all sides wanted the evidence, Sharon wanted it perhaps more fervently than *Time* did; but *Time* had hopes of its own (if not the appendix, then some document or other record, somewhere). And it would, in any case, appear awkward for a news magazine *not* to join in a court's request for information. As for the underlying thriller, it seemed until literally the final days of the trial that there would be no dénouement, that Israel would not, for whatever reason, permit access to the relevant documents in any form agreed to by the parties and admissible in an American court. "I really despair of that, your Honor," Thomas Barr, of Cravath, said early in the trial, when Judge Sofaer suggested that Israel might provide such access; and less than a week before the case went to the jury the lawyers for both sides told the judge that they were preparing their summations on the assumption that access would be denied.

If *Time*'s predicament had, at least initially, to do with inaccessible documents and unverifiable "confidential sources," CBS's predicament was in some ways the reverse. There were countless documents, and numerous sources, named and videotaped, many of whom were prepared, even eager, to appear on the witness stand. Intelligence-agency personnel, former military men—the difficulty was to show what bearing the documents had on any issue in the trial or to prove that any of these sources or witnesses had ever been placed to know the facts he was testifying to. As an intellectual and historical matter, the thesis that underlay "The Uncounted Enemy: A Vietnam Deception" was of course preposterous. It seems clear that in the history of warfare any country that has lost or been forced to withdraw from a war abroad (that is, not in defense of its own soil) has, almost by definition, made the error precisely of underestimating enemy troop strength. The reason for the exception is that people have been willing knowingly to fight hopeless wars in defense of their homes. Normally, whatever the causes, nations go to war expecting to win. When that expectation turns out to be unfounded, they have obviously underestimated the strength of the enemy, relative, at least, to their own. It has been a kind of miracle of our recent history that in the wake of the bitter defeat in Vietnam there have been no recriminations and efforts to attach blame of the sort that followed, for example, our "loss" of China to the Communists. A television program, therefore, that claimed to find, fifteen years after the events in question, that the underestimate and the loss reflected a "conspiracy" was not only a considerable, apparently unconscious lapse into the old mode; in ascribing the leadership of the "conspiracy" to General Westmoreland, and including among its victims the President and the Joint Chiefs, it ceased to make even internal, superficial sense. What motive would a general have to *underestimate* to his commanders the size and strength of the enemy when his every interest and inclination would fall more naturally on the other side: to overestimate, in order to make whatever victories there were heroic and whatever defeats explicable, and to sustain a demand for more troops of his own? The motive, according to the program's producer, Crile, and its star, Wallace, among many others at various points, was "political." The election year, 1968, was coming up. Without the conspiracy to underestimate, the President would have lost. Since the President in the four months of 1967 and the one month of 1968 when the alleged conspiracy took place was Lyndon B. Johnson, General Westmoreland's "political" motive, then, to prevent this loss would have, theoretically, to be based on fear of some Republican dove, like Richard Nixon. And what conceivable motive to include President Johnson himself among the victims of such a conspiracy? No, even before the details, the distortions and misrepresentations (including answers spliced onto questions quite other than the ones they were answers to; persons misidentified to exaggerate their position, rank and competence to answer specific questions; interviewees coached and rehearsed in the desired answers; and so forth), which had been touched on in the Benjamin Report but which emerged most clearly on deposition and at trial, it was obvious that the thesis, such as it was, did not bear even superficial scrutiny. In fact, the notion of Westmoreland as the arch-deceiver was so obviously implausible that Cravath tried early in the litigation to show that the alleged libel was not "of and concerning" General Westmoreland at all, since the phrase "a conspiracy at the highest levels of American military intelligence" could refer only to personnel who actually belonged to "military intelligence." Boies did not pursue this strategy at trial.

But an absurd defamatory thesis—even if it is presented at ninety-minute length, with drums and guns, old footage, music, misleading cuts, the whole arsenal of television's most overwhelming techniques for simulating the authentic—is not in and of itself a libel. Opinions are as clearly protected by the First Amendment as the truth itself is; and each of us is permitted to hold and to publish any number of preposterous views. Westmoreland, like Sharon, still had the burden of proving, not only that specific, defamatory factual statements about him were "clearly and convincingly" (or by a preponderance of the evidence; federal law on this question is unsettled) false, but that they were made with actual malice; that is, with knowledge of their falsity, or reckless disregard whether they were false or not; that is, with serious doubt whether they were true. Since so many "sources" supported the program's allegations, it was going to be awfully hard to show that, false though the program, even in its entirety, may have been, it was produced with actual malice (which Judge Leval, to avoid at least some confusion, preferred to call "Constitutional malice") on the part of anyone at CBS. Not, perhaps, in the particular circumstances, impossible, but hard to overcome the defendants' argument that they could not have been in reckless disregard, because they had sources whom they did not seriously doubt. In libel cases, moreover, plaintiffs at once become, in effect, defendants—in the sense that lawyers for the actual press defendant, in what is called arguing in the alternative, will try to prove that the allegedly libellous statements do not say what the plaintiff says they say; or, even if they do say what he says they say, they are literally true; or, even if they are not literally true, something similar but incomparably *worse* is true about the plaintiff than what the alleged libel said. The program included interviews with nine people who fell more or less in line with its thesis about

Westmoreland; one person (at a length of about twenty seconds) who did not; and Westmoreland himself (portrayed mumbling, unprepared, stammering, and incessantly licking his lips). David Boies, a particularly aggressive litigator even within Cravath, not only elicited from some of the nine witnesses sworn testimony incomparably stronger and more flatly anti-Westmoreland than their statements on the broadcast; he produced many other witnesses to the same effect. His ambition, set forth in his opening statement, was nothing less than to rewrite in court the whole history of the war to conform with what the broadcast said "CBS Reports has learned." He did not, from a legal point of view, need to prove truth; he could not, as a factual matter, prove truth; but with broad attacks and massive depositions he was going to try to. And there remained throughout the trial the almost imperceptible difficulty that, with two arguable exceptions, none of the defense witnesses were able to testify, from personal knowledge, that any ceiling on estimates of enemy troop strength existed, or could remotely be imputed to Westmoreland.

If the Sharon case became a kind of thriller, the Westmoreland case became whatever the droning opposite of a thriller might be. Since much of the trial had, of necessity, to do with dates and numbers (months of 1967 and 1968, number of enemy troops); and since hours, on many days, were occupied in bench conferences between Judge Leval and the attorneys, at the sidebar, outside the hearing of the jury (but recorded, obviously, in the official transcript), the trial seemed at times to approach an order of tedium characteristic precisely of anti-trust cases—which do not seem to unfold in mortal time, and in which no recognizably human issue appears to be at stake. On a not untypical day, November 29, 1984, Boies asked Westmoreland, for example, on cross-examination, a series of questions that began, "Now, the March 25 PERINTREP, which is Exhibit 199A . . . "; continued, "And it is indicated here that that estimate of 113,087 . . . represents a reduction of 405 from the previous month, correct, sir?"; continued further, "And if you added 405 to 113,087, what would you come up with, sir?" To which Westmoreland, perhaps understandably, replied, "Say again, now? Added what, now?" Five questions later, in reply to "And am I correct that adding 113,087 and 405 you come up with

113,492?," Boies elicited the answer "Yes." More than a hundred questions later, Boies having posed in various ways questions about "probable and possible" infiltration rates for the months of September, October, November, December of 1967 and January of 1968, Judge Leval interrupted to suggest that the jurors be given a copy of the figures. Boies distributed copies of a document to the jury and asked Westmoreland, "Do you have the pending question in mind?" Westmoreland said, perhaps again understandably, "I would like it repeated." Whereupon Boies said, "Sure," and did repeat: "This infiltration estimate . . . shows total infiltration, including both possible and probable, estimated as 6,300 for September, 4,300 for October, 5,900 for November, 5,300 for December, and 21,000 for January, 1968, correct?" The entire sequence ends, "I am in no position to answer that question." What the jurors, with their yellow pads, or anyone, can have made of this is far from clear. On the other hand, Westmoreland's very first answer to the very first question posed to him as a witness had also to do with numbers, and seemed to reveal something personal, and perhaps odd, about the plaintiff, the adult, the former general, on the stand. Asked, by his own attorney, "General Westmoreland, how old are you, sir?" he replied, "I am seventy and one-half."

A remarkable feature of both trials, *Sharon* in Room 110 and *Westmoreland* in Room 318, was that both plaintiffs and all the defendants regarded themselves as simultaneously heroic and aggrieved. *Time* knew (or, at least, its lawyers did) as soon as it saw the completed depositions of its own witnesses—Duncan, the chief of correspondents; Smith, the writer; Kelly, the Jerusalem bureau chief; and several others, including Halevy—that there was so far no evidence whatever for its paragraph. It had not, of course, known this at the time of publication. In fact, in the course of Kelly's deposition it emerged that Halevy had told Kelly, at the time of Halevy's Memo Item of December 6, 1982, that Halevy had actually *read* the notes, or minutes, of the conversation at Bikfaya and that his sources had confirmed, the following February, that the substance of the notes, and of the Memo Item, appeared in Appendix B. At his own deposition, Halevy refused to say whether he had read the notes or not, claiming repeatedly that to answer either way might "disclose the identity of the source." The sacred, Delphic, oracular nature of sources was invoked, with a kind of gravity, by several witnesses in declining to answer questions; but this claim of Halevy's was hard to understand. If he *had* seen the notes, of course, his answer might reveal the identity of the source who showed them to him. If he had *not* seen them, however, the source who had not showed them to him might be anyone in the entire world. Halevy did not exactly contradict Kelly's testimony ("His recollection . . . is ten times better than mine"; "I thought that Mr. Kelly gave you too much information"); but in refusing to confirm or deny that he had seen the "newly discovered" notes, or minutes, Halevy was evidently trying to imply that he had seen them, when in fact (as emerged more clearly in his testimony at trial) he had not. *Time* knew at the close of depositions what sort of witness it had in Halevy, and in all the members of its staff who testified. And yet it chose, at great expense of time, and money, and moral energy, to stand by its story that Sharon had discussed with the Gemayels, on the eve of the massacres at Sabra and Shatila, the subject of revenge. The reason *Time* thought itself aggrieved was simple: it was being sued, and it had to undergo, like any other litigant, the ordeal of discovery and trial. The reason it considered its role heroic was less clear. A customary argument of the press (and, more significantly, of libel lawyers) in libel cases is that any retreat from a story as originally published puts in jeopardy the entire First Amendment and threatens the integrity of the entire press—including, in particular, the little publications, unable to defend themselves. One difficulty with this argument is that large publications, and, of course, television networks, are both rich and insured for vast amounts—which is why all libel lawyers are defendants' lawyers; there exist no plaintiffs' libel specialists. Small publications are not. So that even if all large publications were to win their cases, small publications would be in no way protected. Rich libel plaintiffs could still sue them and ruin them on legal costs alone. There exists, of course, no reason why the law should not evolve to establish different standards for small than for large publications. What is "reckless disregard," for instance, on the part of a global, technologically advanced medium, with large resources for checking, might not be "reckless disregard" on the part of a small publication, with a little staff. As for the entire press and the First Amendment, it is hard to see how either can be served by all-out legal advocacy of stories that are false. But *Time* believed its story was not false, and stood by it.

Westmoreland and Sharon felt themselves aggrieved, obviously, by what each maintained was the initial libel, and heroic for taking on the almost insurmountable burden of proving that the stories about them were, clearly and convincingly, false; and were published, clearly and convincingly, with actual malice. As for CBS, it shared *Time*'s view. They were represented, after all, by the same law firm; and Cravath's libel specialist, Stuart W. Gold, participated in writing the motions and legal briefs for both. In addition, however, CBS's witnesses and, to a lesser extent, its chief counsel, Boies, felt that they were taking on the war in Vietnam. The genesis of the program itself had been, roughly, this: In August of 1966, Samuel A. Adams, a young intelligence analyst in the C.I.A., had concluded, on the basis of a visit to Vietnam and some monthly summaries of reports derived in part from captured enemy documents, that the military's estimate of enemy troop strength was too low; his "extrapolation" from the monthly summaries led him to believe that the correct figure for total enemy troop strength was not the 297,000 estimated by the military but 600,000. His arguments, within the C.I.A., were not accepted. They were not accepted, either, at a conference in late 1967, in Saigon, between military intelligence analysts and analysts from the Defense Department and the C.I.A. Adams, a 1955 graduate of Harvard, came to believe that his arguments were rejected as a result of a conspiracy. In 1973, he testified in defense of Daniel Ellsberg; but, for various reasons, which emerged at the Westmoreland trial, he kept his estimates of enemy troop strength vague. In May of 1975, Adams, no longer with the C.I.A., published in *Harper's* an article entitled "Vietnam Cover-Up," which was edited by George Crile, then an editor at *Harper's*. The thesis of the article was summed up in its subtitle, "A C.I.A. Conspiracy

Against Its Own Intelligence." In September of 1975, Adams testified before the House Select Committee on Intelligence, the Pike Committee, in its investigation of American intelligence; but, again, for various reasons, he kept his testimony about estimates vague. For a time, it emerged at trial, Adams had tried to bring Westmoreland to trial for violations of the Uniform Code of Military Justice; and for some years he had been compiling what became known as his "chronologies," and "list of sixty" (actually, eighty), which consisted of handwritten notes of interviews, and plans for interviews, with eighty people who might shed light on his thesis of a conspiracy or a "coverup" in Vietnam. Adams was planning to write a book. By 1980, however, George Crile had moved to CBS, where he had participated in the production of several documentaries. By November 24, 1980, Crile, with Adams' help, had written what is called at CBS a "Blue Sheet," a proposal for a program. The Blue Sheet was sixteen pages, typed, single-spaced; it mentioned the word "conspiracy" twenty-four times and the word "conspirator" five times. Crile's proposal, for a ninety-minute broadcast, with Adams as a paid consultant, was approved by CBS News executives, on condition that Crile could produce interviews with people who would support his thesis. Crile and Adams selected people from Adams' list. A year and two months later, heralded by network commercials and full-page ads, all of which used the word "conspiracy," "The Uncounted Enemy: A Vietnam Deception," produced by Crile, with interviews by Mike Wallace and Crile himself, was on the air.

J ust inside the main entrance, at the top of the broad granite steps of the federal courthouse on Foley Square, the briefcases, parcels and handbags of all plaintiffs, defendants, attorneys, reporters and spectators are checked electronically for weapons, on a conveyor belt of the sort used for security checks at airports. Outside Courtrooms 318 and 110 during *Westmoreland* and *Sharon,* there were federal marshals watching over the sort of electronic arch through which passengers pass before boarding their flights. In one of the rows on the left of Room 318, Mrs. Westmoreland, known to hawk and dove alike as Kitsy, sat each day, in bright sweater and skirt, working on her needlepoint. Mrs. Sharon, who sat in the front row of Room 110, worked on her knitting, but only in a robing room set aside for the plaintiff in that case. The courthouse has many floors and many rooms; but from October 9, 1984, to February 19, 1985, there were few indications that, elsewhere in the building, cases of in some ways more immediate seriousness were going on. The elevators in the courthouse are few and, even for a federal building, inordinately fickle and slow, so that anyone who could would be inclined to avoid them. On one particularly cold morning, about a dozen Oriental men seemed to be exercising a new extreme of courtesy in entering an elevator that had at last arrived on the first floor. As each young man (and they were all young) passed through the doors, the doors would close, literally, upon him; but none raised a hand to ward them off. Each waited to be released, and then stepped inside while the elevator doors closed upon the next. Quite a while passed in this apparently curious ritual, until it occurred to any observer that the newspapers, two days before, had mentioned the arrest of thirteen alleged murderers and gang enforcers for the tongs; and that no one raised his hands against the doors because all of them were in handcuffs. But such intrusions by matters of local, recent, immediate consequence in life and death were rare. Meanwhile, particularly in Room 318, people followed the most arcane, and even unintelligible, testimony with the intensity of fanatics.

This quality of attention seemed to exist even in the Westmoreland jury. Since the "conspiracy to deceive," if it did exist, would consist of two deceptions—arbitrary removal from the Order of Battle of all village self-defense units and other irregular supporters of the Vietcong, and deliberate understatement of the rate of infiltration, in the five months preceding Tet, of North Vietnamese soldiers into South Vietnam—which, when combined, would constitute the grand deception, a false and arbitrary ceiling on estimates of enemy troop strength, to keep the figure below three hundred thousand, almost all the testimony in the case, particularly testimony that addressed dates and numbers, lacked drama, lacked narrative, lacked, the more one thought about it, any reality at all. And yet on January 7, 1985, the jury complained to Judge Leval of "noise" (two reporters, as it turned out, talking) in the third row on the right. Two weeks later, after a heavy snowstorm that put several subways out of service, a juror called the judge's chambers—sobbing, because she had somehow become stranded in a station in Hoboken and would be more than an hour later than the others. With the agreement of counsel, Judge Leval agreed to delay the trial till she arrived. The level of education in both juries was, for New York, unusually high, but not *that* high. On December 5, 1984, the first day of Crile's testimony, Judge Leval received from the jury a note saying that Juror No. 10 had "throwed out" three times, on account of the chicken soup at lunch. The jurors, with their legal pads, were not, in other words, pedants or scholars. But the intensity of interest was greatest by far on the part of members of the most radically anti-war factions of the press. When I asked one of the best of these reporters why he attached such immense importance to the question of whether or not village defense and self-defense units were included in the Order of Battle (a technical matter, it seemed, since when they were not included they were simply listed separately), he replied that the whole point lay here: that the trial would show the world that American imperialism was fighting not an army but a whole people in that war. Like the ideologues on the other side, who thought that Westmoreland's chief counsel, Burt, was right in predicting that the trial would bring about the "dismantling of a major news network," for having undermined American morale and thereby lost the war, the reporter seemed not to have considered the fact that, no matter what the jury decided, the trial would have a politically ambiguous result. If CBS was right, for example, and Westmoreland had lost the war by deceiving his military superiors and his civilian Commander-in-Chief, then the Commander-in-Chief, President Johnson, was inescapably exonerated from responsibility both for the escalation of the war and for its loss. Since there have been, so miraculously, no witch-hunts, as there were after World War II and the Korean war, there may be no serious harm in exonerating President Johnson, and attaching blame to General Westmoreland, if that is what the left, at this moment in our history, wants to do. But what follows from it, as from Boies' position at the trial, and from CBS's position in the program, is that no blame attaches to the very civilian, capitalist, democratically elected Administrations that the left would ordinarily want most to blame. As for the question of including the grandmothers and the children who were members of village self-defense units (or, for that matter, any civilian whose sympathies were with the Vietcong) in the enemy Order of Battle, if the program was right and Boies was right, that these grandmothers and children *must* be included in the Order of Battle, the inescapable conclusion is that these people were in fact army. And if they were army, and enemy army, the opposing army is hardly to blame for trying to kill them before being killed by them. And the argument from My Lai, in all its ramifications, starts to dissolve. If CBS was right, then these "civilians" were Order of Battle soldiers, and what appeared to be an indiscriminate massacre of noncombatants becomes more like an act of war. So there was nothing to be gained by either left or right in the outcome of the case. And what was, oddly, never mentioned by either side, in the ninety-minute broadcast, in the months of trial, or at any time before or since, was that all that was at stake were *estimates.* Not facts. Not counts. Not commandments graven in stone. But "estimates"; the word, like "source" in the other trial, was used as though it meant something either sacred and talismanic or solidly professional, like the words proper to a science. The tragedy, one tragedy, anyway, was that the estimators *did not know* what was the strength of the enemy in Vietnam. President Johnson, as became clear (if it was not clear before) in the course of the trial, and the Joint Chiefs knew as much as General Westmoreland and all the intelligence bureaucracies combined knew. The rate of enemy infiltration, for example, was monitored, electronically, by what was referred to throughout the trial as Source X (the National Security Agency), which was based in Washington. General Westmoreland not only did not, he *could* not suppress those reports, which reached the Pentagon and the White House before they reached Saigon. Judge Leval, in one of the few arguable rulings in the course of the whole trial, ruled that what Johnson knew was not the issue; the issue was whether Westmoreland had intended, no matter how unsuccessfully, to deceive. There is evidence even in the memoirs of

Truong Nhu Tang, a founder of the National Liberation Front and Minister of Justice of the Vietcong, that the President's, the Joint Chiefs' and Westmoreland's estimates of total enemy troop strength, including irregulars, and their appraisal of the military results of Tet were more accurate than those of the defense witnesses, including, of course, Samuel Adams. But Truong Nhu Tang was mentioned nowhere in the trial—though the defense several times quoted, of all people, General Nguyen Cao Ky. And an "estimate," particularly on the basis of facts and procedures relied on by witnesses for both sides (as the lamentable quality of the military and civilian intelligence bureaucracies emerged, almost imperceptibly, at trial), is only an estimate. If the stated thesis of the broadcast, however, had been that Westmoreland led a conspiracy to alter and suppress suppositions and not very educated guesses, there would have been no broadcast; or, even if there had been such a broadcast, there would have been no suit.

Early in the afternoon of Thursday, July 12, 1984, two American attorneys, each a partner in a major New York law firm, appeared at the offices of Maître Michel Distel, on the Boulevard Saint-Germain in Paris. With them they had brought Martha Hess, a certified shorthand reporter and notary public of the State of New York, and Patricia Kinder, a French interpreter, who was duly sworn. The attorneys and Ms. Hess had flown in from New York to take the deposition of one Josette Alia, a journalist and editor of the French weekly *Le Nouvel Observateur*. Ms. Alia having also been duly sworn, there ensued approximately five hours of wonderfully absurdist colloquy, with the two attorneys, counsel for opposing parties, at odds not only with each other but also with the interpreter, who could not resist interjecting her own views from time to time, and even with a person, identified only as "Claire Senard," who seemed, according to peripheral testimony midway through the deposition, to have served as translator between one of the attorneys and Ms. Alia in a meeting at the Bristol Hotel. Even this person, who had not been sworn, spoke up at one point to correct either the interpreter or Ms. Alia—until, the attorneys having agreed that there could be only one "official interpreter," she was duly silenced.

The official interpreter, meanwhile, was frequently and clearly in distress. Asked to translate Ms. Alia's responses exactly, saying "I," for example, when Ms. Alia said "I," the interpreter lapsed frequently into "she." Admonished, at one point, not to make speeches of her own but to translate all, but only all, that she heard from Ms. Alia, the interpreter said, "Surely, but what I am trying to elucidate is what Madame means by the word 'almost.'" When one attorney asked her, in the most tactful terms, only to interpret, and to leave "elucidation" to the attorneys, she replied somewhat huffily. "When she is vague, I will be vague," she said. Shortly after that, however, the official interpreter apparently felt compelled to speak up again. "May I make one small point," she said. "I would hate myself to be caught on the hot and find my own language in five or six weeks' time to be found on the table." The attorney, perhaps unfazed by this utterance, said, "We all understand that, and we want to avoid that very thing." Later still, the interpreter said, "Madame says she doesn't understand what you are talking about." An attorney interrupted. Ms. Alia, meanwhile, said, "Of course I do." Sometimes, in addition to a clear antagonism between the two attorneys ("Rich, try to control your mouth," one attorney said, for example, to the other), there was tension between both attorneys and Ms. Alia over differences between French and American law, or even what constitutes a "defendant," a "judgment" and a "trial." In the course of what, with various breaks and discussions off the record, came to occupy a hundred and three pages of official transcript, Ms. Alia asserted thirty-nine times, in various ways and in response to several kinds of questions, that she did not, could not, and never would divulge her sources. Almost any sort of question might elicit this reply. Asked, for example, whether she had actually listened to a particular phone conversation, not directly but on tape, Ms. Alia said, "I can't answer that question. That is information which if I gave to you would enable you to find out who gave me that information." Obviously, if Ms. Alia had *not* listened to the conversation her answer would enable no one to find out anything of the kind.

An admission to not having heard something can hardly reveal the source from whom you heard it. So the clear implication of Ms. Alia's answer is that she had listened to the conversation in some form. Since the phone conversation in question took place, however, between a head of government and his minister of defense, and since, in an article published in the November 6, 1982, *Nouvel Observateur*, Ms. Alia had been wrong about both the time and the content of the conversation, this implication would appear to be misleading. But to the very next question, "If you tell me whether or not you listened to a tape—just yes or no—would that reveal your source?," Ms. Alia replied serenely, "Yes, of course."

The deposition of Josette Alia was the second (the first was of Sharon himself) in the case that became *Sharon* v. *Time.* The attorneys were Thomas Barr, of Cravath, Swaine & Moore, for *Time,* and Richard M. Goldstein, of Shea & Gould, for Sharon. (Milton Gould was critically ill during most of the year when the case was being prepared for trial. Barr, too, became intermittently seriously ill. Both made complete recoveries.) Ms. Alia was never called as a witness, and her deposition was unusual even for the expensive, wasteful, disingenuous, tedious and ultimately absurdist process that is the modern American legal deposition. The purpose of depositions, as of the other methods of "Discovery," under Rule 26 of the Federal Rules of Civil Procedure, is to enable each party to obtain from the other, before trial, information "regarding any matter . . . which is relevant to the subject matter involved in the pending action"—so that each side will have access to the witnesses and the evidence that the other might present at trial, either to avoid trial (because there is no case) or to facilitate settlement (because the contours of the case are clarified) or to expedite the trial if the case does come to court. Depositions are ordinarily taken, and paid for, by the "hostile" party, and only the "hostile" party may introduce a witness's deposition testimony in court. An attorney for the side on whose behalf the witness will appear is also present, to "defend" the deposition. Each deposition, therefore, entails the presence of one witness, at least two attorneys, and a certified reporter, who administers the oath and makes the stenographic record, before the expenses for travel, and for extra attorneys (if the client can afford them, or if the case involves more than two litigants, or if a witness other than the litigants requires the presence of his own attorney) and (as in the case of Ms. Alia) an official interpreter are reckoned in. Sworn testimony on deposition has, theoretically, the same weight, and is subject to the same rules with respect to perjury, as testimony at trial. But the depositions in a given case amount at best to a sort of rehearsal, or mini-trial (with voluminous records, at considerable expense), composed essentially of mini cross-examinations, which the real trial either repeats or (in the case of dishonest or bewildered witnesses) contradicts. Attorneys make much of these contradictions—and, as part of the completed record of a trial, they sometimes reveal with an extraordinary clarity who is telling the truth and who is not. But juries rarely pay much attention to deposition testimony introduced at trial, and confine their deliberations to what the witness said, and how credible he appeared to them, upon the stand. At worst, depositions, more than the other forms of discovery (sworn affidavits and document production, which do not require the presence of witnesses and paid attorneys), are the rich litigant's best instrument for harassment, obfuscation, and delay.

One completely incidental effect of depositions, however, is to make most civil trials oddly unsuitable to coverage, on a daily basis, by the press. Criminal trials do evolve from day to day; but in most civil trials the record is for the most part already in, and the only persons to whom it unfolds each day are the spectators —and, most critically, the jury. The litigants know in advance almost everything except how opposing counsel will proceed, how the judge will rule on various questions, and what the jury will decide. It was a misunderstanding based on the nature and the demands of daily reporting that led, for instance, to the story, in newspapers all over the world, that the outcome of the Westmoreland case was determined by Westmoreland's surprise and dismay at the testimony, on the stand, of two intelligence officers, one a fellow-graduate of West Point. The outcome, a "Joint Statement" signed by Westmoreland and all the CBS defendants with the remarkable but scarcely noticed exception of Samuel Adams, was undeniably strange. But it had nothing to do with Westmoreland's reaction to testimony of any kind. He knew in substance, from what both witnesses said at their depositions, what they were going to say. Indeed, Boies had quoted extensively from one of them in his opening statement, on the second day of trial.

In both *Sharon* v. *Time* and *Westmoreland* v. *CBS*, the plaintiffs were able, through Shea & Gould and the Capital Legal Foundation, to meet the deposition costs. One fact about both trials, however, explains why Barr should have troubled even seriously to consider as a witness, on *Time*'s behalf, Ms. Alia, of *Nouvel Observateur*. In spite of any special affinity the Cravath attorneys might have with their media clients, and in spite of trying to prove that *more* than what was published or broadcast by their clients was true, in certain respects what the lawyers would want to prove and what their clients would want to claim were inescapably at odds. CBS and *Time* might, for the litigation's sake, oblige Cravath in its argument that the alleged libels were not "of and concerning" the plaintiffs at all; and, though the argument was abandoned early in Westmoreland, every single witness who contributed to the story in *Time* testified that he read and, depending on his contribution, composed, edited or wrote the offending paragraph as "of and concerning" not Sharon at all but Amin Gemayel. Even a cursory reading of the paragraph, and particularly the sentence beginning, "Sharon also reportedly discussed with the Gemayels the need . . . to take revenge"—with its clear grammatical construction: subject, verb, indirect object, object—might make this position difficult to sustain. *Time*'s own press release heralding the story included the words "Sharon" and "urged." But defense lawyers are not grammarians or practitioners of textual criticism. And every *Time* witness who had anything to do with the paragraph as published—from Halevy, the reporter, through Kelly, the bureau chief; Helen Doyle, the fact checker; William Smith, the writer; and Richard Duncan, the chief of correspondents—dutifully testified, under oath, that he or she had always understood what little news there was, if any, in the whole passage beginning "*Time* has learned" to concern not Sharon himself but some entirely other person, a Phalangist, if not Amin, then some other Gemayel. So far, it seemed, attorneys and press client could agree. More difficult to reconcile were *Time*'s journalistic interest and a position most helpful to its lawyers: that the story and, particularly, the paragraph at issue *were not news.* If they were not news, if everyone had known for some time that Sharon discussed revenge with the Gemayels, then there was no libel—or, at least, there would be great difficulty in proving actual malice. Far from publishing, for instance, with "reckless disregard," *Time* had simply repeated what was common knowledge, information that had already been published elsewhere, which it had no reason seriously to doubt. And that is where Ms. Alia came in. Because she had published in the *Nouvel Observateur* of November 6, 1982, more or less the same sort of story that appeared the following February in the paragraph in *Time.*

How radically this contention violated every natural journalistic instinct, particularly Halevy's pride in his own "scoop," is revealed at virtually every stage of deposition and trial testimony on this point. On the one hand, *Time* and its attorneys felt that they had to argue that the paragraph was investigative reporting of the highest order, which could not have been obtained without Halevy's confidential sources; on the other hand, they had to claim that they had relied upon information already published, of which they had no serious doubt. Whether a witness in a lawsuit accurately reflects the person outside the courtroom can never really be known; but Halevy, at least in his capacity as a witness, was not a self-effacing man. To a question, on September 25, 1984, the fifth day of his deposition, whether he had ever in his journalistic career published a story that turned out to be untrue, he replied that he recalled no such event; and "To the best of my knowledge, all my information, in fifteen years of reporting out of Israel, out of the Middle East, and out of other parts of the world, all my information I gave to *Time* magazine, all my stories, all my cables, all my ideas, and all my suggestions, were accurate, were ahead of time, were on top of the story, and were exact." There followed what for any other witness might be a particularly awkward colloquy, about an episode, in October of 1979, when five "sources" Halevy claimed for a story about Prime Minister Begin's health so convincingly denied every element of the story that *Time* ultimately published a retraction. Halevy, saying that he had a "vague" recollection of the episode, responded with heavy sarcasm, "As we all know, the man [Begin] is still very healthy, in terrific condition. . . . He is running his party, operating as a healthy human being." (He responded in a similar way at trial, referring to Begin's denunciation of the paragraph at issue in the lawsuit: "I survived it. That's all. Look where he is now and look where I am now." Where was Begin now? "Very sick, secluded in his apartment . . . very sick, Mr. Gould, very sick." It did not seem to occur to Halevy that between the time of the first episode, in 1979, and the time of his deposition and the trial five years had passed.) Normally, however, in his least self-effacing mode, Halevy is most expansive. Asked, for instance, whether in the course of his military service he received any commendations or awards for bravery, he says, "No, sir. I escape all ceremonies." But he volunteers, "Forgive me, I have a terrific memory for numbers, probably part of my education," and proceeds to reel off phone numbers. He tells of a secret nocturnal visit to his home by a source whom he characterizes as an Israeli general, who says that only "you are known to have the guts" to write truthfully about affairs in Israel; and of a lunch at the Commodore Hotel in West Beirut when no fewer than eight high Israeli officers ("Everybody at the hotel saw me talking to them. Everybody at the hotel. . . . Present there were many of the sources I mentioned. Maybe I disclosed something to you which I did not intend") sought him out to confide in him. He says that one of his "sources"—after the publication of the paragraph; after the filing of the lawsuit; in fact, in the very course of the trial itself—not only reconfirmed to him that his paragraph was accurate but also asked him whether he had the courage to maintain the source's anonymity. He says he replied that he thought he could manage. He says that when the Kahan Report came out "it says, in a very ego-sided point of view, 'Whatever information you learned, Mr. Halevy, is accurate,'" and that the report as published "confirmed in a steel form" his Memo Item of two months before. Whatever one makes of this testimony—and whatever it implies about what it means to be a correspondent, in a foreign country, for a major news magazine —it is clear that it must have been particularly difficult for Halevy to fall in line with the position that his scoop was nothing new. And, in fact, he could not quite bring himself to do it. He testifies repeatedly that he learned the facts in his Memo Item of December 6, 1982, more than three weeks before he sent the telex—learned them in "mid-October, early November." He does not claim that he spent the time in checking. It is simply not in the nature of the "investigative reporter" Halevy believes himself to be to wait weeks, or even days, after acquiring information before filing it; and one wonders at first why Halevy should lay such stress upon having waited. Then one remembers that Ms. Alia's article appeared in *Nouvel Observateur* on November 6, 1982, more than three weeks before Halevy filed his Memo Item, and the thing becomes clear. He wants to establish, for the record, although no one seems to notice, that he *knew* the story before Ms. Alia did.

For the rest, Halevy and all the other defense witnesses must simply oblige the attorneys' and the magazine's ambivalent interest, in showing that the story was simultaneously investigative, of the utmost immediate importance, and in essence just a reprint, nothing new. And for that, within Cravath's conception of thoroughness, Ms. Alia's *Nouvel Observateur* was not enough. *Time* must claim other sources, other publications: domestic publications; *Stern;* a Dutch newspaper. While it was hard to imagine *Time*'s staff poring over French, German and Dutch papers, and while there were certain lapses (asked whether he was familiar, for example, with the *Neue Zürcher Zeitung,* Kelly said, "I have heard of Zurich, I don't know the newspaper, sir"), most of the defense witnesses testified that they had read and relied upon these publications, which, though they did not specifically mention any discussion of "revenge," more or less implied that Sharon had virtually incited the Sabra and Shatila massacres. But even foreign and domestic publications were not enough. The attorneys argued, and the witnesses testified, that they had read the Kahan Report, *as published,* to say exactly what *Time*'s paragraph said—only, as it were, "between the lines." And, finally, in one relatively daring step, the attorneys argued, and the witnesses testified, that *Sharon himself* had said, practically in the same words, what the paragraph said—specifically, in his own public testimony before the Kahan Commission, on October 25, 1982. What Sharon had actually said, as part of an answer to a direct question from Justice Aharon Barak, one of the three members of the Kahan Commission, was this: "Revenge exists, without a doubt. Exists revenge. Amin himself, at the funeral, to the best of my recollection, at the funeral [of Bashir Gemayel] used the word 'revenge.' The word 'revenge' also appeared, I would say, also in discussions among us." Almost every *Time* employee who had anything to do with the paragraph at issue said, under oath, that he had read some version of Sharon's public testimony before the Kahan Commission, and that he had always understood the "us" in Sharon's "among us" to mean among Sharon and some Phalangist or other Lebanese.

This was a daring argument, on the part of attorneys and witnesses alike, for several reasons. Quite apart from the fact that a public admission on October 25, 1982, by Sharon himself that he had, on the eve of the massacres, discussed revenge with the Phalangists would have been front-page news the following day (and that *Time*'s story "Sharon Takes the Stand," in its issue of that week, made no mention whatever of such an admission or of the words themselves); quite apart, too, from the fact that the Kahan Report, as published, makes it clear that the discussion of revenge to which Sharon referred took place among Israelis, at a meeting of the Cabinet, the question arises why, in the view of *Time*'s journalists and editors, the Kahan Commission, which did assign to Sharon, among others, "indirect responsibility" for the massacres, would make no mention of such a discussion between Sharon and the Phalangists—or why, for that matter, the commission should relegate to a secret appendix information to which Sharon had testified in public several months before. Leaving aside, as well, the question why something that Sharon had publicly admitted in October should become for *Time* the following February a scoop on which countless other publications based their stories, this opened the way to one of the most peculiar developments of the trial. Halevy himself testified, at the trial and at his deposition, that he had read both Sharon's public testimony and the Kahan Report in Hebrew. He even ventured to claim to find "huge discrepancies" between the original Hebrew and English translations of what Sharon actually said. At his deposition, he testified firmly and categorically that Sharon's "among us" implied, in Hebrew, "among Sharon and the Phalangists."

Q. Does not the word *etslenu* mean also ourselves?
A. No.
Q. Not at all?
A. *Etslenu,* ourselves, not at all. . . .
Q. Does it mean in our place?
A. No, sir, it does not . . .

Also:

Q. Mr. Halevy, what was the basis, sir, for the statement in your December 6th telex? . . .
A. First of all, on top of everything, it is Mr. Sharon's public testimony before the Kahan Commission, during which—and I remember that sentence—I think the copy of the Kahan Commission you received from us, that sentence is underlined. There is a sentence—I am not sure I'm quoting it correctly, I don't want to mislead you—There is a sentence . . . Mr. Sharon says, "The matter of revenge was discussed among us." There is a very clear reference . . . that he is referring to meetings with the Phalange or with the Lebanese officials.

No other *Time* witness claimed to read Hebrew. Halevy's testimony on this point had the entirely incidental effect of making a young official translator, Laurie Kuslansky, one of the most important witnesses of the trial.

Having made the argument that *Time* had relied for its paragraph not only on Halevy's vital confidential sources but also upon other publications, upon the Kahan Report as published, and on Sharon's own public testimony several months before (Halevy himself got so carried away by this defense litany, or rote, that he testified at one point, in his deposition, that he had relied on all of the above sources, published, confidential and "you name it," and, at another, in the trial itself, upon all of the above and "from so many things that it's almost unbelievable"), the defense had to make yet another argument more congenial to the lawyers than to the journalists. In trying to establish that the paragraph did not say the defamatory things that Sharon claimed it said, the defense had to argue that all the publications that picked up and relied upon *Time*'s scoop unaccountably misread it. Every publication that, like *The New York Times,* for instance, of March 1, 1983, attributed to *Time* the information that in the conversation at Bikfaya Sharon "urged [the Phalangists] to take revenge" simply and inexplicably got it wrong. This was especially difficult to argue in connection with *The New York Times,* because the same piece, of March 1, 1983, quoted Duncan, *Time*'s chief of correspondents, to the effect that *"Time* stands by its story." All the defense witnesses had, however, to testify that while *Time* had relied for its story upon other publications, every publication that subsequently based its own story upon *Time*'s paragraph misunderstood the paragraph to say something defamatory about Sharon.

If the attorneys and their media clients in both *Sharon* v. *Time* and *Westmoreland* v. *CBS* could be, in certain key respects, at cross-purposes—because CBS, too, needed to argue both that its story was a historic scoop and that it simply paraphrased earlier publications, including the Pike Committee Report, and contained really nothing new; and also, to a lesser extent, that the broadcast, as interpreted by Westmoreland and by publications that took the program's thesis up, had been misunderstood—there were signs that, in the strange heat all litigation brings to bear on things, the very process of litigation fosters the most profound misunderstandings in the world. The depositions in *Sharon,* like nearly all Cravath depositions, were of an aggressiveness and incivility that have come to constitute one modern litigating style. But a particular exchange in the course of Sharon's own deposition seemed to illustrate the extreme of incomprehension that a lawsuit can create even in men most familiar with and professionally at ease within the law. Sharon's deposition occupied six days. The first session, on June 15, 1984, a Friday, took place at the offices of Cravath, and it bristled with such animosity, mainly between the attorneys ("Mr. Barr: What in the world does that have to do with anything? . . . If you don't keep quiet— Mr. Gilbert: Mr. Barr, don't point your finger at me"; on the other hand, "Sharon: We are not in a hurry. We are not in a hurry. We have time. We have time. . . . O.K. I enjoy being here with you, you are very polite, very nice, wonderful room, wonderful atmosphere . . ."), that it had to be adjourned within less than an hour and to be resumed the following Sunday, in the courtroom of

Judge Sofaer. Even the judge's presence did not entirely subdue the almost unremitting hostility of the attorneys; and certain aspects of Friday's session, not apparent from the transcript of the session itself, were brought to light:

> Q. Is the question confusing or you just want to hear it again?
> A. Mr. Barr, you cannot confuse me. Even when you were sitting with your legs on the table on Friday, you didn't confuse me.
> THE COURT: It is a common habit in this country, General.
> THE WITNESS: I beg your pardon, your Honor.

Three months later, at 8 a.m. on September 5, 1984, the deposition was resumed, in Judge Sofaer's courtroom. Depositions in the presence of the judge are in themselves highly unusual. Normally, they take place in the offices of opposing counsel. Yet four of the six days of Sharon's deposition took place in the courtroom of Judge Sofaer. And again the Cravath style set the tone of the entire day. Stuart Gold, the firm's young, bearded specialist in libel, had seemed not so much to question as to bait Sharon, asking him again and again, in increasingly mocking terms, precisely what he meant by "blood libel":

> Q. I assume, General, you weren't accusing me personally, right, is that correct?
> A. No, not you personally; I am accusing the *Time* magazine . . . not that *Time* magazine and not any other publication will dare to do it again, to me or to anybody else.
> Q. I don't want to steal your thunder, General, but you are not the first foreign official—
> THE COURT: Keep yourself out of this, Mr. Gold.

The day also brought one of the lawsuit's few moments of rather sombre and unlikely humor. Gold had just asked Sharon whether he felt that his reputation had been damaged by the article "in the Arab countries." Sharon replied, perhaps understandably, "I don't understand the question." Milton Gould, his chief counsel, interrupted. "Your Honor," he said, "I am prepared to stipulate that we suffered no damages in Libya." Judge

Sofaer, by no means a humorless man, was just this once unprepared. "In *Libya?*" he said. But the key, in its own way touching
or appalling, exchange took place when the deposition was
resumed on November 9, 1984, the week before the trial began,
at the offices of Cravath, Swaine & Moore. From eight-forty-five
that morning until late afternoon, the unbridled rudeness of the
attorneys ("Oh, God"; "Baloney"; "No, I want you to be quiet";
"You find a lot of things hard to believe. That is a congenital
problem"; "I will do it, Rich"; "You are really tedious"; "You
are being preposterous"; "And you are being insulting"; "I am
deliberately being insulting"; "I would like you to be quiet")
made it clear why these officers of the court—all attorneys are
officers of the court—were better off, with this deposition, in the
presence of the judge. And then the remarkable exchange began.
Barr had just confronted Sharon, in the form of questions, with
what Cravath, in its thoroughness, had assembled: a long series
of derogatory comments about him, by the press, by colleagues,
by military superiors and subordinates, by prime ministers and
political friends and enemies, throughout the course of Sharon's
adult life. Sharon, having been shown piece after piece, in various publications, had just said that *Time*'s paragraph "is, I
would say, worse than anything else that has been said" when,
after a few more lines of quarrel between the attorneys, this colloquy occurred:

A. And I would like to add to that . . . you can laugh as much as
   you want, because you know, Mr. Barr, that you are defending
   a lie.
Q. Look, General, let me tell you one thing. Don't you accuse me
   of unprofessional conduct. Shut up. You can walk around—
A. You are defending a lie, Mr. Barr.
Q. I am not defending a lie. . . .
A. I would like to say, just to add one thing.
MR. BARR: You explain to the general to stop making personal
   attacks.
MR. GOLDSTEIN: He has not made one. Don't you point your finger
   at him and don't raise your voice at him.
MR. BARR: Richard, you are making a fool of yourself.
MR. GOLDSTEIN: We will let the record speak for itself.

MR. BARR: You tell the general that he is not here to accuse me of unprofessional conduct.

MR. GOLDSTEIN: He has accused you of defending a lie. That's what this lawsuit is about.

MR. BARR: No, it is not. The lawsuit is not about me defending a lie. Let me tell you something in words of one syllable. If he will step out of this room, out of this deposition, and go before these people and accuse me of deliberately defending a lie in a context where I can sue him for libel, I will. As long as you are here in this deposition, you can do that with impunity. If you step outside this room and do it—

Apart from the obvious ways in which the incivility of this exchange is extraordinary even within the context of this or any other lawsuit, the most remarkable thing about it is simply this: that a highly respected and capable attorney should become so incensed at what he regards as an imputation to him of "unprofessional conduct" that he finds it necessary not only to adopt this tone but actually to threaten to sue the plaintiff in a libel suit for libel. "Defending a lie" is in his view an actionable accusation of "unprofessional conduct." It does not seem, in all good faith, to occur to him that the plaintiff, the general himself, regards himself, in the paragraph in *Time,* and then in Cravath's own conduct of the litigation, as having been actionably accused of nothing less than a lifetime of lies and war crimes, and having the "evidence" for such an accusation attributed to the official, forever secret finding of a tribunal appointed by his government. The same irate, offended and combative stance was taken, throughout both trials and after, by the press defendants and their witnesses almost without exception. It was as though the very notion that a news magazine or a network might be mistaken, in what one of the judges called "the gravest possible charges one can level at a professional soldier," were in itself a kind of libel; as though the profession of journalism, as well as the profession of law, lacked, in all good faith, any sense of proportion, or even comprehension; and as though a remark like "You are defending a lie, Mr. Barr," in the course of an arduous deposition, from which one might, but more likely would not, draw an inference of "unprofessional conduct"—it is, after all, unarguably part of the business of lawyers in our system to defend, if not lies, then liars—were in any way comparable to the paragraph, or the ninety minutes, and the gravity of the charges that were read by or broadcast to millions by the press. The deposition of Sharon in the offices of Cravath that day continued:

THE WITNESS: Mr. Barr, don't dare to talk to me like that.

MR. BARR: And don't dare to talk to me like that. . . .

MR. GOLDSTEIN: We will take five minutes, and I will see if the general is in a position to continue.

MR. BARR: We will continue now.

MR. GOLDSTEIN: We are going to take five minutes. . . . I insist that we take a break now in light of your behavior.

MR. BARR: In light of your behavior and the general's loss of control of himself, you take a break.

THE WITNESS: Mr. Barr, don't talk like that. I never lost control.

MR. GOLDSTEIN: You got it. The deposition is concluded. I am asking you as your attorney—

THE WITNESS: I like to tell you, Mr. Barr. I never lost self-control. . . . I have been through the most difficult situations. I never lost self-control.

And then, as if to underscore, in an almost touching way, the defendant's attorney's absolute failure to understand the plaintiff's case, these words of conciliation:

MR. BARR: General, let me tell you something. I am sorry that you and I have exchanged harsh words. There is no reason why you and I should fight with each other. I am here representing a client. I have an obligation to do that. I would not intentionally or deliberately represent a lie. I resent that, I am sorry that I resent it. I am sure you didn't mean to say it in the way it sounded to me, and I am sorry that I reacted emotionally to that. I thought you reacted emotionally too and I am sorry if I provoked that. We both have something that is important to do and we ought to do it calmly and quietly, and I will try to do that.

Reading these words, it is almost unimaginable that the speaker, who "would not intentionally or deliberately represent a lie," and "resents" even the suggestion that he might do so, but feels "sure you didn't mean to say it in the way it sounded to me," is a man who has already taken the position, and hopes to prevail with it, at great expense and in open court, that the man to whom the words are addressed is not only a liar and perjurer but a murderer of women and children. And whose own "resentment" has brought them all to court. In any event, the conciliatory moment is quickly past.

> MR. GOLDSTEIN: I suggest that we take a brief recess and we will see if we can continue.
> MR. BARR: Do as you please.

There is a ten-minute recess.

> MR. GOLDSTEIN: Let us proceed.
> MR. BARR: Do you want to say something.
> THE WITNESS: Yes.
> MR. BARR: Please do.
> THE WITNESS: After hearing your statement, I am willing to proceed.

The lawyers, more politely than at any earlier time, discuss technical and procedural matters for a few moments. And then the deposition (having lasted from 8:45 a.m. to 4:15 p.m., not a long time as depositions go) is ended for the day.

What we expect from the courts is, broadly, justice. What we expect from witnesses is true testimony, under oath. What we expect from press accounts is true testimony of another kind, subject to certain limitations, of timeliness and deadlines, of the abilities of the reporter, of the necessity, in all reporting, to select and to compress—otherwise, each story, in literal and full transcription, would unfold in real time; that is, indefinitely. One thing we do not, or are not legally entitled to, expect from press accounts is justice, in its aspect of fairness. Journalism has a professional obligation to be, within its own limitations, true, but no legal obligation whatever to be fair. What we expect from lawyers is victory in combat according to certain rules, which used to include courtesy to the point of courtliness. What we expect from generals is victory in combat of another kind. One question, in *Sharon* v. *Time* and in *Westmoreland* v. *CBS,* was whose sense of truth, the court's, the lawyer's or the journalist's, was going to prevail; and in one sense there were, in both cases, two juries out, the actual jurors and the press, which was going to have the final word. As witnesses, the generals in both contests faded, oddly, into virtual inconsequence. There were only six important witnesses in *Sharon.* For *Time:* Halevy, the reporter; Kelly, the Jerusalem bureau chief; Duncan, the chief of correspondents; and one Robert Parker, who drew up the press release that began "Sharon said to have urged," and who testified, forthrightly, that what the business people at *Time* do each week is to ask the editors "what do you have that is promotable this week." ("If other media picked that up, with attribution to *Time,*" his boss, Brian Brown, had said, in a deposition that was read into the record of the trial, "this is a way of publicizing the magazine. . . . It is getting the space or the air that money cannot buy.") According to Parker, *Time* had once kept a file of stories in other publications which were picked up from *Time*—and had discontinued, and perhaps lost, that file in early 1984. For Sharon: Ehud Olmert, the member of the Knesset; and, finally, Laurie Kuslansky, the official translator. In *Westmoreland,* too, though many witnesses were called, there were few who mattered. For CBS: Crile, the producer; Adams, the paid consultant; George Allen, Adams' superior in the C.I.A.; Colonel Gains Hawkins, the officer who had been in charge of Order of Battle estimates between February of 1966 and September of 1967; and General Joseph A. McChristian, who had been in charge of all military intelligence in Vietnam from July of 1965 to June of 1967. For Westmoreland: Robert McNamara, Walt Rostow, Robert Komer, Paul Nitze, all of whom, as advisers in various capacities to President Johnson, could testify as to what information reached the President and the Joint Chiefs; George Carver, Allen's own superior at the C.I.A.; General George Godding, Hawkins' immediate superior in military intelligence; Colonel Danny Graham, the only official to be interviewed on camera in opposition to the program's thesis (Graham was the one who appeared on camera for about twenty seconds); and General Phillip Davidson, who succeeded McChristian as chief of all military intelligence in Westmoreland's command.

In libel suits brought by public officials, it is not uncommon for the plaintiff to put on the stand, as part of his own case, "hostile" witnesses; that is, witnesses for the other side. It is the most obvious, and sometimes the only, means of establishing, on the part of those very witnesses, "knowing falsity" or "reckless disregard." Judge Leval had, however, imposed a time limit, a hundred and fifty hours, on each side for the presentation of its case. Burt, on behalf of Westmoreland, began with his own witnesses, moved on to one from CBS, and returned to a witness of his own, before running nearly out of time. Among the first of these witnesses, Rostow and Komer could testify that the controversy over enemy troop strength had been presented in full to President Johnson, both directly and by way of Ellsworth Bunker, who at the time was the United States Ambassador to Vietnam; Godding could testify that all sides of the controversy had been presented to Admiral Ulysses S. Grant Sharp, Westmoreland's immediate superior in the Pacific, and to General Earle Wheeler, head of the Joint Chiefs. Rostow and Godding also testified that though neither of them had appeared on the broadcast, they had told these things, in interviews, to Wallace or to Crile. Two of Burt's most effective witnesses, however, were Carver and Davidson. Carver, of the C.I.A., who was not interviewed on the broadcast, could testify that, far from having "capitulated," as the broadcast put it, to military intelligence, in a joint conference in Saigon in September of 1967, he had actually *proposed,* on behalf of the C.I.A., the estimate of enemy troop strength that was adopted jointly by the military and the C.I.A. Davidson, as the chief of military intelligence in Saigon from June of 1967 to May of 1969, and the only intelligence official high enough to be in constant and direct contact with Westmoreland during the months of the alleged conspiracy, would have had to be the *arch*-conspirator "at the highest levels of American military intelligence." He was not, however, interviewed for the broadcast, either. Crile claimed to believe that Davidson was "on his deathbed" at the time—which made all the more impressive Davidson's own testimony about the events of 1967, and about his own good health and his accessibility during the whole period when the broadcast was being produced.

McNamara had originally been presented as a witness solely to Westmoreland's reputation, for veracity, integrity and so forth, and to Crile's state of mind, with respect to actual malice, at the time the broadcast was produced. But, in the first of many mistakes attributable in part to his inexperience as a litigator, Burt inadvertently opened the door for Boies, on cross-examination, to reach broader issues and to try to impeach McNamara's credibility. McNamara had testified, for instance, that what the program had characterized as a "conspiracy" were in fact good-faith, "honest differences of opinion," and "a difference in [the] judgment of honest men"; also that the actual data were unimportant, and that there existed "cross-checks," so that any particular mistaken estimate would make no difference anyway. He confirmed as well that the controversy over estimates was known to the President and the Joint Chiefs; and that he had told these things, in what he had been assured was an off-the-record interview, to Crile. On cross-examination, however, Boies introduced certain statements that McNamara made to Congress and the public in 1967, and then elicited McNamara's testimony that he had reached the view earlier, "no later than mid-'66," or "as early as the latter part of '65," that the war could not militarily be won. Boies attempted to show a contradiction between McNamara's public statements and his real beliefs (with the clear implication that the public statements were dissembling), in order to call into question the truth of McNamara's testimony at the trial. McNamara explained, however, in one of the few moments of real historic interest in all the testimony about the war, that in his official capacity he had never made a secret of his dim view of American military prospects. In August of 1967, he had, for example, testified so candidly before a subcommittee of the Senate Armed Services Committee that Senator Strom Thurmond, he said, had called him a "Communist appeaser" for making a "no-win statement," and had suggested angrily that the only conclusion to be drawn from McNamara's appraisal of the military situation was that we should "get out . . . at once." The Senate subcommittee hearing, however, was in closed, or executive, session. And the point of McNamara's testimony was this: that at the time of the hearings Henry Kissinger was in secret contact, through intermediaries, as a private citizen but on behalf of the Johnson Administration, with Ho Chi Minh; and that there was within the Administration a hope that if the United States stayed on a bit longer militarily a political solution might be found. As Secretary of Defense, McNamara felt obliged to inform neither the press nor a Senate subcommittee of what the President already knew: the connection between the secret negotiation and McNamara's views. His testimony on this point was, not explicitly but in passing, a reminder that the press when it is not told something, like the intelligence bureaucrat when his view does not prevail, tends to think that it has been in some sinister way conspired against.

The witness, however, who set the tone, and turned out to exemplify the defense strategy of the whole case, was first called by Burt as a "hostile" witness: George Crile. Crile had been married for some years to the stepdaughter of the writer Joseph Alsop, and had known in a social capacity both McNamara and Paul Nitze. He had secretly tape-recorded, it emerged rather late in the process of discovery, his phone conversation with McNamara (and had lost or accidentally erased one of the tapes); he had also discussed his conspiracy theory with Nitze—who testified that he had told Crile, among other things, that the theory was nonsense, that Westmoreland had no motive to fabricate, and that the military estimates were, if anything, "too high." (Boies tried to impeach Nitze's testimony as well; the purpose of his cross-examination, he acknowledged to Judge Leval in one of the conferences at the sidebar, was to show that Nitze was "lying" in his testimony about Crile.) As producer, Crile had been most directly responsible for the program, in its entirety and in its details. It was Crile who wrote the script for Mike Wallace's on-camera interview with Adams, without revealing on the broadcast that Adams was a paid consultant. Crile chose to interview

Allen, of the C.I.A., not Carver; Hawkins and McChristian, of military intelligence, not Godding or Davidson; Graham at a length of about twenty (in fact, exactly twenty-one) seconds. Crile had made the decision to cut the words "but they do have the capability of stepping this up" from an answer Westmoreland gave in the course of an interview, in 1967, on *Meet the Press*—to leave the impression that Westmoreland had given a final, and deceitful, estimate of troop strength in that answer. Crile had written the script that characterized as "head of M.A.C.V.'s delegation" to a joint conference of civilian and military intelligence at C.I.A. headquarters, in Langley, Virginia, in August of 1967 one Colonel George Hamscher—lending a note both of authority and of confession to the words of Hamscher, a minor officer based in Honolulu and a member neither of that "delegation" nor even of M.A.C.V. It was Crile who spliced an answer by Hawkins, "These figures were crap," which had been given to a question about estimates made by the South Vietnamese before 1966, onto the question of estimates adopted in 1967 by the joint conference of civilian and military intelligence. It was Crile who, dissatisfied with the first filmed interview with Allen, took Allen to the editing room and showed him other interviews, and then reinterviewed and refilmed him ("Where am I? What do you want me to say, George?" and "I'm sorry, George, I don't know what you want me to say. I don't know what you're expecting me to say," Allen keeps saying on the outtakes; Crile replies, "Come to the defense of your old protégé, Sam Adams"); and who, having rehearsed Adams as well, wrote Wallace a note, after the filmed interview with Adams: "It looks beautiful. Now all you have to do is break General Westmoreland and we have the whole thing aced." And it was Crile, finally, who cut the specific denials of four people (McChristian, Hamscher, a C.I.A. analyst named Joseph Hovey and a Commander James Meacham) that what they regarded as unjustified altering of estimates reflected a conspiracy of any kind, and who nonetheless stuck by his characterization of the events in question as a "conspiracy."

It is not the business of courts to look over the shoulders of editors, or of juries to second-guess even the most arguable of editorial decisions. Still, it might seem that, after all these and other decisions and practices emerged in the Benjamin Report and on discovery, Crile would feel that some of the decisions at least *were* arguable. Instead, on the afternoon of December 5, 1984, his first day on the stand (and, coincidentally, Halevy's last full day, also as a "hostile" witness, on the stand two floors below), Crile answered with traces of derision the questions put to him by Burt. On December 10th, his second day, he took part in one entirely characteristic exchange: asked what he had meant by a sentence he had written about Westmoreland's having deceived his Commander-in-Chief, he replied, with unmistakable condescension, "I meant what I said, given what I meant, Mr. Burt." On December 12th, in response to a simple question that required a yes or no, "[Allen] says the [accurate] numbers are in there, correct, sir?," he began, in a scathing and patronizing tone, "Mr. Burt, I think I can help you in understanding this," and proceeded, for eight paragraphs, without giving any answer to the question. On December 10th, Crile incurred from Judge Leval a rather long and stern rebuke, which included these words:

> Let me explain to you in clear and unmistakable terms that that is not a proper role for you to be playing as a witness. You are to answer the question that is put to you. You are not to use the opportunity to be on the stand to make speeches or use the question that is given to you as an opportunity to say things that help your case, which are not responsive to the question.
>
> I hope I will not have to repeat the instruction further.
>
> Those several instances were in no way, by any stretch of the imagination, called for by the question; they were simply volunteering on your part to say things that you thought were helpful before the jury.
>
> It is not proper to do that in answers to questions. Simply answer the question that is put to you. . . . Understood?

Crile replied, "I understand." But the admonition had occurred outside the presence of the jury. By December 12th, his answers, including the eight paragraphs where there should have been just yes or no, incurred a rebuke in open court:

Your role as a witness on the stand is not that of a debater, and although it may be tempting to you to respond fully to all of what you see as the implications of a question, your proper function is simply to answer the question, and you will have the opportunity to be questioned by your own lawyer subsequently in a manner that will permit you to bring out other things that you might want to say.

The words and the attitude of a judge, state or federal, are of enormous consequence to the jury. In all but the rarest cases, jurors trust the judge completely for the duration of the case. Federal judges tend to have a special instinct for the press protections of the First Amendment. Both Judge Leval and Judge Sofaer were acutely aware of the importance of protecting speech, particularly speech that claims, as did both *Time*'s paragraph and CBS's ninety minutes, to report abuse of power, and were conscious as well of their own authority in the minds of their respective juries. Both judges were especially restrained, even kindly, in their few rebukes to witnesses. But, in spite of repeated mild admonitions from Judge Leval, Crile did not so much run away with as override Burt's questions, rarely troubling to answer, simply saying what he chose to say. Burt was not only unable to cut him off; he made the additional mistake of spending seven full days of the valuable hours allotted for his presentation on largely unfocussed questions to this witness, who in the hands of a more experienced litigator would have had precisely (if he had been brought to answer with precision) a lot to answer for.

Also, with his first "hostile" witness Burt gave signs of an undercurrent that began subtly but eventually determined the actual outcome of the trial: the unusual and developing relationship between himself and the opposing counsel, Boies. In the rare instances, for example, when he made timely and well-founded objections (in the course of Boies' cross-examination) or motions to strike (in the course of unresponsive answers to questions of his own), Burt began, increasingly, to glance not toward Judge Leval but toward Boies, as though in anticipation of a reaction from opposing counsel rather than of a ruling by the judge. Nonetheless, the case against the truth of the broadcast was at that point

such a strong one—with witnesses who ranked above Westmoreland testifying that no intelligence estimates had been concealed
from President Johnson or the Joint Chiefs; and military witnesses
directly below him, and others, high in the civilian C.I.A., testifying that no estimates had been, on his orders or otherwise, suppressed—that the derisive runaway witness and the growing deference of plaintiff's counsel to defendant's counsel did not appear
to matter much. Judge Leval's controversial position, that the
issue was not whether the President and the Joint Chiefs had in
fact been deceived but whether Westmoreland had intended, and
conspired, however unsuccessfully, to deceive them, left something for the jury to decide. His single other controversial ruling
was that, since journalism has no legal obligation to be fair, the
Benjamin Report, which addressed, among other issues, fairness,
was inadmissible and had no bearing on whether Crile or the other
CBS defendants had proceeded with Constitutional malice. This
left the jury to decide as well whether Crile's and the other CBS
defendants' decisions to ignore selectively what they had been told
by McNamara, Nitze, Rostow, Carver, others (if the jury believed
those witnesses who said they had been told it) constituted "knowing falsity" or "reckless disregard" or, on the contrary, mere
exercise of editorial judgment, whose legitimacy it was not the
business of courts or juries to decide. For the moment, however,
Westmoreland's case was going very well.

From mid-October of 1984 through mid-February of 1985, for
the duration of *Westmoreland* v. *CBS* and *Sharon* v. *Time*,
more than a hundred reporters were accredited for, and in more
or less regular attendance at, one case or the other. A strange sense
of moment and of urgency was reflected not only in the presence
on the courthouse steps each day of camera crews waiting, often
shivering in their parkas, for one of the principals either to enter
or to emerge but even by a yellow "Out of Service" sticker pasted,
for several weeks, over the slot for coins in one of a row of
telephone booths on the first floor, just outside *Sharon*. The phone
was in good working order. A reporter for one of the wire services

had put the sticker there to assure his own access to a phone when there was a general rush for the booths at every break. "Very few civil cases are decided by advocacy," Milton Gould said during a break, midway through the Sharon trial, to a reporter who had asked him how radically the outcome of the case upstairs might be affected by the fact that plaintiff's counsel seemed over-matched. "Because the facts control. In criminal cases, it's different. But most civil cases are decided by incontrovertible fact." Judge Leval, too, had said, very early in the trial upstairs, that the case would not be decided by lawyering. At another point, however, Gould said, "My kids," meaning his young partners and associates, in the months when he was ill, "performed a miracle of lawyering": and, later still, that a turning point in the preparation of Sharon's case had been the day when he persuaded Sharon to admit that letting the Phalangists enter the camps at Sabra and Shatila had been, on Sharon's part, a mistake. Sharon had protested that not even the Kahan Commission, when he had appeared before it, had required him to acknowledge a mistake. "But in the tortuous intricacies of American libel law," Gould said, persuading Sharon "transformed this case from a contest of shams to a contest of mistakes." There was more than one sense in which Sharon's suit and Westmoreland's became, paradoxically, one of the best things that could happen to the American press. Neither suit should ever have been brought. Once brought, neither suit should have been so aggressively defended. Because neither the ninety minutes nor the paragraph should have been broadcast or published, either. Whether it was Cravath, or the press defendants, or some unexamined, combative folly the clients and their law firm embarked upon together, the refusal to acknowledge, or even to consider, the possibility of human error caused both CBS and *Time* and their attorneys to spare no expense, and experience, apparently, no doubt or scruple, in transforming both suits into a contest not of mistakes but of legal and journalistic shams. The trials, as they evolved, had important implications for journalists, print and television, and for their audiences and readers. But the question was what accident or principle caused these cases, or shams, to take the form they took, or even to come before the courts at all.

In the fall of 1979, after it published David Halevy's story "Fears for Begin's Health," *Time* had, it emerged rather late in discovery, undertaken an investigation—as much to its credit as the Benjamin Report, triggered by the piece in *TV Guide,* had been, more recently, to the credit of CBS. Within six years, however, the magazine had changed so radically in its view of its own obligations that it not only abdicated any responsibility to inquire whether the paragraph at issue in the lawsuit was accurate but seemed positively embarrassed, in fact, tried actively, to a point very near the borderline of legal ethics, to conceal the results of the 1979 investigation, or even the fact that any investigation had taken place. The story had said that, according to confidential sources, a stroke two months before had so severely incapacitated Begin that he was unable to govern; and that three neurologists, including one named American, had been summoned to examine the Prime Minister, in secret, in a laboratory somewhere in Israel. Begin himself, among others, had so vociferously denied the story that Dean Fischer, then *Time*'s Jerusalem bureau chief, had checked with all five people Halevy claimed were "sources" (with the exception of one, whom Fischer characterized as "a close friend of Halevy's," and "a tipster"), and found that one had not even spoken with Halevy, and that another said the story was "fantastic," while all, including the American named specifically in the story, said that it was false. But on the first day of his deposition, September 11, 1984, Richard Duncan, *Time*'s chief of correspondents, replied, for example, to a question whether Fischer had got a "different version" from Halevy's and had told Duncan so, "I don't recall that. That people told him something—told him that they had said to Halevy something different than Halevy said they had told him?"

Q. Yes.
A. I don't recall that.

Also, within the first hour of the first day of Duncan's deposition, there occurred this colloquy:

Q. Do you maintain any ledgers or files of any kind with respect to the performance of reporters, correspondents?
A. No.
Q. So, to your knowledge, no documents exist at *Time* magazine with respect to the evaluation of particular reporters?
A. That is correct.

Within a few moments more, however:

Q. Does *Time* maintain personnel files for its reporters?
A. I maintain files for the correspondents. . . .
Q. [Does what the file contains] sometimes relate to the performance of the reporter?
A. It could be.

And then:

Q. Do you recall what is in the personnel file of Mr. Halevy?
A. No, I do not.

Richard Goldstein, who took Duncan's deposition (which was defended by Paul C. Saunders, another veteran of Cravath's defense of I.B.M. in anti-trust), immediately renewed an earlier request for the personnel files of all *Time* employees who had contributed to the paragraph at issue in the trial. Cravath, on behalf of *Time,* renewed an objection, that to find and produce the documents was "overbroad" and "unduly burdensome." As it turned out, the files took less than an hour to compile. Duncan was obviously proceeding in the absolute confidence that the documents would never be produced. Judge Sofaer ruled that *Time* must turn them over "prior to scheduled depositions" of witnesses placed to testify about them. Cravath waited until less than two hours before the last such deposition was at an end. At the trial, however, both the personnel file itself and Duncan's answers about it, and about the Begin health story, came back to present a major problem for *Time* in its defense. Because it turned out, from one letter in the file, that, alone among *Time*'s eighty-eight current correspondents (and perhaps among the correspondents in its history, certainly among those Duncan could recall), Halevy had, in 1980, been put on "probation"; and the file contained as well a memorandum from Duncan to *Time*'s three top editors which read, in part:

> At this moment, on the basis of the information given to me by Fischer, and of my talks with Halevy, I believe our story is wrong. Inescapably, that conclusion then requires a further decision as to whether Halevy was either (a) inexcusably shoddy in his reporting, or (b) intentionally misled us, or (c) was the victim of an incredibly well-orchestrated disinformation plot. . . . Begin's personal protest is not routine, and I consider that it essentially discredits the story. . . . Halevy's case rests on establishing that there is, indeed, as he says, a huge coverup. It is possible but I'm afraid he must prove that case . . . with much better evidence than he has for the original story.

Also:

> I have talked with David Halevy and he will be filing what he promises to be dramatic confirmation of the story late Thursday or early Friday.

Halevy never did file "dramatic confirmation" of the story; and a few weeks later *Time* published a sort of retraction. But the point is not only that *Time* should be at pains to conceal this essentially healthy self-examination (Duncan's memo also included a summary of the specific denials by all the "sources" Halevy claimed); it is that *Time*, through Duncan, through Kelly, the bureau chief, through all the many witnesses who testified, for example, that Halevy was an "excellent" reporter, one of "the top four or five" of *Time*'s investigative correspondents, should feel that it had to litigate, as it were to the death, over a single paragraph rather than to inquire, for its own sake, for economy's sake, for the honor of journalism, for the trust and the information of its readers, whether the paragraph, as published, was correct. Because the problem, as it emerged in court, was not that a reporter should once have been put on "probation," or that *Time* had once conducted an investigation and discovered a mistake. The problem was that *Time* assumed so aggressive a strategy in the litigation that it tried to conceal its own earlier, praiseworthy acknowledgment of fallibility, and thereby raised serious questions about the honesty of its witnesses in the present case. It is understandable that Duncan would want to protect the confidentiality of his personnel files; also that he should misunderstand the rules of discovery and testify on a misguided assumption that those files would never come to light. But to testify at his deposition that he did not recall anything about Halevy in those personnel files; and to offer a description of a walk, in May of 1982, with Halevy along the banks of the Nile, in the course of which, Duncan claimed, he actually criticized Halevy for being "too factual," and for "hitting hard with news significance," and not giving enough "interpretive material"; and then to become extremely vague in his recollection of an earlier walk, in Athens, in 1980, after the Begin health story and the retraction (about these matters, and throughout his deposition, Duncan has a remarkable density of "I don't recall"), raised serious questions about his veracity at trial. The personnel file, for example, contained another letter, dated February 13, 1980, from Duncan to Halevy, which began, "Dear David: This is the letter I promised you confirming our conversation in Athens"; went on to discuss the terms of the "probation"; and enumerated certain "conditions," which Halevy had accepted, "to correct that situation." One of the conditions was "A more obvious effort on your part to insure that what you report to *Time* . . . is printable, reliable information, reflecting *not just informed speculation* but the most likely true situation"; another was "A consistent effort on your part to report, and also to suggest, the 'meat and potatoes' everyday (or every week) stories from the bureau, not just specials and exclusives"; and a third was "multiple sourcing, when at all possible," on all stories. The difficulty was not that these letters, memos and files existed, or that the events reflected in them had occurred. It was that Duncan should claim so clearly to recall what was not really a criticism at all ("too factual," not enough "interpretive material") from one conversation and to have forgotten, or to recollect only vaguely, what would convey the flatly opposite impression (too little "reliable information," too much "just informed speculation") from another conversation, which was so clearly documented in his files.

There is no doubt that publications less serious than *Time* might never have conducted the internal investigation, which resulted in Duncan's memorandum and his letter (and that broadcasters less serious than CBS would never have produced the Benjamin Report); it is also true that less responsible publications, faced with discovery in a lawsuit, might have destroyed what files they could, and responded to specific document requests with the claim that they had no files. But, short of that, *Time* and, to a far lesser degree, CBS made every effort to conceal their own honorable attempts at self-examination, to the very borderline of what a jury could believe, and even of what the law of discovery permits. (Duncan, for example, it emerged at trial, went, immediately after the close of his deposition, to look at the files and memorandums, which he had just claimed, under oath, so vaguely and, as the trial revealed, inaccurately to recall.) And the problem in *Sharon* went further still: the press witnesses tried to justify their apparent absolute, even righteous, lack of interest in the factual truth of their paragraph, as published, with an increasingly odd conception of the law itself. Witness after witness, having said, as though making a modest disclaimer, "I am not a lawyer," proceeded to explain that once suit was brought, all responsibility for investigating or attempting in any way to check a story shifted entirely to the attorneys. Asked, for instance, on December 13, 1984, his first day on the stand, whether he or anyone else at *Time* had made any effort, from the time of Halevy's original Worldwide Memo Item of December 6, 1982, to the present, to learn the identity or check the reliability of Halevy's sources, Duncan replied, "We have not, at *Time.*" Also, "It has been my longstanding impression as a reporter . . . that it was not correct"; "It would have been improper"; "Once I was sued, it wasn't wise for me to have that particular knowledge"; "Nor did I wish to know"; "That was at the time when the lawyers were taking this thing out of the hands of the journalists, as far as we were concerned"; finally, "Some reporters go to jail. . . . I guess the shortest answer would be, I thought the fewest of us who might be liable to go to jail should be liable." Quite apart from the ignorance this showed on the part of people highly placed, after all, in the profession of journalism about the very shield law they invoked so frequently at other times—indeed, the specific intent of the law is to *enable* journalists to check with "sources," whose names, in cases of this kind, they can neither be compelled nor be sent to jail for refusing to reveal—there was the note of drama, even of heroism. One might expect from the leader, in an occupied country in time of war, of a brave little group in the resistance just this sort of statement: the fewer who know, and thereby risk jail or worse, the better. It was as though the press defendants, CBS and *Time,* both apparently sincerely, considered themselves in just this way embattled—having, also apparently sincerely, no conception of their own size and strength. And in *Sharon* it was as though the whole aura of mystification that surrounded the "confidential source" attached as well to the attorneys, leaving the journalists with two oracles, and two bases for a professional obligation not to inquire.

"I, as chief of correspondents, did not [inquire]," Duncan replied, in court, to yet another question, "because at that point the role to conduct that kind of investigation had passed from me to the lawyers. The lawyers were starting a very big investigation, which continues to this day." The position, legal, moral, intellectual, journalistic, of the press defendants, especially in *Sharon,* was essentially embodied in that answer. The little band of sometimes stoic but at other times complacent and even flip resistance fighters hired counsel. Their attorneys, committed to the most aggressive and thoroughgoing modern style of advocacy, did undertake "a very big investigation," trying to prove that, far from being instances of knowing falsity or reckless disregard, the defamatory statements were substantially and literally true, and were even, in effect, understatements: something more, and worse, was true. The "very big investigation" in *Westmoreland* consisted largely of trying to elicit, from persons who had appeared on the broadcast more or less in support of the program's thesis, statements far stronger and far less ambiguous than their statements on the broadcast; also of trying to find other witnesses who might support the program's thesis; and, finally, of massive subpoenas, depositions and requests for document production, on the scale of a major suit in anti-trust. In *Sharon,* however, the "very big investigation, which continues to this day," turned out to consist only secondarily of this last form of discovery—though it included what one judge in Washington dismissed as a "sweeping, un-focussed request" for documents from agencies of the United States government, which "makes absolutely no effort to demon-strate relevance," and an attempt to subpoena an Israeli general (who was temporarily in Washington), which another judge dis-missed as "unprofessional." The "very big investigation" con-sisted more importantly of the research involved in gathering, from publications of all kinds, such items as the stories in French and Dutch newspapers and magazines, and the transcript of Sharon's public testimony, on October 25, 1982, before the Kahan Commission—on which all *Time* employees who had contributed to the paragraph could claim they had relied. (The thoroughness of Cravath's investigation could not, in all probability, have over-looked something as nearby and accessible as Duncan's personnel files, which made all the more mystifying the attorneys' permitting him to testify about their contents in such a misleading and, as it happened, ultimately damaging way.) But the predominant ele-ment in the "very big investigation" by the attorneys in *Sharon* was simply this: an attempt to confirm what *Time* said, by confirming that Halevy's "confidential sources" had said what Halevy said they said. The sense in which the investigation, as Duncan put it, "continues to this day" was that *Time* claimed, through both its witnesses and its attorneys, that the investigation *by the attorneys* after the publication of the paragraph did confirm it. On at least four occasions—once right after Sharon brought suit; once after Halevy had read Sharon's deposition; and twice in the course of the trial itself (once when the jury was actually deliberating)—*Time* claimed to have reconfirmed that the para-graph was true. The difficulty, as it turned out, was that the only confirmation the lawyers' "very big investigation" yielded came from Halevy's "sources," or, more precisely, from what Halevy, at each of these post-publication stages, said his "sources" said. As though this position, sincerely and adamantly held, were not in itself sufficiently circular and odd, it was carried a step further. Halevy at one point claimed for what he had "learned," after publication, on behalf of the attorneys, the work-product privilege:

> A. This is the work product of Mr. Barr, your Honor. . . . So I think, for the last twelve months, I worked for Mr. Barr, and for Cravath, Swaine & Moore, and . . . they wanted my knowledge . . . And we talked to a lot of people, to a lot of sources.

And the attorneys claimed, in effect, the journalistic shield. In the end, Judge Sofaer did sustain an objection; the shield, after all, protects only who "sources" are, not what they said. But this was on the last of Halevy's seven days on the witness stand. On the second, in consultation with his attorneys, he had already given an answer that caused the judge to comment, "This situation is even more puzzling, where a person invokes a privilege over something he had previously *said himself.*" And the attorneys' "investigation," such as it was, turned out to yield only a small series of dire intimations, cloaked in "work product," derived again from "confidential sources," by the same Halevy, saying the paragraph, as published, was truer than he had ever known it was:

> Q. Do I understand you to say that since the article was prepared you have learned more information which makes the paragraph in the article totally irrelevant, is that what you said?
> A. I didn't say that.
> Q. Well, sir, let me read you this, reading from page 752 of your deposition. . . . "A. Oh, no, oh, no. I think you misunderstood me. Since that article was prepared I learned more information which makes this paragraph look totally irrelevant. . . ."
> Now, sir, would you tell us what more information you learned which would make the paragraph totally irrelevant?
> [Five successive unresponsive answers.]
> THE COURT: Why did it make the paragraph irrelevant? That is the word you used. Was it an inappropriate word, you think?
> THE WITNESS: I think I still stand behind that word. Since the lawsuit was filed I think we approached more sources. We

got ahold of more minutes, notes. . . . I don't know everything that was done by Mr. Barr and his team. I think a couple of things—

THE COURT: Just testify about yourself, what you know.

THE WITNESS: I said it there, that this is the work product of Mr. Barr, your Honor.

MR. GOLD: Can I address that for a second, your Honor? Certain material we do believe constitutes our work product that Mr. Halevy did help gather. . . .

THE COURT: I don't understand it. Is he saying that these are materials that he will not reveal to us? Is that what you are saying? Was it covered by the work product privilege?

MR. GOLD: I am not sure, unless I can speak to the witness, the full extent as to what he has in mind.

[More questions and unresponsive answers.]

THE COURT: He wants to know *what did you come up with,* that is all.

THE WITNESS: . . . I did not go to any meeting alone, without the lawyers present. So you want me to talk now about meetings where the lawyers were present? With pleasure.

THE COURT: Mr. Gould doesn't want you to talk in terms of lawyers being present or not being present. You are introducing this element about your lawyers being present. I wish you would leave that out of it. Your lawyers are representing you here. They are representing Time Inc., here. They are not witnesses in the case. What you should just tell him is *what did you find out?* What information did you develop? . . .

MR. GOLD: With your Honor's permission, can I speak to the witness to find out the extent of the material?

MR. GOULD: I object to it.

THE COURT: Sustained. This is a very simple question. You say the story became irrelevant because you found out so many other things, presumably. He just wants to know what other things you found out.

[Two full pages of questions and unresponsive answers.]

Q. Now, sir, you did not learn anything more about the visit of Sharon to the Gemayel family, which is referred to in the paragraph, did you? . . .

A. No, sir.

Q. And you did not learn any more about what was in Appendix B?

A. No, sir.
[Etc.]

This verged, obviously, on farce; and it is possible that when journalists and lawyers combine their particular certainties, totems and obfuscations, as well as their notions of what the truth, or even a fact, is and its uses, the result is almost inevitably farce. But even without these "privileges," these chimerical licenses and restraints, the position became this: A story is filed; a publication believes it and, without further investigation, prints it; the person whom the story most directly concerns disputes it; the publication, still without further investigation of any kind, stands by the story and refuses to retract it; the publication is sued; now claiming a positive duty not to investigate, the publication continues to stand by its story, and leaves what investigation there will be, if any, to its lawyers. The lawyers are advocates; they have no interest in the results of an investigation, except for its effect on their client's interest in the case. In the real world, the client's journalistic interest in being accurate may be in absolute conflict with its legal interest in court in prevailing in the litigation. (The lawyer's obligations as an officer of the court, under the adversary system, may be inescapably in conflict with his obligations to his client; but this is a matter that legal philosophers tend either to argue, without any prospect of resolution, or simply to deny.) The press client's choice, to pursue this position throughout the litigation, is considered by the defendant and by his colleagues indispensable, in some way, to the defense of the First Amendment. Part of this development seems to be the result of processes by which a sound, even a noble, position—that the press should be free to publish, and free from harassment or oppression, after publication, by men in power—slides into cant; and a small chapter of modern legal history might be called the cant of the libel bar. But part of it has to do as well with the peculiar powers, capacities and limitations of the press at this historical moment; and to whom or what, if anyone or anything, it considers itself accountable. As it happens, there has been in recent years a problem of accountability in the military as well. Disasters, whether of unpreparedness, incompetence or corruption, used to be followed, immediately and invariably, by courts-martial, inquiries to assign responsibility. Some-times the outcome was not what would be recognized in a civilian court as justice, but there existed in the military at least the notion that *someone* was accountable—a notion that appears to have vanished, in the absence of courts-martial, since at least the disas-trous episode of the rescue mission to Iran, and until at least as recently as the calamity in Beirut, of marines insufficiently pro-tected, and blown up in their beds. It was to the press, in print and on the air, that everyone, including the military, had seemed in recent years accountable, with the reporter frequently as counsel; the anchorman or editor as judge; and the court, each living room. In *Sharon* and *Westmoreland,* the press, in what should be one of its highest and least arguable functions, to report on the abuse of power by men (in this case, military men) in power, went somehow awry, and found itself called to account before two juries in defense of principles that appeared, gradually (and in the course of what one of the judges called "this all-out litigation strategy"), less and less compatible with its interests not as litigants but as press.

O ne peculiarity of transcripts of trials and depositions is that almost nobody ever reads them. Attorneys read them, in their more or less daily segments, for the day-to-day conduct of the case. Other attorneys, perhaps, later read them, in search of arguments to raise upon appeal. But the purpose of a trial is, of course, to get a dispute resolved and over with. The jury is specifically precluded from knowing anything but what is pre-sented to it in court, on a quotidian basis (and what it chooses, in the course of its deliberations, to read or hear again); once a verdict is reached, there is almost nothing to be gained from reading the completed record. The transcript either supports the verdict or raises an uneasiness that the trial should have laid to rest. Though it is essential to our system that official transcripts of trials and depositions be on file in their respective courts, there exists no branch of legal studies which is occupied with transcripts at the level of trial. The transcripts, in all the many courts, local, state and federal, would be so many and voluminous (the records of the trials alone, in *Sharon* and *Westmoreland,* run to four thousand one hundred and eighty and nine thousand seven hundred and forty-five pages) that it is not clear where such a branch of studies could begin. And so, official and necessary as they are, an accumulation of all the individual biographies of our legal system, they remain, in their completed form, unread. A study, to some small depth, of the transcripts of depositions and the trial in *Sharon,* and of certain events at the trial in *Westmoreland,* reveals with a clarity, perhaps greater than that of the litigation as it unfolded day to day, just what the personalities and issues were, and what was decided by the end.

T he lore had it that the Sharon case ended in a kind of moral victory for Sharon, reflected in certain of the jury's verdicts and in *Time*'s concession that there was no reference to any discussion of revenge between Sharon and the Gemayels in Appendix B—a public-relations setback of considerable proportions for *Time.* But also that *Time*'s position (that the paragraph was still "substantially true"; that the attribution of the "disputed material" to Appendix B was a "relatively minor inaccuracy"; that evidence of the discussion of "revenge" existed somewhere; and that *Time* had been denied "due process" by Israel in the search for that evidence) had been vindicated, in some way. The lore also had it that the Westmoreland case ended in an absolute rout of Westmoreland, in that he was so daunted by the testimony of two witnesses, General Joseph McChristian and Colonel Gains Hawkins, that he abandoned what he had come to realize was a hopeless case. The "due process" argument was one more legalistic obfuscation, an attempt, for public-relations purposes, to use a precise and important phrase from Constitutional law in circumstances where it had no meaning and no application. There is no sense in which it is possible to say that a litigant in a case before an American court has been denied (or, for that matter, has been granted) "due process" by a foreign government. And it was, after all, *Time* that initially claimed access to the "notes," or "minutes," of the meeting at Bikfaya between Sharon and the Gemayels (and to Appendix B), by way of Halevy's "confidential sources," whose identities it refused, under the shield law, to divulge. It could hardly claim that "due process" had been denied it in reaching the same "sources" from whom it claimed already to have "learned." In his Opinion and Order of November 12, 1984, Judge Sofaer put it very simply: "*Time* cannot deprive itself of using information it has and claim at the same time that it has been denied due process" in its search for that information. What Cravath seemed to want to say was that *Time* had been treated, in some general way, unfairly by the State of Israel in Israel's refusal to grant access to the entirety of its secret archives—where *Time* hoped to find something, anything, as compromising as its paragraph about Sharon. But there was, legalistic obfuscations aside, something inescapably circular about *Time*'s fundamental claim. "I have to believe it," Kelly had said at one point in his deposition, and he repeated this at the trial: "I have not seen Appendix B. And I am totally unconvinced it is not in Appendix B. So I believe it is in Appendix B."

Similarly, at trial, Duncan:

Q. At the time . . . did you believe that [Halevy's] reporting was unreliable?
A. No.
Q. Why not?
A. Why did I not believe it was unreliable?
Q. Yes, sir.
A. Because I continued to believe it was reliable and I continued to believe that it was reliable reporting. We continued to rely on his reporting. That is the best evidence.

These little circles of belief (a favorite word of both Kelly's and Duncan's was "logical") characterized *Time*'s position to the end. *Time* believed it because *Time* had said it; and if there was no other evidence for it the unmistakable implication was that Sharon, the Israeli government, the Kahan Commission, Justice

Kahan, and, finally, even Judge Sofaer, were involved in a coverup.

The lore was correct in depicting the outcome of *Westmoreland* as a rout, but mistaken about its causes, its meaning, and its terms. The Joint Statement with which, on February 19, 1985, the lawsuit ended read:

> General William C. Westmoreland and CBS today jointly announced the discontinuance of the Westmoreland suit against CBS, Mike Wallace, George Crile, and Sam Adams.
>
> The suit pertained to a CBS News broadcast "The Uncounted Enemy: A Vietnam Deception," broadcast on January 23, 1982.
>
> The matters treated in that broadcast—and the broadcast itself —have been extensively examined over the past two and a half years both in discovery and then through documents and witnesses presented by both sides in Federal Court.
>
> Historians will long consider this and other matters related to the war in Vietnam. Both parties trust their actions have broadened the public record on this matter.
>
> Now both General Westmoreland and CBS believe that their respective positions have been effectively placed before the public for its consideration and that continuing the legal process at this stage would serve no further purpose.
>
> CBS respects General Westmoreland's long and faithful service to his country and never intended to assert, and does not believe, that General Westmoreland was unpatriotic or disloyal in performing his duties as he saw them.
>
> General Westmoreland respects the long and distinguished journalistic tradition of CBS and the rights of journalists to examine the complex issues of Vietnam and to present perspectives contrary to his own.

Even the most cursory reading of these paragraphs shows that they contain no concessions whatever on the part of CBS, and that Westmoreland could have obtained such a statement not only without ever bringing suit but even if he had brought suit and lost. Also, the most elementary principles of draftsmanship would at least have substituted the word "dishonorable" for "unpatriotic or disloyal" (the statement as it is barely exonerates Westmoreland of something not even the program had accused him of: treason); deleted the phrase (unworthy of both parties in its condescension) "as he saw them"; and added a paragraph to the effect that each party had agreed to bear its own legal costs. The statement, nonetheless, would remain irremediably trivial. Blandly to dismiss as a matter of "perspectives" an outright allegation of "conspiracy" to deceive not only dissolved in euphemism the central issue of the program and the case, it inadvertently brought an ironic focus to the words "CBS News broadcast" and "the rights of journalists." Because, though the program may have been produced within the CBS News department, and even purported to present a major scoop (that Westmoreland's "conspiracy" to deceive had led to a military defeat at Tet, and to the ultimate loss of the war), the program was clearly not, in any conventional sense, "news." Nor were its producers and interviewers "journalists." And the scoop, or, as the statement would have it, the "perspective," was demonstrably wrong: Westmoreland led no such conspiracy; Tet was a public-relations catastrophe but not a military defeat; and though the war was lost, the loss could hardly be attributed to a conspiracy or a defeat that never was. An example of the sort of testimony, on just the matter of Tet, with which the trial "broadened the public record" occurred on February 8, 1985, between the day of McChristian's testimony and the first day of Hawkins', in another colloquy, between Westmoreland's chief counsel, Burt, and the defense witness Crile:

Q. And did you believe, Mr. Crile, prior to the broadcast, that Tet was a terrific military victory for the United States?
A. [Four paragraphs, containing neither yes nor no.]
Q. Mr. Crile, did you tell any executive at CBS, after the broadcast, that in a war of attrition Tet was a terrific victory for our side?
A. [Three paragraphs, containing neither yes nor no.]

The witness was shown notes of a conversation between him and CBS executives, in which he was identified by the initial "G."

Q. Did you *say those words,* Mr. Crile?
A. [Two full pages, which contain neither yes nor no but include a strange insistence that the transcript "has three dots."]

Q. "G," that is George Crile, isn't it?

A. I presume so.

Q. [Quoting "G" in the notes] "If you're talking about a war of attrition, *Tet was a terrific victory for our side*"?

A. There were three dots there, Mr. Burt.

Q. Three dots? Thank you, Mr. Crile.

A more experienced, and, by this point in the trial, presumably less exhausted, litigator would have elicited from Crile no paragraphs, nothing about what he "presumed," no remarks about "dots" or other punctuation, but a simple and, on the basis of the notes, undeniable "Yes." It was clear, however, on the "broadened" record, that even Crile himself had not believed that element of the program's thesis which ascribed to the "conspiracy" a military *defeat* at Tet.

But in the lore it was not Crile or any of the other CBS contributors to the program who so demoralized Westmoreland. It was McChristian and Hawkins, those two former subordinates, one a fellow-graduate of West Point. The exigencies of news reporting, particularly daily reporting under deadline pressures, could not help contributing to a myth, or at least an overly hasty explanation, of what had led to the Joint Statement. From a plaintiff's point of view, the statement, or a settlement of any kind, came at the worst possible moment—namely, at the height, and nearly at the end, of almost six weeks' presentation of the defendant's case. If he was going to settle at all, a better time, obviously, would have been earlier, at the end of his own, very strong presentation; or later, after the summations of both sides to the jury; or later still, while the jury was deliberating; or even after the verdicts had come in. As it was, the "discontinuance" of the case was announced in the course of a three-day holiday weekend, Washington's Birthday, which meant that the jurors were exposed to three days of television and newspaper commentary about the meaning of Westmoreland's "capitulation"—whether it repeated, in some way, the American experience in Vietnam; what were its ramifications for First Amendment freedoms; and so forth—before the agreement was actually announced to them in court. And even then, it was by no means clear what the verdicts would have been. Interviews, after the last day of *Westmoreland* v. *CBS,* revealed that most of the jurors (height of the defendant's case and three days' coverage notwithstanding) believed Westmoreland, liked Boies, disliked both Crile and Burt, but simply had not made up their minds. In any event, before McChristian and Hawkins took the stand Westmoreland was still suing; afterward, or, more precisely, in the middle of Hawkins' cross-examination, he was not. So the explanation *ought* to lie in the fact that they testified, and in who they were and what they said. Of course, Westmoreland and his attorneys had known for months, from their depositions well before the trial began, what both McChristian and Hawkins were going to say; and if Westmoreland had somehow missed it he would have been reminded when Boies used a videotape of McChristian, saying virtually the same things, in his opening statement of the trial. The lore of the unanticipated betrayal, however, not only made better, simpler sense; it made, in another way, better, that is, more sentimental, copy. The "discontinuance" and the statement had, however, almost nothing to do with McChristian or Hawkins—or, for that matter, with Westmoreland.

McChristian had been J-2 M.A.C.V. (that is, chief intelligence officer in General Westmoreland's command) from July 13, 1965, until June 1, 1967, when, in the realization, by his own account, of an old dream, and not (as the CBS program had suggested) as a form of exile or demotion, he became Commanding General of the 2nd Armored Division, at Fort Hood, Texas. He was later promoted further, to Chief of Intelligence of the United States Army. In 1971, he retired, to Hobe Sound, in Florida. At first, as a witness, under Boies' direct examination, McChristian seemed forthright and well informed, with a trace, perhaps, of vanity. He testified, for instance, that in his very first week in Vietnam he had founded C.I.C.V. (Combined Intelligence Center, Vietnam)— which, it seemed he could not help adding, was "one of the *finest* supports of *combat intelligence* that was *ever developed* in support of our forces in wartime." In view of the outcome of the war in Vietnam, and in comparison with, for example, the breaking of German and Japanese codes in the Second World War, there was an intimation of something both comic and frightening in that claim. There were intimations as well, in McChristian's early testimony, of the quality of "intelligence" he had in mind. "All of your reports, all of your studies," he said, rather typically, at one point, "go to your estimators. Your estimators have access to all types of intelligence, whatever it may be; and then they, taking into consideration the objective of the estimate, come up with their estimative procedures." Also, "They used the total estimate of enemy strength in the production of what we referred to as the estimate of the enemy situation, which is the apex of all of your intelligence activities"; and, "The intelligence officer is not only responsible for the enemy, but he is responsible to report on the weather, and the terrain and the enemy . . . but I won't get into it. They aren't as germane." Boies seemed serene with testimony of this sort, and the jury sat, as usual, with its yellow legal pads; but the primary reason the defense had, apparently, for calling this particular witness, and the only substantive testimony (germane, as the witness himself might put it, to the central issue of the trial) that the witness seemed placed to give, was this: that about two weeks before his departure, on June 1, 1967, from Saigon for Fort Hood he had given Westmoreland, in the form of a cable, a briefing on revised estimates of enemy troop strength, which, McChristian said, he had proposed sending, over Westmoreland's signature, to both Admiral Sharp's command in the Pacific and the Joint Chiefs, in Washington. According to McChristian, Westmoreland had not only "blocked" the cable: "He looked up at me, and he said, 'If I send that cable to Washington, it will create a political bombshell.' "

Q. Sir, I want to ask you, are you absolutely positive General Westmoreland used the term "political bombshell" during that meeting?
A. Yes, I am. I am as sure of it as I am seeing people in front of me right now. I was so surprised by it that there were enough words said there that *burned themselves right into my memory,* and there were not many, but that was part of them.

There would, of course, be nothing inherently improper in a commander's using the words "political bombshell" in reacting to the suggestion of a subordinate, or in his taking the time to inquire independently into the basis of the subordinate's entirely new statistics—and McChristian's estimates were, according to documents and other witnesses, in fact transmitted within days to Admiral Sharp and the Joint Chiefs. But Westmoreland had testified in court some weeks before that the words "political bombshell" were "not in my lexicon." McChristian seemed to be calling into question Westmoreland's veracity on this mildly electrifying point. McChristian's interlocutor on cross-examination was not, however, Westmoreland's chief counsel, Burt, but David Dorsen, a widely experienced Washington attorney—who had served, for example, as assistant chief counsel to the Ervin Committee at the time of Watergate. Dorsen's low-key, almost gentle style seemed, deceptively, to verge upon the ineffectual as, in marked contrast to almost all the other attorneys in the lawsuit, he built up a case to be used later, in summation to the jury, rather than for immediate, transitory effect. This courtroom style is remarkably unsuited to press coverage (and the summations, of course, never came); but under Dorsen's cross-examination McChristian did not fare well. Seeming not to want to address, for the moment or perhaps at all, the question of the "political bombshell," Dorsen embarked on an apparently innocent line of inquiry, which he had previously used on other defense witnesses, notably Sam Adams, to quietly devastating effect. McChristian had already testified, in support of his view of the superlative quality of American intelligence in Vietnam, that Order of Battle estimates were "updated" not just monthly, or even weekly, but "daily, if information warranted." "General McChristian," Dorsen began, "if you had information on enemy strength that was not in the . . . Order of Battle summaries, that was relevant to a mission of an American fighting unit in the field, did you provide that information to the American unit?" The meaning of the question, which seemed to require a simple yes or no, was plain: Would the witness, a professional soldier, even granting (or at least supposing) that information was being suppressed (or "blocked"), on the orders of Westmoreland, from his military and civilian superiors in Washington, withhold that information as well from the American soldiers actually at risk of being killed? No intelligence official (even those who claimed to have acquiesced in the deception of superiors about

enemy troop strength) could quite bring himself to say he had kept
the truth from fighting units. And yet the estimates relayed to
Washington and those conveyed to fighting units were the same.
Dorsen's previous yes-or-no question had elicited from McChristian an answer of six unresponsive paragraphs. "Here again, Mr.
Dorsen," McChristian now replied, "we are skating around hypotheticals and not talking specifics . . . but we are getting in a
nebulous area, and I think it could be misleading, and I think it
would behoove me to ask you to please give me the context of what
you're talking about." The answer, such as it was, seemed wary
enough (and the vocabulary was entirely, perhaps lamentably,
characteristic not only of McChristian but of most defense witnesses who were former officials of intelligence); but McChristian
did not seem intellectually equipped to sense the specific nature of
the trap in this whole line of questions:

Q. Was there ever an occasion where you, to your knowledge, or
your staff, to your knowledge, withheld relevant information on
the enemy from the American forces in the field?
A. Did I personally—
Q. Or your staff, to your knowledge, fail to convey to American
forces in the field relevant information on the capabilities of the
enemy, whether or not [it] was in the . . . monthly Order of Battle
summary?
A. Mr. Dorsen, here again I want the context of that explained to
me, to be able to give an accurate answer.

Dorsen, sweetly but inexorably, made ever more clear the "context" of the simple question—to which, of course, he had not yet
received the simple "Yes," "No" or "I don't recall" upon which
a lawyer with a perhaps more bullying style would have insisted.
Did either McChristian or his staff acquiesce in the deceit (by
which McChristian claimed to have been surprised, in the "block-
ing" of his cable) to the extent of keeping soldiers, as well, in
ignorance, with the result that they were killed?

A. I personally flew in the airplanes . . . and I communicated to the
units on the ground and sanitized the information. . . . We had

a way of doing it and sanitizing it, and it was definitely in line with my instructions to my staff throughout that intelligence must get to the commander, who can do something about it, in time to do something about it.

Also,

And be specific on what you are talking about.

Dorsen having elicited, however ramblingly, from McChristian (as from other defense witnesses) that the "conspiracy" to withhold "estimates" from the White House did not extend to withholding them from soldiers in the field (and since the size of the enemy contemplated in those "estimates" was the same), the "conspiracy" crumbled, by implication, from the ground up.

Dorsen left the subject. He asked instead whether McChristian had happened to "learn, on your last day in Vietnam, that there was going to be a reorganization involving certain responsibilities for intelligence operations."

A. That's the end of the question?
Q. Yes.

And McChristian, having begun what appeared to be another rambling disquisition, about a dinner held in his honor at the American Embassy in Saigon with "key people, military and civilian" ("I was highly honored by this, and they were all very kind to me"), suddenly focussed on the question—not to answer yes or no but to reveal that at the Embassy dinner he had indeed learned that there had been a new study, and that although his plane would leave Saigon at noon the following day, he had asked to see it.

> I was scanning this thing very rapidly, and the constant thoughts that were going through my mind is, ". . . I wouldn't do it that way, this is wrong, this will destroy what I have been building . . ." I had a very, very negative reaction to that study. Of course, another thought kept going through my mind, "Why wasn't I involved in this?"

Distinct questions of bureaucratic turf were beginning to emerge. In response to the same yes-or-no question, McChristian embarked on another narrative, to the effect that, having learned that the study was prepared under the direction of Ambassador Komer, he had rushed first to the office of Komer himself (to whom he said, "I want you to know that it has not been coördinated with my staff. It has not been coördinated with me," and announced his intention to take the matter to Westmoreland); then to the office of Westmoreland (to whom he said, "Sir, I have just read this study. It was not coördinated with my staff. It was not coördinated with me"); then he had rushed back to his own office, grabbed his hat, and gone to the airport at Tan Son Nhut for the journey home. "And I assure you that I felt like I had been kicked in my stomach when I left there." This testimony had travelled a considerable emotional distance from "your estimators," and "their estimative procedures," and "hypotheticals," and "nebulous area." Two questions later:

Q. And is it correct that you developed an animosity toward Robert Komer as a result of that?

A. That is not correct, Mr. Dorsen. I have never taken animosity. I was very hurt. . . . Did I feel that I should have been involved in that study? Absolutely. Did I feel that I could have contributed to it? Absolutely. [Then an almost unintelligible ramble.]

Q. Isn't it true, General McChristian, that you loathed Robert Komer and you loathed [your successor] General Davidson?

A. No, sir, that is not true. I don't have that type of temperament in my body to loathe somebody. . . . *I loved every single minute of my service.* . . . The next man to come in, it's best for him to do. Did I feel I should have been in on it? Yes. [More unintelligible ramble.]

Embedded in the ramble, responsive in no way to the original question (which, again, required, after all, only yes or no), were these sentences concerning General Davidson: "I never considered, like some people have reported, that we were rivals or competitors. That was no concern of mine whatsoever." Another sort of attorney might have pressed McChristian on some of the more emotional elements of his testimony (whether, for example, the moment when he felt as if he had been "kicked in my stomach" was contemplated in his having "loved every single minute of my service"); Dorsen, however, like some kindly though implacable therapist, continued in his own mild style.

> Q. Didn't [General Davidson] undo some of the things that you did in Vietnam, and you resented it, General McChristian?
> A. He undid, so I have been told, but I wasn't there. I don't know what he did. I had no resentment then. I have no resentment now. I made no effort to find out did he change anything I set up. . . . It was not my concern.

So far, whatever else it might reveal, the questioning seemed to leave untouched the matter of the "political bombshell." The word "loathe," a few questions back, however, had appeared so uncharacteristic of Dorsen's general manner and vocabulary that it seemed certain to be based on something other than his own surmise. And so it was. Immediately after the name "McChristian" in Samuel Adams' "list of sixty," upon which Adams and Crile had drawn for the production of the program, were the words "loathes Komer and Davidson." Cravath, of course, knew of Adams' list and notes (had, in fact, possession of them); so it came as no surprise when the witness, asked whether he knew of "any basis that Mr. Adams would have" for making such a note, should recover his composure sufficiently to reply, like a lawyer (or, more precisely, like a well-coached witness), "I can only testify to what I know, Mr. Dorsen, not what somebody else knows." Adams' notes, however, went on to quote McChristian purporting directly to quote Westmoreland. McChristian first denied having quoted Westmoreland to Adams, then briefly resumed his preoccupation with "context" ("I don't recall saying that. I'd have to see whatever context you have, Mr. Dorsen"), and, finally, denied that he had ever quoted Westmoreland to Adams or to anyone till now, when he was "sworn and under oath."

This (and perhaps something else by now in the demeanor of his witness) led Boies to request a bench conference, at the sidebar: because if McChristian's testimony on this point was accurate, then two of Boies' primary witnesses were at odds: Adams in attributing to McChristian a direct quote from Westmoreland, and McChristian in denying that he had ever quoted Westmoreland until he was obliged to, in this lawsuit, under oath. Boies argued long and hard (in the bench conference, outside the hearing of the jury) against the admissibility, on technical grounds, of Adams' notes to impeach McChristian's testimony. The argument was unsuccessful. It was followed, however, by a ten-minute break, and when McChristian resumed the stand he seemed to have resumed as well his early confidence and speaking style:

> If General Westmoreland was interested in the intelligence . . . if he was interested in the criteria, the methodology, the definitions, certainly he should be asking me. But he didn't ask me any of those questions. All he stated was that he was concerned that if he sent [the cable] it would create a political bombshell and to leave it with him.

Though this answer was in no way responsive to the pending question (which would, again, have required a simple yes or no), McChristian dismissed as "hypotheticals," which he disdained to answer, all questions whether Westmoreland might have held the cable up for study and then passed McChristian's estimates on to his superiors (as, it was clear from other evidence, he had): "You would have to show me the context of that, Mr. Dorsen, for me to know." And he seemed content repeatedly to ascribe to Westmoreland the phrase "political bombshell," which must by now have been as ineradicably engraved upon the jury's mind as the witness claimed it had been, since that day in mid-May of 1967, upon his own. Then, to two simple yes-or-no questions about whether he had said (in a tape-recorded interview with Don Kowet, of *TV Guide,* of which he now had before him the verbatim transcript) the words "No, absolutely not" (in answer to Kowet's "Did you have the feeling, at any time, that you were being asked to suppress information?") and "I did not" (in answer to Kowet's follow-up "You did not?"), McChristian replied, "He didn't ask me for the criteria, he didn't ask me about the definitions, he didn't ask me about the methodology."

Q. Do you recall whether [Kowet] asked you whether you felt you were being asked to suppress information, and you told him that you did not?

A. Mr. Dorsen, I don't recall specifically. I may or may not have said something like this. But I would like to see the context, please. . . .

Now, the question, please.

Q. Whether Mr. Kowet asked you "Did you have the feeling at any time that you were being asked to suppress information?" and whether you answered "No, absolutely not," and whether Mr. Kowet said "You did not?" and you said "I did not."

A. O.K. I want to put this in proper context.

Q. Could I ask you first, General McChristian, whether you recall whether you said that to Mr. Kowet?

A. I want to put it in proper context first, and I will answer specifically. [Increasingly unintelligible gabble.]

Then, mildly and as if it were a matter of no consequence, Dorsen began to change the subject:

Q. Now, you testified, I believe, that the words "political bombshell" are burned in your mind, in your memory, is that correct?

A. Yes, sir, that's correct.

Q. Didn't you tell George Crile, when you were being videotaped, that *you didn't recall the precise words* that General Westmoreland used?

A. I would like to see that in context. I don't believe I said that.

But, of course, McChristian had said precisely that, and Dorsen had the videotape and the verbatim transcript. A few moments later, still to the question had he said the words or hadn't he, McChristian replied, in a sequence that (allowing for the absence, in the peculiar circumstances of the case, of melodrama) precedes, in soap operas, the disintegration of a witness on the stand:

A. At this time I again was trying to avoid—

THE COURT: I am sorry. I have to interrupt you. You are simply to answer the question that's asked of you. . . .

A. . . . . This was not something I was giving under oath. . . . I tried to avoid quoting General Westmoreland. . . . I knew, without quoting him, that he had said "If I send this to Washington it will create a political bombshell."

Q. You wouldn't have lied to Mr. Crile, though, would you have?

A. I would not lie to anybody.

Q. You remember Mr. Crile asking you, "Do you remember *any of his words?*" referring to General Westmoreland, and whether you said, "I *can't recall* his exact words at this time, but that is my strong impression . . ."?

A. Can you show me that, please? [Pause] Yes, at this particular time I was aware of what General Westmoreland had stated, and I was not telling him the exact words.

Q. You did tell—

A. I was giving him the gist of the facts that did happen. . . . I was of the opinion that if he sent it back to Washington it would create a political bombshell. . . . I may have said that. . . . Here I wasn't quoting it. This is basically the same thought, same words, I might say again, Mr. Dorsen, when this—

THE COURT: I'm sorry. If you are answering the question that was asked, you may answer it. But if you are providing comments, that is going beyond the question.

A. I will hold up.

This small exchange, about the words "political bombshell," attributed so firmly to General Westmoreland, and so ineradicably "burned . . . right into" the memory of the witness, effectively disposed of the matter, not so much on the spot (since Dorsen did not stress it) but for later, for the summation to the jury—which, of course, because of the Joint Statement and its timing, never came.

All these colloquies were interspersed with objections (unusual in number even for Cravath) and bench conferences; but the subsequent testimony, on cross-examination, of this witness, who (as the lore would have it) so demoralized Westmoreland, became even less impressive as it went along. It developed, for example, that McChristian was concerned not so much to get the contents of the cable with the revised estimates to Washington as to be the person delegated to present them there himself:

Q. Do you recall testifying [at your deposition], General McChristian, that you said, "General, let me take this back to Washington when I go, and let me brief them on what we are doing?" Do you recall whether you testified to that *under oath,* General McChristian?

A. [Some preliminary, rather sullen muttering and waffling.] I'm saying that I may have said this. You'd have to show me the context of it.

Boies spoke up with an interruption, not on the merits but, presumably, just to remind McChristian, as lawyers sometimes do tend to remind a faltering witness, that he was not alone. Then:

Q. And correct me if I am wrong, General McChristian, that this is one of the times that you said you *couldn't be sure* or positive *what* you said to General Westmoreland, is that correct?

A. I tried to put it in context. [Several paragraphs, containing neither yes nor no, of particularly maundering disquisition.]

Q. Are you saying, General McChristian, that as far as you know, there very well could have been a briefing *by your staff* of Admiral Sharp, containing all the materials in the cable you presented to General Westmoreland, and *you just may not have known about it?*

Dorsen had by this time conclusively established that McChristian's staff had in fact conducted such a briefing for Admiral Sharp, on May 19, 1967. Whether McChristian himself was there remained unclear. McChristian said he had "no recollection" of having been there, and added, "I have no knowledge of such a briefing having taken place at that time, no."

Q. Are you saying—let me ask you this, General McChristian, did you make any *affirmative effort,* in the last two weeks you were in Vietnam, *to find out* whether the material that was in your cable *was communicated* to any of General Westmoreland's *superiors,* military or civilian?

A. The fast answer to your question is that I have no recollection of having looked into that or any other ongoing action in my staff.

In this seemingly flat, frequently rambling and unresponsive testimony, McChristian had unwittingly taken away all that he had seemed, as a defense witness, to offer: he had not remembered, at the time he was interviewed for the broadcast, the "political bombshell," which he claimed had been burned into his memory; he had cared so little about the revised estimates, in the cable he had presented to Westmoreland, that the moment he found he was not being delegated, personally, to forward the information he lost interest in it—did not trouble, for instance, to brief fighting units (or even understand the meaning of questions about whether he had done so), or to find out whether members of his own staff had briefed Westmoreland's superiors with precisely the information McChristian had proposed. Suddenly, in an almost absent-minded way, Dorsen produced a letter, signed by McChristian, and dated May 21, 1967, to Ambassador Komer calling Komer's attention to the appointment by Westmoreland of a new committee, "to review this new estimate [of irregular forces] as well as the infrastructure study," in what had become known as the McChristian Report.

Q. Isn't that *exactly what you wanted,* General McChristian?
A. Wait a moment. I haven't finished answering. . . . I asked nobody about this committee. . . . I knew nothing more about it. [Almost a new order of defensive ramble.]

But the letter was, after all, over McChristian's *own signature.* Finally, Dorsen raised one other, relatively minor matter: McChristian's having protested, after the broadcast, the "improper" splicing of one of his own answers not to the highly abstract and hypothetical question he had actually been asked but to a concrete, specific question, about Westmoreland, that he had not been asked at all. Dorsen asked whether McChristian ever "came to the opinion that an answer of yours to a hypothetical question had been edited" to appear to be an answer to a real one. McChristian, aware that almost two years after the broadcast he had signed a sworn affidavit to precisely that effect, interrupted:

Came to the what?

Objection from Boies, who did not want anything from the affidavit introduced, or, failing that, wanted to give the witness time to think. Bench conference. Objection overruled. But Dorsen, whose litigating method did not include reducing the other side's star witness to too obvious a self-serving and less than honest fool, abandoned the matter of the affidavit anyway.

In trying to resuscitate his witness on redirect examination, Boies began by asking McChristian why he had shown "some reluctance," in the videotaped interview with Crile, to quote Westmoreland's "exact words."

> A. . . . . I just didn't want to have any dirty laundry taken care of in public.

But then, entirely in the Cravath spirit, Boies went perhaps too far. He tried to introduce what purported to be McChristian's handwritten notes of a telephone conversation with Westmoreland, in 1982, after the broadcast was complete. Objection—this time from Dorsen. Bench conference:

> THE COURT: If you plan to offer this, why do you think you should be allowed to offer it?
> MR. BOIES: Because, your Honor, the plaintiff has put in issue this witness' credibility . . . this witness' alleged loathing for Mr. Komer and Mr. Davidson.
> THE COURT: What does that have to do with this?

The bench conference, in which Boies tried to demonstrate what relevance notes of a telephone conversation, in which neither Komer nor Davidson was mentioned, between McChristian and Westmoreland, *after* the broadcast was complete, might have to the question of the witness's credibility in claiming not to have loathed Komer or Davidson ever since 1967, took a long time—during which, of course, the jury and the courtroom spectators heard nothing. Boies pursued his position so aggressively that he evoked from Judge Leval, on the record, such comments as these:

> THE COURT: . . . Mr. Dorsen brought out that he lied, that he said to Kowet or somebody, or to Kowet and to Crile, "I don't

remember"—it was one of those things where, according to Mr.
Dorsen's argument, "You're either lying now or you were lying
then, because you then said you don't remember the exact
words, and today you say, 'They are etched into my mind, I
could never forget them.'"

And, later:

THE COURT: I don't think I would have a problem with it if the only
thing that was involved was the question whether the witness
made it up or not. . . . But the problem is that the particular piece
of evidence [McChristian's 1982 notes] has a more prejudicial
effect than just supporting the witness's credibility as against an
attack of recent fabrication, because it puts down in writing a
statement attributable to General Westmoreland which General
Westmoreland denies . . . which is quite a different thing than
the basis for your offering it, which is to explain why he,
McChristian, gave a weaselly answer or a false one to Kowet
[and to Crile].

These are strong words to elicit from a judge, even at the
sidebar; and Boies proceeded, in open court, to take up a line of
questioning that provoked the judge to summon him (with the
words "Are you contending that this was covered by our discussion at the sidebar?") to another bench conference, where
there were further comments awkward for his version of the
case:

THE COURT: You don't challenge, do you, the proposition that
General Westmoreland had a perfect right to delay the sending
of that cable, if the purpose of the delay was for General Westmoreland to acquaint himself with reasonable speed with the
information underlying it and making a judgment of its accuracy, do you?

After a somewhat grudging concession on this point ("If the
court has a problem with the . . . question, I will pass it, because
it's not a matter of enormous significance"), Boies immediately
introduced an argument that he should be allowed to elicit from
McChristian his views of Colonel Graham (the intelligence officer

who appeared on the broadcast for twenty-one seconds): "And I think I am entitled to do that."

> THE COURT: Wait a minute. In order to bring out what? Mr. Dorsen asked his views of Davidson and Komer, seeking to elicit that he had a hatred of Davidson and Komer . . . whether the purpose was one or the other or both of suggesting that either it led the witness to lie about them . . . and about General Westmoreland, or . . . to simply an error of judgment in his appraisal of all of this.
>
> Now, that was suggesting a *bias* on the witness' part that affected either the honesty of his testimony, or the accuracy of his testimony even assuming honesty. Now, what's your purpose in asking his appraisal of Graham?
>
> MR. BOIES: I believe that will support the accuracy of the witness' appraisal of what was going on.
>
> THE COURT: Is he going to say negative things about Graham?
>
> MR. BOIES: I think so, your Honor.
>
> MR. DORSEN: General Graham didn't arrive there for weeks and weeks [after McChristian left Saigon], for one thing.
>
> THE COURT: I don't understand.
>
> MR. BOIES: Your Honor, I will pass the Graham question.
>
> THE COURT: All right. . . .
>
> MR. BOIES: It's not of enormous significance.

It was Boies' style in bench conferences to argue fiercely and articulately for a position (often that he was "entitled" to do something, or that it would be "unfair" for opposing counsel to do it), and if the ruling went against him, to say that the whole question was "not of enormous significance." The phrase seemed a way of shrugging off the natural litigator's disappointment that *any* ruling should ever go against him, and of diminishing the importance of the ruling; it was also an instance of the Cravath style of having, in all discussions, and even after the judge himself has spoken, the last word. At one point in the same bench conference, Dorsen, apparently incensed by Boies' efforts to introduce yet another piece of what Dorsen considered, and Judge Leval agreed, was inadmissible evidence, said, "Of course, the [Order of Battle] wasn't increased. The question is whether it was done *dishonestly"*—which was, of course, the whole point of the program, and, for that matter, of the lawsuit. And the striking point about these bench conferences, so near the closing days of trial, was that, at the sidebar, as in open court, Dorsen, far from failing, as did Westmoreland's chief counsel, Burt, to make timely and apposite objections (and further still from being so apparently in awe of Boies as to look, as did Burt, not toward Judge Leval but toward Boies for rulings), again and again prevailed.

When this particular bench conference was over, Boies resumed trying to resuscitate his witness. He read from a note McChristian had received, in March or April of 1982, from Westmoreland:

> Joe, here is the letter I mentioned on the telephone. CBS has maliciously, or through ignorance, confused my demurring in increasing the [Order of Battle] without further analysis with your constant theme that the enemy had the capability to pursue a war of attrition, to which I fully agreed.

What this meant to the jurors with their yellow pads was difficult to imagine. Perhaps some, with their graduate educations, might have extracted from Boies' reading of it at least the meaning that (1) General Westmoreland had demurred (or declined) to increase, without further analysis, the Order of Battle, to the "new estimates" proposed in McChristian's cable of mid-May of 1967, and (2) General Westmoreland had fully agreed with McChristian's view that the enemy could sustain a war of attrition, with the result that (3) a declining, without further analysis, to increase estimates, coupled with an agreement that the enemy was strong enough to sustain a war of attrition, equalled— Well, the question was what it equalled. An intention to deceive? And, if so, whom? Boies almost immediately abandoned the subject of this at best ambiguous note and asked instead whether "in or about June of 1984" Westmoreland had telephoned McChristian and "told you, in words or in substance, that you were both expendable": "A. Yes, sir . . . Q. And was that in connection with this lawsuit? A. Yes, sir." Leaving this further mystery, in all its dramatic language ("both expendable" to whom, for what, and in what way?), unresolved, Boies said simply, "Your Honor, I have no more questions." Or not so simply.

THE WITNESS: May I explain something on these, your Honor? [It seemed, for a moment, that McChristian was about to resume, this time perhaps on point, his language of "estimators," "criteria," "nebulous area," even "context."]
THE COURT: No. No speeches. Only answers to questions.
MR. BOIES: Your Honor, let me just ask one question. I think I know what the witness has in mind, and I probably should clarify that, with the court's permission. [And it became clear at once that the witness' question had been, in no sense and by no means, spontaneous.]
THE COURT: All right.

It turned out that Boies' question was whether the notes and letters from McChristian's files had been produced "pursuant to a subpoena in this case."

Q. Was that subpoena served on you by *plaintiff's* counsel, if you recall?
MR. DORSEN: Objection, your Honor. . . .
THE COURT: Sustained.

The objection was sustained because the question was irrelevant and had no legal meaning: in discovery, documents are *always* produced in response to opposing counsel's (and, obviously, not one's own counsel's) subpoena. But the witness, having preserved in a way that could not have escaped the jury's attention (and his counsel, having abetted him in this by introducing a question whose answer would be inadmissible) that small, deceptive implication of honor—that he would not have betrayed the confidence of his fellow West Pointer and former commander unless he were here and, under oath, obliged to— left the stand.

A normal day in federal court begins at ten and ends by five, with an hour's break for lunch. It seems, in short, to occupy less than six hours, on each of five weekdays, and to be interrupted not only by weekends and holidays but by other delays and recesses called for various reasons by the judge. In reality, however, litigation on the scale of *Westmoreland* and *Sharon* occupies a twenty-four-hour day and proceeds throughout a seven-day week. The judges meet, in chambers or in the robing room, with the attorneys, and then draft and issue rulings. The attorneys draft briefs on various points on which the judge will rule. In addition, the attorneys review every evening the transcript of the day's proceedings, and prepare their strategies, questions and even witnesses for the following day. For law firms with the resources of Cravath, Swaine & Moore or Shea & Gould, with their quantities of experienced attorneys and recent graduates of law schools, the pressures of litigation are to some degree distributed. When the main team of litigators has completed its day in court, a night team is available, from 10 p.m. till 6 a.m., for briefing points, highlighting and collecting sections of depositions and trial transcripts for the major attorneys in the case to peruse before the next day in court begins. Dan Burt, however, having never tried even a minor jury case before, had no major law firm or night team behind him, either. Apart from Dorsen, he had a few young attorneys from here and there (including a skilled young black attorney, Anthony S. Murry, who was by far the most distinguished historian in the case), and the occasional advice of one other experienced litigator, George Leisure; that was all. Even Boies, with his formidable experience and aptitude for litigation, gave signs of feeling the case's extraordinary pressure; he often perspired clear through the jackets of his suits. But Boies took off an occasional weekend, gambling in Atlantic City. Burt, accustomed to working on his own, and apparently not quite trusting even his own associates, engaged in increasingly frequent conversations with Boies about his own conduct of the case, and became perceptibly more taut and defensive with other people, as the trial progressed.

Though Colonel Gains Hawkins was CBS's only military witness equal in importance to General McChristian, the morning of Hawkins' testimony in Room 318 of the federal courthouse (February 12, 1985) began in a more than usually stupefying way. Judge Leval made a little opening joke ("You have waited a long time for this, and you're now going to get to hear . . ."), and even Boies said, "I know it is not as exciting or as interesting as having people live, but where we could not bring the people live, we nevertheless thought their testimony was important, and that's particularly true of Colonel Russell Cooley," whereupon, with Victor Kovner, Crile's chief attorney, playing the role of Cooley on the stand, Boies and Kovner began to read, to the jury and into the record, "the balance of the Cooley deposition." Colonel (at the time Major) Cooley, it turned out, had arrived in Vietnam in October of 1967 and within days received the impression that his immediate boss, Colonel Everette Parkins, had been "fired" for estimating the rate of North Vietnamese infiltration into South Vietnam at twenty thousand a month—a figure considered far too high not only by other American intelligence analysts at the time but also by every competent source, American or North Vietnamese, in the fifteen years between the alleged "conspiracy" and the time the broadcast was produced. Parkins, Colonel Charlie Morris (who did the alleged "firing") and four other people present at the event explicitly denied Cooley's (and the broadcast's) account. But although Cooley's vocabulary was entirely consistent in reflecting the quality of *thinking* in those people entrusted at the time, and, no doubt, to this day, with "intelligence"—

That was outside our functional area . . . The fact—I think you're getting into a wordplay here, and that's what he's doing, is whether he includes the unit by nomenclature or how it's caveated in the document. . . . I think you're mixing apples and oranges here. Let me make it clear . . . I've referred to this as our methodology, of enemy strength calculations . . . what I have referred to in several cases here as a system of guerrillas coming, you know, as a slop factor. . . . In the parlance of the word "slop," this means that that was another of these areas that typically got hit, because it made it very, very easy to come back and say, well, the guerrillas just aren't as high because we want the figures to be lower—

the *content* of his deposition contributed almost nothing to the case. At the sidebar, when Boies had finished his reading, Judge Leval considered whether he might find it necessary to point out, for example, that Colonel Cooley could not properly be described as Boies had described him, as an "infiltration analyst," since his field of intelligence was not infiltration; that Cooley did not know, one way or the other, why or whether Colonel Parkins was or was not "fired," since Cooley had not been there at the time, and could only testify concerning "rumors" about it; that Boies should not be permitted to leave the jury with the impression that "we could not bring people live" in cases where Cravath, for its own reasons, preferred a deposition, read into the record, to a witness, present and subject, under oath, to cross-examination; that Cooley's parenthetical remark (which had appeared also in the testimony of several other Cravath witnesses) "And, again, I've got to say I think history bears this out" should be stricken from the record, of Cooley and all other defense witnesses. In fact, though Judge Leval immediately instructed the jury that some of Cooley's testimony was inadmissible, the only mildly illuminating element of what Cooley had to say was inadvertent, and concerned the transaction that occurs between witnesses and attorneys before cases come to court. Cooley was testifying about his impression that Colonel Danny Graham had dishonestly "altered the data base"; that is, the figures, reflecting estimates of enemy troop strength before Tet, which were stored, and of course continually altered, in the computers of American military intelligence in Vietnam.

Q. O.K. Let me ask you what exactly do you mean by the phrase that you used several times in that answer, "alter the data base"?

A. I'm quoting it, parroting back your words, as well as what we've seen in some testimony here.

Q. Do you have a definition of your own, or—

A. "Alter it" obviously means to change it.

Q. O.K. But all changes of the data base are not per se nefarious, are they?

A few questions later, witness and attorney were "parroting back" the words "per se" and "nefarious" as well, but this particular exchange continued:

A. Well, I think if we're going to split words here, there are several ways you can alter it, O.K.? One is with merit and the other is without merit, if you want to put it in a very broad sense, O.K.? One says we're just going to alter it just because we think, and the other says we're going to alter it because *we have hard intelligence* to back it up.

This exchange, in the course of the deposition of a relatively minor witness (who had nonetheless been one of the eight people, besides Adams, who appeared, more or less in support of the program's thesis, on the broadcast), whose testimony was simply read into the record (though its salient points, such as they were, might subsequently be stricken as inadmissible), and who never actually took the stand, was an almost perfect distillation of the travesty at the heart of the program and of the case: the intelligence bureaucrats firmly believed that their own "estimates," in a guerrilla war, after all, and in an alien country, constituted, as opposed to the other fellow's, "hard intelligence," and that any disagreement or rivalry with other bureaucrats was never what McNamara, of the Defense Department; or Carver, of the C.I.A.; or Davidson, McChristian's successor as chief of American military intelligence in Saigon; or Graham, the intelligence officer of the twenty-one-second interview, and Godding, the actual head of the M.A.C.V. delegation to the August, 1967, conference at Langley, along with other high military and civilian officials, would characterize as good-faith "honest differences" or "a difference in [the] judgment of honest men." It was, rather, nothing less than evidence, as Cooley's deposition would have it, of "per se nefarious" conspiracy.

In the afternoon, the second (as the fable had it) formidable military witness, Colonel Gains Hawkins, took the stand. Hawkins had been Order of Battle chief in Vietnam between February of 1966 and September of 1967. In 1970, he retired from the Army. Since 1981, he had run an old-age home in the town of West Point, Mississippi. "Order of Battle per se," Hawkins was soon explaining, "is the military forces of any country." Within minutes, in the second paragraph of his answer to a yes-or-no question, he added, with unmistakable pride:

> When I arrived [in Vietnam], the Order of Battle, monthly Order of Battle summary, was about *a quarter of an inch thick,* and when I left there, a little better than eighteen months later, it was about *an inch—a little better maybe than an inch thick,* because our requirements had grown during that time along with our capability to process and to produce Order of Battle intelligence.

Sam Adams and attorneys from Cravath had travelled fifteen times, since early 1983, to Hawkins' old-age home in that small Mississippi town to prepare Hawkins for his sworn testimony on his deposition and at trial; and at first he seemed rather like a candid, boozy anecdotalist and a well-rehearsed, clownishly beguiling witness. In fact, on direct examination Hawkins seemed so eager to oblige that he often finished his answers to Boies' questions with a question of his own: "You're focussing strictly on the guerrillas, sir, on the irregulars, sir?"; and, "Does that get you where you need to be?" Within a short time, however, he showed an irrepressible need, almost aimlessly, and without limitation, to prattle. "[The estimates] were somewhat lower, but they did not make a difference in the magnitude. . . . You take a hypothetical figure of 100,000, that figure, using the techniques and methodologies, could actually be 105,000 or it could be 95,000. It is an order of magnitude, nothing more, nothing less." And, "This is our methodology. This is our criteria. There is the best that I can do." And, in another mode:

> A. [In captured documents] the system, they had sort of an overlap system . . . reduced the—you know, the lying possibility there. I never found a document in Vietnam which I thought

was intentionally forged. Some were perhaps a little bit, maybe optimistic, as were some of ours, but I think it's the analyst's problem to take in all of these documents, and put them together, and meld this and extract this information and meld it together and develop the picture of the—the composite picture of the enemy, and that is where the integrity comes into the act.

It's like a journalist sometimes, but that's not my business, but integrity—

THE COURT: Colonel Hawkins, I think you are getting beyond the question.

THE WITNESS: I'm sorry, sir. I am wrapped up in the subject. If you would tap me on the shoulder, I will shut up.

And:

A. . . . a program called Operation RITZ, R-I-T-Z, which was directed at the guerrillas, the irregulars, and a program called Operation Corral, just like in corral, which was directed at the political, political infrastructure, to develop valid strength figures on what General McChristian referred to as the political Order of Battle strength. Does that get you where you need to be?

Q. Yes, Colonel Hawkins.

A. Or whatever.

Q. Yes, Colonel Hawkins. You gave me what I needed to know, and you also went to the political Order of Battle, which was going to be my next question.

A. I'm sorry. I just get overworked, you know, enraptured with this.

Two questions later:

A. In the RITZ program, that collected information on the guerrillas, the self-defense, and the secret self-defense. The whole schmear.

One question later still:

A. Yes, yes, yes, indeed, indeed. I misunderstood your question at first.

In addition to "the methodology" and "the criteria" (always used in the singular) and "meld [also "amalgamate"] this and extract this information and meld it together," the odd Yiddishism "the whole schmear" recurred in Hawkins' testimony. So did the extreme eagerness to oblige reflected not just in "Does that get you where you need to be?" and "Yes, yes, yes, indeed, indeed" but also in the virtual shrug of submissiveness embodied in the answer (which also recurred in Hawkins' testimony) "Or whatever."

No matter how rambling and technically inadmissible Hawkins' answers to Boies' questions were, the persona of the amiable cornball on the stand made it difficult for opposing counsel, Dorsen, to raise objections—without himself appearing to be an ogre or an unamiable spoilsport. The two principal substantive reasons for Cravath's having called Hawkins as a witness were that at one briefing in May and another in June of 1967 Hawkins had received the impression that Westmoreland had rejected, as "politically unacceptable," new and higher estimates of the number of irregulars to be included in over-all enemy troop strength; and that at the joint conference of civilian and military intelligence officials at Langley in August of 1967 he received the impression that there had been a military "command position" that estimates of total enemy troop strength were not to exceed three hundred thousand. But despite Cravath's and Adams' fifteen visits to him in Mississippi Hawkins' memory and capacity to focus soon began to fail him. Very early in his rambling testimony, the witness heard a sympathetic but rather firm instruction:

THE COURT: Let me just interrupt to say that, as you now get into areas of testimony that have been the subject of particular debate in this case, I want you to be sure to limit your answers to exactly what is asked.

THE WITNESS: Yes.

THE COURT: If you are asked about a conversation, state your best recollection of what was said at that conversation. Of course, I understand that you can't be expected to remember word for word what was said seventeen years ago, but your efforts should be to tell the substance or the words of the conversation as closely as you can, rather than telling what emotional effect it might have had on you, what you felt. Limit your answer to the question that is asked, rather than straying beyond into other matters.

But Hawkins, it seemed, could not help, indeed, quite revelled in, "straying beyond." From his briefing of May, 1967, Hawkins claimed to recall that Westmoreland had said, "in substance," that the new estimates were "politically unacceptable":

A. . . . and I repeat, the substance of the other statements was "What will I tell the President? What will I tell the Congress? What will be the reaction of the press?" And there was another statement that I did not mention before, which was, in substance, "We'd better take another look at these figures."

But in response to questions from both Boies and Judge Leval his memory simply would not quite stay fixed. Four rambling answers away, for instance, from a question whether he remembered who else was present at this May, 1967, briefing, he said, "Yes, there were other people there. But I cannot recall who these people were." A few questions later:

Q. Did General Davidson [McChristian's successor] indicate to you why these higher estimates were unacceptable?
A. In substance, for the political impact they would carry. I never heard any criticism of our methodology. In fact—may I carry on from here?
THE COURT: No. Stick to the question, please.
THE WITNESS: I'll shut up.

Of the June, 1967, briefing, Hawkins could remember only one thing: that Ambassador Komer had said, "in words or in substance," "This is Byzantine." But what was "Byzantine" he did not recall. Since the May and June briefings were the only two direct contacts Hawkins had with Westmoreland, his testimony was not very illuminating about the central figure in the case. In due course, however, Hawkins testified that he *himself* gave orders to his subordinates "to reduce their enemy-strength estimates" before the joint conference at Langley:

Q. Did you believe those orders were proper orders, sir?
A. They were not, sir.

The difficulty with this exchange was that while the "orders to reduce" estimates of enemy troop strength which Hawkins claimed to remember may "not" have been "proper orders," they were, by Hawkins' own testimony, orders given only by Hawkins *himself;* and Hawkins, of course, was neither the "conspirator" in the broadcast's thesis nor the plaintiff in the case. No matter how many times Boies reformulated his question (after objections from Dorsen, and a suggestion of possible reformulations by Judge Leval), Hawkins was unable not only to connect any ceiling on estimates of enemy troop strength to Westmoreland but to find a basis for any such ceiling in "orders" by anyone above himself.

Q. Colonel Hawkins, when you gave the intelligence officers to whom you gave orders to reduce their enemy-strength estimates, were you carrying out the orders or instructions of anyone else?
A. Yes.

It seemed, here at last, that Hawkins would respond with a straight, comprehensible, unwaffling and perhaps (from Westmoreland's or, at least, some superior's point of view) devastating answer. But:

Q. Whose—?
A. I worked directly, for the most part, with Colonel Charlie Morris . . . and I ordered the appropriate officers to make the changes, and I made some of the changes myself.

So the answer was, again, not responsive to the question, was, in fact, yet another preposterous evasion; the answer to who ordered whom was only, again, Hawkins ordering some nameless persons. And, as throughout the months of trial, there seemed no consciousness on anybody's part that what was "changed," or "reduced," or "altered," was not solid, verifiable fact but "estimates"—based on what some witnesses liked to call "extrapolations" or, perhaps more frankly, "guesses." Suddenly, Boies appeared to have reformulated the question in an odd way:

Q. Did those estimates that you presented . . . at the August, 1967, conference represent your best estimate of enemy strength?

Which elicited an odd answer:

A. No, sir, they did not. They represented crap.

And, of course, what Boies was trying to do, with the witness's enthusiastic and, for the moment, precise, coöperation, was to justify retroactively one of the broadcast's more egregious elisions: the splicing of Hawkins' characterization of *South Vietnamese* estimates of enemy troop strength *before 1966* onto the question of the figures Hawkins had presented, in August of 1967 to the joint conference at Langley, on Westmoreland's behalf. This tactic provoked an objection from Dorsen and, in the ensuing bench conference, a remark from Judge Leval: "I don't think it's a proper issue what Crile did with the film tape. It is what it is, and it's visible to everyone. . . . The issue is what he told Crile." So, hoping to elicit from Hawkins that he had used about the August, 1967, estimates at Langley, somewhere, off-camera, the word "crap," Boies soldiered on, with a question that, perhaps, he came to wish he had not asked:

Q. Were you also interviewed by Mr. Crile, other than on film?
A. I must have spoken in person and on the telephone with Mr. Crile about ten, eleven, or twelve times, from about the time I sat in his apartment in that overstuffed chair with the tufts out, and between the time that the documentary was aired. In fact, he came to my room— Am I going too far, sir?
THE COURT: No.
THE WITNESS: In fact, the interview was conducted in the afternoon. It lasted about two, two and a half hours. I was—the CBS staff had delivered tickets for my wife and I to attend a play that evening. The title of the play, ironically, was "Ain't Misbehavin'."
THE COURT: I think perhaps now you are going a little too far.
THE WITNESS: I called Mr. Crile and told him that I would like to relinquish these tickets, because I was mentally and emotionally exhausted, and that I would just rather stay in the hotel that

night and have two or three martinis and a dinner, and he came
over and we spent an hour or two talking, and I think I opened
up to him more then, because I was pretty tight. I mean, not
martini tight.

And here the impression of the boozy anecdotalist seemed not
altogether unconfirmed. Four questions later (including two by
Judge Leval), Hawkins, whose mind had wandered once—"Sir,
I'm sorry. This is unforgivable, but I was involved in thinking, and
I will try not to do it again. I would like to have the question
reread"—finally gave the answer at which all this arduous questioning was directed:

> A. I told Mr. Crile, in effect, that they were crap, the figures that
> we brought to Langley were crap.

After this small triumph of advocacy, the courtroom was sufficiently exhausted to welcome Boies' suggestion of a break. When
the witness returned, fifteen minutes later, however, presumably
refreshed, it turned out that what had always been missing was
still missing: any link between the orders Hawkins claimed to have
given to his subordinates and some order, by any military superior
of Hawkins', which might, in turn, be linked to any order by
General Westmoreland himself. From "crap," then, the key,
sought-after words became "command position." Hawkins testified readily to his "understanding" that there existed a "command position," and that his "understanding" of it was "that
there was a ceiling of 300,000 and we would not exceed that
ceiling." But from that moment on his testimony proceeded, or
deteriorated, to the point where Judge Leval began to find it
necessary repeatedly to intervene.

> THE COURT: It seems to me that it would be necessary for you to
> bring out what that understanding was *based on* for it to be
> proper testimony.
> Q. Colonel Hawkins, a moment ago you testified that it was your
> understanding when you went to the August, 1967, Langley
> conference that there was a . . . command position not to exceed

a total enemy-strength number of 300,000. Do you recall that?

A. Yes, sir.

Q. What was your understanding based on, sir?

A. It was based upon all of the instructions that I had received, everything that I had done before I got to Langley, with all the papers and with the slides that we had presented to show a command position not in excess of 300,000. [Further unresponsive ramble.]

MR. DORSEN: Your Honor, I object. I think I would like to move to strike the prior answer on the ground that there is no foundation that this witness has demonstrated for a command position.

THE COURT: I would agree that the prior answer did not demonstrate a foundation.

After several tries, Hawkins produced this:

A. The first indication I had from General Westmoreland was the May and June briefing, which I briefed to him figures in excess of 300,000, which were not accepted, and I believe I have testified earlier as to the substance of General Westmoreland's remarks at that first May briefing in regard to these higher figures and what impact they would have. Should I—?

THE COURT: You may continue to answer the question.

THE WITNESS: May I continue to answer the question?

THE COURT: As long as you limit yourself to the question.

A. Later on, I had several contacts with General Davidson and Colonel Charlie Morris.

In response to the very next question, whether the "substance" of what General Westmoreland had said to Hawkins at the May briefing did "lead you in whole or in part to conclude what you have testified you concluded," Hawkins replied with uncharacteristic brevity:

A. Definitely did.

But that's *all* Hawkins said, and Boies was in the increasingly obvious position of trying unsuccessfully to tie anything Hawkins said he "concluded" to anything said, even "in substance," by any of Hawkins' military superiors, including, of course, General Westmoreland. Cross-examination had not even begun, but Hawkins, for all his eagerness to oblige, was nattering uncontrollably:

Q. What did General Davidson say to you, in words or in substance, if anything, that led you to reach any conclusion about a . . . command position?

A. In substance, the only— I don't recall the conversations except in substance, but the substance was we were going to attrite this enemy, and eventually, after several conversations of this nature, I told General Davidson that—and Colonel Morris—that "Look, this is the way we have developed this Order of Battle estimate, this is our methodology, this is our criteria. . . . Now, if you want a different figure you need to change the rules of the game."

Until he reached:

And this was the beginning of the reduction of the figures. I abdicated my position as Order of Battle chief, because I realized that I was—

THE COURT: Just a second. . . . The jury will disregard the last few words of the answer.

Because, of course, Hawkins had again replied with what he himself had said ("this is our methodology, this is our criteria," etc.) in answering the question of what was said to him. Boies struggled on, but the witness continued, in his own manner, to testify that he himself had ordered reductions, he himself had reduced estimates, until Boies' failure to elicit that he had done so *on the basis of some higher order* began to look like a not entirely ingenuous effort to conceal, by the sheer amplitude, repetitiveness and apparent candor of Hawkins' own confessions ("I abdicated my position," "I ordered the appropriate officers to make the changes, and I made some of the changes myself"), that there *were* no such higher orders. Finally, pretending that he had, after all, elicited from the witness a link to the key words "command position," Boies announced that he was turning to another subject. Judge Leval, however, immediately interrupted, to summon both counsel to a bench conference at the sidebar.

> THE COURT: I don't think you have covered it. I think Mr. Dorsen's objection, as it now stands, is a proper objection. . . . I just wanted to point out to you that in my view you have not laid an adequate foundation for his testimony that there *was* a command position.
>
> MR. BOIES: . . . What I asked him was what his understanding was as to whether there was a command position, and it seems to me he is clearly a competent witness to testify what his understanding was, and his understanding . . . is relevant in and of itself.
>
> THE COURT: Well, it's of marginal relevance.
>
> MR. DORSEN: And great prejudice.
>
> THE COURT: It's of marginal relevance and great prejudice, unless his understanding was based on *communications from upstairs.* . . . He testified that he had these conversations with Davidson and Morris, but he only gave his half of the conversations. . . . He said, "The whole history of my preparation led me to believe this," but he didn't say what it was in the history of that preparation that could have communicated that message. . . . The other thing is that the events of the second briefing of General Westmoreland—I don't think he has testified to what happened at the second briefing. . . . The principal relevant point is . . . whether orders *were coming down* that constituted a command position, rather than [what] he understood . . . I think it's a point of such importance that it deserves being presented as clearly as possible, what that conclusion is *based on*.

But the witness, many questions later, was recounting yet again ("I . . . told him, 'Son, this is the command position. I hate to do this to you . . .' I went through his methodology, and I directed him"), in his seemingly rambling, bumbling way, what he himself had said and done. Boies managed, at last, at least, to get Hawkins to claim that he had said the same sort of thing to Crile:

> Q. Did you discuss with Mr. Crile, in 1981, who was responsible for the dishonesty of . . . enemy-strength figures?
>
> A. I told him it went back to Westmoreland himself.

But the very next, in fact, the key, question—

> Did you discuss with Mr. Crile *why* you believed that it went
> back to General Westmoreland himself?—

elicited another senseless and maundering reply:

> Because General Westmoreland had established a ceiling, and
> that no competent intelligence analyst can function under the ceil-
> ing that had been established.

Because, of course, precisely the point at issue was that in
Hawkins' entire testimony there was still no evidence whatever
that Westmoreland or anyone else had informed Hawkins
that any ceiling did exist. Within a short time (and still before
cross-examination had even begun) the witness was confusing
McChristian and Westmoreland, in an increasingly clownish
prattle that wandered further and further from any specific question and from any point at issue in the trial:

> A. I briefed General McChristian on the 29th of May. I briefed
> General Westmoreland on the 28th of May. Not briefed, excuse
> me, sir, I retract that. I did not brief General McChristian
> on the 29th of May. I received the Legion of Merit pinned to
> my chest on the 28th of May and I was very proud of it at the
> time.
> Q. Who pinned that on you, sir?
> A. General McChristian, sir . . . Counsel for the plaintiff found the
> letters and pointed out that—thank you, sir.
> Q. Counsel for the who?
> A. For the—what do you call it—General Westmoreland.
> Q. For the plaintiff?
> A. For the plaintiff, yes. Whatever.

At one point, Judge Leval had to interrupt:

> A. I skimmed a few off the top . . . not a dramatic sudden increase
> . . . what we called a book increase . . . I skimmed some off the
> top, a few thousand, sir, in these categories, because I was not
> able to believe—

THE COURT: No, no.
THE WITNESS: Excuse me.

At another point, there was a small epiphany:

Q. Were the numbers that you briefed on the 14th of June lower than the numbers that you had briefed on the 28th of May?
A. They were somewhat lower, but they did not make a difference in the magnitude. When I'm talking about magnitude, I would like to explain, you take a hypothetical figure of 100,000, that figure, using the techniques and methodologies, could actually be 105,000 or it could be 95,000. It is an order of magnitude, nothing more, nothing less. You can skim 2,000 off of it, or you can add 2,000 to it. It does not disturb the order of magnitude. This is the nature of the skimming which I did when I returned with the briefing the second time.

Within moments, Judge Leval sustained an objection (which Dorsen had not yet made) and a motion to strike (which he had): "The jury will disregard the answer and the question." And a moment later, in a bench conference at the sidebar, Boies said the prior question and answer were "not of great concern" to him, "because that's already in the record earlier." Dorsen said, "I move to strike it, then." Boies, seeming to forget for a moment that he was not judge but counsel, said, "It's too late. It's in about two or three other times and—" And Judge Leval interrupted, with evident dismay, "Does he not have *any* recollection to summarize *what was said?*" The judge went on to say that there was so far no basis at all for Hawkins' repeated testimony that there was a "command position" establishing a "ceiling of 300,000." "It's just floating there, unsupported." Dorsen argued that Boies was continually eliciting from the witness some totally baseless conclusion, obliging Dorsen to "get up time and time again" with an objection, and that though the objections were sustained, and Hawkins' answers were stricken, Boies simply elicited them again, the same baseless conclusions; that, though these questions and answers were again objected to, and stricken, "it makes it look like it's more and more powerfully persuasive, because I have objected, had something stricken, and he then continues." Judge Leval remarked that the day before was the last day of Hawkins' deposition: "Has he testified, on his deposition, to a basis for it, for his believing that there was a command position?" Dorsen pointed out that all Hawkins could remember from his second briefing of Westmoreland was "something not by General Westmoreland but by Robert Komer, who said 'This is Byzantine.'" Some more argument, and then:

> THE COURT: I don't care if you laid even a minimal foundation for the proposition that he was under orders, a command position order, to stick to a 300,000 man ceiling. He hasn't said a word —he never mentioned 300,000 except in [one unresponsive] answer. There's absolutely nothing in it, and I mean, you know, I thought at first that it wasn't a serious problem because I assumed that there must be a vast amount of basis for it. Maybe there isn't. I assumed that he must have had conversations with General Godding. . . .
>
> MR. BOIES: I will now go directly to his conversations with those people, although I do say to you that this is the . . . Order of Battle chief.
>
> THE COURT: I know. When he says command position—he's not the commander—that means a position that comes down from the commander. *What this case is about is the commander.* This case is not about whether the . . . Order of Battle chief acted dishonestly.

While it is true that all this took place at the sidebar, out of the hearing of the press as well as the jury, and that day-to-day coverage of trials simply does not include bench conferences, there was something in these remarks by the court that made almost farcical, quite apart from the farcical aspect of the witness himself in open court, the notion that this particular witness, Hawkins, was one of two so formidable as to make Westmoreland abandon his case. And the cross-examination of Gains Hawkins had not yet begun. As the increasingly appalling quality of what was called "intelligence" in the Vietnam years became apparent yet again, in the testimony of this nearly final witness; and as the implications, for those young men whose life and death depended on these bureaucrats, with their "techniques," and "methodologies," and "skim[ming] . . . a few thousand," "off the top," and "book increase," and "order of magnitude, nothing more, nothing less," dawned, in all their tragic, mindless clarity, this serene, complacent cornball maundered on. Asked simply to state, for example, the substance of his conversations with General Davidson, he drifted through eight paragraphs, which included:

> Body counts were coming in a lot of times without any identification. There was no way to tell whether these people were guerrillas, or self-defense, or just farmers out there with a buffalo, or the 256th Regiment, or whatever the hell they were, and so I made a note— you don't just tell a—a young colonel just doesn't tell a brigadier general, "Sir, you're full of stew";

and

> I couched it in very polite terms, the kind of terms to use with a superior officer, that "Sir, this study is not feasible";

and

> It was relating to what the press was going to make of these figures . . . and finally *I told* General Davidson and Colonel Morris that, "Look, this is the way we have been doing it all these months. This is our methodology. This is our criteria. There is the best that I can do."

And, of course, the answer, such as it was, was couched again not in terms of what Hawkins had been told *by* any superior officers but what he had said *to* them. In spite of the fact that one's heart sank yet again, because, inadvertently embedded in these answers was the awful truth that this Order of Battle chief, defending his bureaucratic turf, simply (like all his subordinates and colleagues) did not *know,* in all good faith, dead or alive, who *were* the enemy, and who was the farmer with his buffalo; and in spite of the fact that this witness was, in effect, making the perfect argument not just against the war but against the very thesis of the broadcast (what the program chose to call "conspiracy at the highest levels" revealed instead this rank and utter mindlessness at every echelon below), these were the men produced on the witness stand, as they had served in the military, for what Boies called their "expertise."

And suddenly Hawkins' worst moment, on direct examination by defense counsel—a moment that made no sense except on the basis of his deposition. All the witness seemed to be saying, in the second paragraph of what appeared to be just another of his usual answers, was "I tried my best to protect these main forces. It didn't really make any difference, because it distorted the intelligence anyway, because you had to have all of it to have a complete Order of Battle, but I felt sort of like the lady—" when Judge Leval, with evident horror, interrupted.

THE COURT: No, no.

MR. DORSEN: I move to strike the last part of the answer as not relating to a conversation with Colonel Morris or General Davidson.

THE COURT: You mean the last part, "I felt like—"?

MR. DORSEN: Yes.

THE COURT: "I felt like" is stricken.

This exchange, in open court, would be totally mystifying were it not for what Hawkins had said at his deposition, and what Hawkins and his counsel were under strict instructions not to say again, in court. Hawkins had said that the regular enemy soldiers, the "main-force units," were his favorites, that the irregulars meant much less to him; and that, "like the lady at Auschwitz," who had to choose which of her children would live and which would go to the gas chambers, he had kept his favorite, his figures for main-force units, and let his estimates of irregulars die. It was to cut off the "lady at Auschwitz" metaphor that Judge Leval interjected his horrified "No, no," and ordered the "I felt like" stricken as well. Only two questions later, however, the witness was saying, "I don't recall figures too well," and one was reminded that, rather than some monster of coarseness, perhaps rather even than some utter fool, he was only the lawyers', and also the press's pawn, trying to oblige, but failing again and again even in that.

Now Boies was trying to elicit from Hawkins the testimony that his immediate superior, General Godding, had given him some sort of order to keep a ceiling of three hundred thousand on estimates for the joint conference at Langley in August of 1967. The witness vaguely nattered on: "He [Godding] was my immediate boss, and I was chief of the Order of Battle"; "He was the man carrying the—really the command image, if you understand what I mean."

He had still said nothing that linked Godding to orders or a ceiling or a command position. He was just beginning to ruminate, on the basis of letters he wrote, in 1967, to his wife ("Yes. She saved faithfully every one of them"), whether he himself or Godding had left Langley for Saigon first when:

THE COURT: Insofar as you were testifying about the fact that General Godding was your chief at Langley—as to *that,* you're testifying from your recollection; is that right?
THE WITNESS: Not from my recollection, sir, but from what I read in one of the letters.
THE COURT: You don't—
THE WITNESS: Not my pure recollection.
THE COURT: You do not remember—
THE WITNESS: I do not remember precisely the event. I obtained it from reading through my letters.

So that Boies had to start all over:

Q. Do you remember, from your own recollection, attending the conference at Langley in August of 1967?
A. Oh, yes.
Q. Do you remember . . . whether General Godding was there or not?
A. Yes.
Q. And do you remember . . . that General Godding was your boss?
A. Yes.

But by this time it was clear that the witness remembered nothing; and that in spite of Adams' and Cravath's fifteen visits to him in Mississippi and in spite of the rehearsal in yesterday's deposition, in spite of Boies' coaching him, as it were, right there on the stand, the best Hawkins could do, no matter how many times and in how many ways he was asked about General Godding, was to say that he did "not remember the details of the conversation, but the substance was that there was a command position." And, *finally:*

The substance of the conversation was that the figures that we would agree with for the purpose of the estimate would not exceed 300,000.

But this was too little, and it came too late; it still gave no intimation of an order, and it could not pretend to establish a link to Westmoreland. Then (in one of the few moments of the trial when Judge Leval was not entirely alert), Boies tried, and for the moment got away with, a tactic, against which, in the end, an objection was sustained (and for which, and for the whole conduct of his direct examination of Hawkins, he would incur, the next day, the court's relatively long and severe rebuke) aimed, as were Boies' last questions, purely and directly at the next day's press:

MR. BOIES: May I have just a moment, your Honor?
THE COURT: Yes.
Q. Colonel Hawkins, you have made some serious charges today, about yourself and about others?
A. Yes, sir.
Q. I want to ask you whether you are absolutely certain that those charges are true?
MR. DORSEN: Objection, your Honor.
THE COURT: Overruled.
A. Yes. I feel certain about the charges—
Q. Do you have any animus or ill will toward General Westmoreland?
A. No, sir, none whatsoever.
Q. Do you have any animus or ill will to the United States Army?
A. No, sir. *I carried out these orders as a loyal officer in the United States Army.*

This time, of course, Dorsen's objection was sustained. The whole point of this witness's testimony, and counsel's failure, lay precisely in the fact that there *were no orders,* as far as Hawkins knew. The judge, of course, understood this. Both lawyers understood it. In due course, as became clear in Dorsen's cross-examination and in the judge's remarks at a robing-room conference the next morning, the jury would have understood it. But there was no news value in a sustained objection. And Gains Hawkins' last line that day was perfectly crafted for, and duly featured in, the press.

The following day, February 13, 1985, in effect the last day of the trial, began, in Judge Leval's robing room, with a conference between the judge and the attorneys:

THE COURT: Yes, Mr. Dorsen. You asked for a conference before trial?

MR. DORSEN: That's correct, your Honor. I am here to object and move to strike certain things, and in general I want to express my objection to the whole manner in which the examination was conducted. . . . then saying was the briefing accepted or not accepted, [and making] a statement that incorporated the use of the word "orders," which I think was totally inappropriate.

THE COURT: Fill me in. What was that? Remind me.

MR. DORSEN [after reading yesterday's exchange, right through Hawkins' last line and Boies' "I have no more questions, your Honor"]: And, not insignificantly perhaps . . . that is the last question and answer quoted in *The New York Times* today, without reference to the fact that the objection was sustained and the matter stricken.

THE COURT: I am sorry.

MR. DORSEN: The last question and answer, using the word "orders," appeared at the conclusion of the story in *The New York Times* today, without any indication that the answer was stricken, and I think that is potentially prejudicial, your Honor. [Some colloquy concerning objections to Hawkins' earlier testimony.] I moved to strike it and, as the record will reflect, Mr. Boies overruled my objection, but I don't think your Honor passed on it. Mr. Boies said it was too late, and I do not believe it was too late. [More colloquy] I do not know what the court would be prepared to say on that subject, because it is highly prejudicial, coming at the end, for him suddenly to inject the word "orders" . . . immediately following a question and answer concerning Westmoreland. I just think that's terribly prejudicial.

And it's not as though this witness' position and familiarity with the evidence is unknown to counsel. I think the record will show . . . that this witness has been prepared to an incredible extent, including something like ten trips by Mr. Adams or Mr. Adams' attorneys to West Point, Mississippi, lasting two days or longer. . . . I think that it would be hard to conclude that adequate precautions could not have been taken.

I also note for the record that the witness, I believe, was starting to tell a story that I specifically brought to Mr. Boies' and the court's attention, about a certain lady who had a problem, which Mr. Boies said "Well, it won't come up on direct" and I believe it was about to come up when the court cut Colonel Hawkins off.

Also, your Honor, based on the current state of the record, I do not believe that there is a foundation for Colonel Hawkins testifying to a command position. . . .

I am also concerned that it's potentially prejudicial, on the other hand, if the testimony is stricken. I am going to be in the difficult spot of perhaps having it elicited again.

Boies argued very strongly against all of these objections, and, in what should have been a very telling intimation of the highly unusual bond that was developing between him and Westmoreland's chief counsel, protested as well that Dorsen "declined to advise me, prior to this conference, as to what he was even going to raise, something that *even Mr. Burt* found unusual when I brought that to his attention this morning." It is distinctly odd for chief counsel of one party to take to chief counsel for the other his complaints about the current conduct of the case, unless the complaints concern a very young and inexperienced associate, whom chief counsel might then set to rights. It is odder still for chief counsel for one party to quote to the judge, in the presence of associate counsel of the other, some view that associate counsel's own chief colleague allegedly holds about associate counsel's current conduct of the case. Boies, however, continued:

> I think that what Mr. Dorsen is plainly attempting to do is he is attempting to confuse the jury about an examination that he obviously finds, and I think properly finds, very harmful to his case, but he is attempting to do that in a way that simply is not permitted. To, at the beginning of the cross-examination, instruct the jury to disregard or to limit portions of the direct examination that were given the previous days seems to me to be highly prejudicial and very inappropriate.
>
> Both sides have from time to time been confronted with testimony that they didn't like that was stricken. The court will recall Mr. Carver [George Carver, of the C.I.A.] bursting out with "It's a lie," which I might note was also totally reported in *The New York Times*, even though it was stricken. There have been a number of other outbursts, including outbursts by the plaintiff that were stricken and duly reported in *The New York Times*.

These were extremely important issues for Judge Leval, at this point, to resolve. (Hawkins' answer had been, in any event, in no sense an "outburst.") He agreed with Boies that to give the jury limiting instructions, for the striking of testimony, just after direct examination and just before cross-examination, might be procedurally incorrect. On all other matters, he seemed to agree with, and to intend at the close of Hawkins' testimony to rule for, Dorsen.

> THE COURT: I also agree with Mr. Dorsen, and I said something to this effect yesterday at a sidebar conference, that I did not understand for the life of me the manner in which the examination, the direct examination of Hawkins, was conducted, to elicit . . . his conclusions first and afterwards proceed to lay the foundations that might or might not be capable of supporting the conclusions that he had expressed.
>
> It was done in that fashion on two or three subjects, as I say.

On the instructions that he gave to his subordinates, what he said to the subordinates was given first . . . The same thing was true of "command position."

I was wondering after court why on earth you proceeded in that fashion, Mr. Boies. I was wondering whether you were concerned about his *ability to remember.* I haven't read these depositions. You say to me that in his deposition he has gone through five and six and ten times and is capable of testifying again and again to all the foundation stones that are necessary for the conclusions he expressed. . . .

I was wondering whether you proceeded in that fashion because you were worried that his memory might be so spotty, or might go in and out, so that you wouldn't get the answers that you needed. I did find it a confusing examination. I found it confusing possibly to the plaintiff's prejudice.

[Discussion off the record]

I had the insecure sense towards the end of the examination that probably the necessary foundation stones had been laid after the vault had been hanging up there in the air for quite some time unsupported. . . .

I don't think that a briefing is a place at which figures are accepted or not accepted. *That's not the function* of a briefing. And I don't think from what I have heard that the figures were either accepted or not accepted at the briefing. What happened was that the figures were briefed and . . . Mr. Komer said a Komer-like thing about something to do with Byzantine. . . . So the figures were perhaps not accepted, but they were not not accepted, either.

I don't think that Hawkins, furthermore, is *qualified to say* whether General Westmoreland or General Davidson [who succeeded McChristian as chief of intelligence in Westmoreland's command] or anybody else . . . at that briefing reacted in agreement or in disagreement with the figures that had been briefed. . . . So I think that the instructions Mr. Dorsen is asking for are proper instructions. . . . I would guess that Mr. Dorsen, on his cross-examination, is going to . . . try to bring out the fact that Hawkins was never told by General Westmoreland that there was any command position. . . .

Now, maybe at the end of the cross-examination, I should make the rulings that are requested, or at or during the redirect or something.

For the outcome of the case, or, at least, for the reception of Hawkins' testimony, the words of the judge in this robing-room conference should have marked a critical juncture. Virtually all of Hawkins' evidence, such as it was (about the two briefings of Westmoreland, about the existence of a command position), would, in all probability, have been stricken at the end of Hawkins' testimony, in rulings—which, of course, because of the Joint Statement and the "discontinuance" of the lawsuit, never came. The robing-room conference went on for some time longer. After Boies made some arguments (prefaced by "The Court: I think that this— Mr. Boies: Your Honor, I don't mean to interrupt the court. Before this is through there are some things I would like to respond to, on the record"), the judge went further:

> THE COURT: Part of Mr. Dorsen's objection was that by eliciting the conclusion first you had put him in the position unfairly of having to object and then invite, as a response to his objection, a pounding, calling attention, in a particularly dramatic way, to the laying of the foundation after the conclusion. . . . It's not a matter of *amount* of foundation. . . . Nowhere in his testimony had he said anything to the effect that he received an order with a suggestion that it was a command position that 300,000 was the limit.

As for Hawkins' single answer, arrived at with such difficulty the day before, regarding a conversation with General George Godding:

> If you ask about a conversation with anybody, that includes locker-room scuttlebutt as to whether there's a command position. It's not the same thing as a conversation which from the commander gives an order that can be construed as a command position.

The main point about this pivotal robing-room conference was that, while bench conferences and robing-room conferences (like sustained objections) are somehow rarely covered even in the legal press, and not at all in conventional journalistic publications, the plaintiff himself and, more particularly, his attorneys had every

reason to know (as the press, seeing only what Judge Leval characterized as "calling attention, in a particularly dramatic way," to
testimony that might subsequently be stricken, did not) how this
supposedly most daunting witness's testimony was going at the
height of the defendants' case. And that was not very well.

Soon after Dorsen began his cross-examination, the courtroom
was reminded of just what sort of, in some ways, inimitable witness Hawkins was.

Q. Colonel Hawkins, isn't it your belief that the Communists, in
connection with the Vietnam War . . . were great liars and that
they liked to brag?

A. I think that the Communists were just like Democrats and
Republicans in that way, that they all do some lying now and
then and you find some once in a while that will tell you the
truth. I am a chairman of the executive committee—

THE COURT: I think you're going—

THE WITNESS: Excuse me, sir.

A. I think that in some instances they are great liars and that they
like to brag, just like other people. But I will *caveat* that, sir.
. . . I'd say most of the documents that we saw seemed to me to
be authentic.

Several questions later:

A. They weren't forgeries and they reflected accurately—you had
to put— Mr. Dorsen, as an intelligence analyst, you had to put
all of this stuff together. You have to collate it, as we say, take
your bits and pieces and compare them. . . . That's why we had
to confirm the probable and the possible, and that's why intelligence gets into these areas, because you don't have the information that an auditor has when he makes up your tax return,
except, you know, for a little lying, cheating here and there. I
mean, it's intelligence. That's why it's intelligence, sir. . . . There
is judgment and integrity involved, sir.

In the next question, Dorsen inquired whether the witness had
"ever described" one of his intelligence categories as "equivalent
to a guess."

A. I don't remember having ever made that statement. It's possible that I could have used somewhat loosely the term, yes. It would depend upon the circumstances.

It turned out that Hawkins had started at some time, and was perhaps still working on ("Yes, sir, I am writing about it"), a book, *The Enemy Order of Battle in the Republic of Vietnam, 1966–67.* "Q. And did you state that if it's 'possible,' we're just guessing? A. Yes, I had that written in in longhand at the top—if it's 'probable' we are almost certain, and if 'possible' we're just guessing."

Hawkins had embarked, perhaps with the understandable defensiveness of witnesses on cross-examinations, on some of the arcana of "the Order of Battle shop" in American intelligence ("the criteria that we would use, the methodology that we would use . . . It gets to be a pretty much involved thing, Mr. Dorsen"), interspersed with small, almost comically appalling indications of what the quality of the American intelligence bureaucracy in the Vietnam years really was:

Q. What was the function of the Collections Division?
A. Simply put, the Collections Division receives the requirements from the Production Division and goes out to collect the information that is needed to draw up plans, and so forth and so forth.

Having elicited, almost by the way, an admission that Order of Battle analysts "would not rely on body counts" for estimates of "the size of enemy losses in Vietnam in 1967" (the admission was important only because Adams had said, and Boies had argued in his opening statement, that an element of the "conspiracy" was to measure enemy losses by counts of bodies, multiplied by estimates of wounded, and that there should have been, according to those body counts, no enemy left), Dorsen proceeded to lay for Hawkins the small, courteous trap he had used for McChristian: Would Hawkins' analysts not forward their most accurate estimates to American soldiers in the field?

A. Yes . . . this was the reason that these reports were compiled. They were not compiled just to put in a library . . . but for subordinate units in the field. . . . I had myself on visits into the boondocks conversations with various analysts. . . . Yes, it's a sharing of information at all echelons. Otherwise, intelligence does not have its full impact throughout the arena.

Here, with a kind of proud, affable prolixity, Hawkins made (as had Adams and McChristian) what amounted, in the circumstances of the case, to a key admission: that their own best information went to American fighting troops. But, once again, since the information received by troops in the field was, on the basis of documents, inescapably and demonstrably the same as the information forwarded to the White House and the Pentagon, there can have been no "conspiracy," for there was simply no deceit. There was always, of course, the possibility that these witnesses were being less than honest in their accounts of having conveyed information to the troops; but a witness who said he had *withheld* his best estimates from those people at greatest risk of death in Vietnam would have appeared a kind of monster, and not a credible witness in the case. Having made with yet another witness that key point, to be reserved for that summation to the jury which, in the event, was never made, Dorsen went on in an almost elaborately harmless way:

Q. I would like to change the subject slightly, Colonel Hawkins. Am I correct that an Order of Battle for guerrillas was a new experience for the Army in 1966?

A. As far as I know, guerrillas was a new experience for the Army in 1966 and 19—yes, in 1966.

Q. You say you are unaware of any prior effort to incorporate guerrillas into an Order of Battle?

Judge Leval asked Dorsen whether his questions were confined to the experience of the American Army:

MR. DORSEN: Thank you, your Honor.

Q. Colonel Hawkins, is it your testimony, and correct me if I'm wrong, that as far as you recall, preparing an enemy Order of Battle for guerrillas was a new experience for the U.S. Army in 1966?

And Hawkins, not yet seeing where this line of questioning would take him, answered "Yes," before babbling happily on about another defense witness, "Mr. George Allen, whom we analysts regard as the granddaddy of Vietnamese Communist Order of Battle," while the point was made, less through the answers than through the questions: that the Vietnam War was the first war in which the American Army prepared an Order of Battle for guerrillas; and that there should be a controversy concerning whom to count, and whether and how to count them, followed naturally from the fact that American military intelligence had never counted them or included them in an Order of Battle before. Soon the witness began to lose his way almost entirely, and to testify as though he were not just a witness for the defense but a defendant in the case.

> Q. On the hamlet level, is it the case that the guerrilla, the hamlet guerrillas, were part time, as you understood it?
> A. No, sir. No, sir. . . . I'd have to consult my Order of Battle summary, but I thought most of the guerrillas were pretty well part time, sort of loose organization. They could have been full time—well, it's hard to say. When you're talking about full time or part time, they are there to do the job . . . and you get into this business about full time and part time. Sometimes it gets things kind of screwed up.

This sort of answer was, of course, both unintelligible and internally inconsistent; and the reason appeared to be that the witness could not figure out which answer would be best for his own party in the case.

> I think, being a country boy, you know, I'm from the country, I am bred in the country. . . . I mean, the idea was to take all of this information and amalgamate it, to put it all together, but I would— General McChristian's philosophy, which I supported . . . There was at least some degree of patterns. This is what always helps an analyst. I mean, if an Order of Battle analyst could find a structure . . . if he could find a pattern, he's going to keep it, because he's going to find out what you are. . . .

THE COURT: Colonel Hawkins, I think you are getting a little too close to the microphone, and it reverberates.

THE WITNESS: I'm sorry. I was too far away before.

A. Again, sir, I think you would—I would have to classify the hamlet guerrillas . . . I wouldn't buy that until I went back and saw what that was, because I don't remember—we had it figured out at the time, and I would have to go back and refind that mission. The books are there. It's spelled out very clearly in our Order of Battle summaries, just what our—just exactly how we described these things, and . . . I don't think I could repeat word for word from memory at this time, in 1984 [sic, the date was actually February 13, 1985], just precisely how we did it. It's there. It's there in the books.

Q. Didn't you give the answer to that question in your deposition, Colonel Hawkins?

A. Probably off the top of my head and probably unprofessionally and probably made a few errors . . . in my deposition, in describing it.

Q. Could you turn to page 302 of your deposition, Colonel Hawkins?

In answer to yet another yes-or-no question, Hawkins began to read aloud.

MR. DORSEN: Your Honor, I move to strike the answer. I was directing the witness' attention to line 10.

A. Oh, all right.

Q. I will come to self-defense forces later.

THE COURT: The jury will disregard the answer.

A. All right.

With this "Oh, all right" and "All right," the previously convivial witness was beginning to appear recalcitrant, and even sullen: "I will have to compare that statement [in my deposition] with what is actually stated in the . . . Order of Battle . . . to determine whether I was making an accurate statement or not."

A. Double hatting was when you had a political personality who also occupied a military position. . . . This is Communist practice, Communist philosophy, sir, with Vietnam, Russia, and anywhere else.

Q. Colonel Hawkins, wasn't there a problem double counting people?

A. Yes, it was a problem. But I think we spent a whole lot more time on it than we should have spent. *I think the figures are insignificant. It is the principle,* the principle . . . The infrastructure is not normally a word which is used on the sidewalk, or used at the family dinner table. . . . It was—an infrastructure is a sort of a euphemism.

The "figures," then, part of the very "estimates" that underlay the broadcast and the case, were, according to Hawkins, anyway "insignificant." With another mild opening ("Q. Colonel Hawkins, I would like to change the subject . . . A. Yes"), Dorsen asked another apparently harmless question: Didn't Hawkins believe that military intelligence in Vietnam was "closer to the problem of estimating enemy strength than was the C.I.A."? And the witness replied rather proudly, if ramblingly ("They had some smart analysts there, but they just did not have the manpower. It took a tremendous amount of manpower to do the whole schmear"), in the affirmative. Then a surprising question: Hadn't Hawkins urged McChristian to "stonewall" the C.I.A., in preserving military intelligence's own turf concerning estimates? "I don't —I did not—I don't think I regarded it as stonewalling," the witness said, and started mixing up the names of McChristian and Westmoreland again: "I urged General McChristian, 'Let's don't cave in. Let's hold off. Let's stand fast and let's do our own studies.' What words I used at that time, but this is the meaning that I think I was trying to give to General Westmoreland [sic], and I believe this is what he understood it to be." So, again, the phenomenon of bureaucratic turf, this time between military and civilian intelligence, made its appearance in the case. And Hawkins went on:

A. I thought we should take whatever time was necessary to do the job right. And the war was slow, Mr. Dorsen. The war moved at a glacial pace. No matter how we tried to speed it up, it was a sort of glacial pace there, and there was so many—let me tell

you this, Mr. Dorsen. In 1966 and 1967 there was so many—
every journalist, every politician, every military bureaucrat,
every civilian bureaucrat who came to Saigon, who was concerned in Washington with the problem, had what was called a
gut feeling about the—

THE COURT: I think you've gone beyond the question.

THE WITNESS: Excuse me, sir.

Q. Let's get back to the term "stonewall." Haven't you used the
term "stonewall" to describe what you urged General McChristian to do in either late 1966 or late 1967?

A. It is possible. If you have a document there that says I used the
word "stonewall," I'm sure I used the word "stonewall."

Q. Could you turn to page 74 of your deposition, Colonel Hawkins? . . .

[Pause]

A. I have read the entire page, and I am proud of what I said here.

Q. Would you characterize what you were urging General Mc-
Christian to do [as] in effect stonewall the C.I.A.?

A. You are stating one word there, sir, and it does not state the
entire context of the page.

With the word "context," the witness was, of course, back in the
special world of his mentor, the preceding witness, McChristian.

Soon the witness was testifying about visitors to Saigon, coming
from the United States, journalists and others, "expressing views
on the size of the enemy":

They were—yes, the size of the enemy, the intentions of the
enemy, what he was going to do, what I refer to as gut feelings,
which were based, upon my estimation, from stomach gas and
nothing else.

Then Dorsen, over heavy objections from Boies, was reading
from a letter, dated May 4, 1967, from the witness to his wife:
"Looks like it may *break open this year.* Can't see that the VC and
the [North Vietnamese] *can take many more big losses.*" And, of
course, the accuracy of Hawkins' memory concerning his estimates, in 1967, of enemy troop strength and capacity to prevail
was called immediately and radically into doubt. If his contempo-

raneous account to his own wife reflected his belief that the war was about to "break open" because of the enemy's inability to sustain "more big losses," his recollection, almost twenty years later, that estimates of an *increased* enemy were being, with his knowledge and coöperation, suppressed could hardly stand.

Q. While you were in Vietnam . . . did you brief the visitors on the higher . . . estimates?

A. I don't recall briefing visitors on the higher . . . estimates. . . . The only briefings that I recall giving myself were the two briefings . . . given to General Westmoreland, on the 28th of May, I believe we established, and on June 14th, I briefed a Mr. Stewart Alsop, who was a reporter, now dead, at one time, but it had nothing to do with this estimate.

Q. A minute ago, Colonel Hawkins—

THE COURT: Just a second. When you speak low you're not close enough to the mike, and when you speak loud you're a little too close.

The reason for this now grating inability of the witness to adjust his voice to the microphone appeared to be that he was no longer able, as he had been on direct examination, to bask in his new public persona (reflected in the previous day's press coverage) on the stand.

Suddenly, Dorsen asked the witness whether he had participated in the drafting of the cable, in mid-May, 1967, which McChristian had proposed that Westmoreland send, with increased estimates of irregular enemy troop strength, to Washington. "I have no recollection of that cable, sir. There were so many cables that I was involved in preparing, during the eighteen months over there, I can't pick out from my mind and say that I have a recollection of this particular cable." Busy as he may have been preparing "so many cables" during his eighteen months in Vietnam, it seemed unlikely that the witness would have forgotten a cable of such apparent importance to the broadcast, to McChristian, and to the defendants' position in the case. What had begun to be called into question, besides the witness's memory and qualifications to testify, was, finally, his veracity:

Q. And you have no recollection as to whether on May 19, 1967, you participated in the drafting of a letter to Admiral Sharp [Westmoreland's immediate superior in the Pacific] on the subject of revised enemy strength figures?

A. No, sir. I have no recollection of that.

Q. Colonel Hawkins, you testified about a briefing on May 28, 1967. Do you recall that testimony?

A. Yes, sir.

Q. And wasn't there a briefing about ten days earlier given to Admiral Sharp?

A. I do not recall such—participating in such a briefing, sir. . . .

Q. Colonel Hawkins, I would like to step back a second and ask you whether, prior to May 19, 1967, the preceding few days, you learned that Admiral Sharp was going to visit [Saigon].

A. I may have known about such a visit. I think perhaps it's reflected in a letter that I wrote to my wife. . . .

Q. By coincidence, it's Exhibit 213F, Colonel Hawkins.

A. Yes, sir. We are both familiar with my letters, Mr. Dorsen. My wife probably doesn't remember as much.

Q. Could you look at Exhibit 213F, Colonel Hawkins? Does that refresh your recollection as to whether you understood on or about May 17, 1967, that Admiral Sharp was going to visit [military] intelligence?

A. This is very interesting, sir. I don't remember reading this right recently, but it clears up some of your questions, sir, you have been asking me.

Q. We did give you your letters back, didn't we, Colonel Hawkins?

A. Yes, sir. I have the entire packet. If you had not sent them back you would have heard from my wife.

Q. Colonel Hawkins—

A. They weren't gems.

THE COURT: Let's get to the next question.

Like the war, like the trial, the pace of the disintegration of a witness's veracity is glacial, and then suddenly precipitous. Hawkins had admitted, for example, during his deposition, that at the time of the Ellsberg trial he had become "antagonistic" toward Sam Adams, because Adams "sort of led me to believe that he mistrusted General McChristian, and that turned me off cold"; more significantly, that when he was to appear as a witness in the

Ellsberg case "I was ready to commit perjury," because "I despised that Ellsberg fellow." ("Q. Did you lie to the prosecutor or to the agents who came and saw you? A. Yes, sir. I don't know how starkly lying it would be. I guess, when you came right down to it, identify it, I lied about what happened in Vietnam.") But Hawkins would have been well prepared by counsel, perhaps even eager, for questions about the Ellsberg matter. Dorsen simply reserved it for the moment and went on:

Q. Colonel Hawkins, does Exhibit 213F refresh your recollection that, on or about May 17, 1967, a visit by Admiral Sharp . . . was anticipated?

A. Yes, sir. That is indicated in this letter. . . .

Q. I am asking you whether it refreshes your recollection as to whether or not you did participate in any briefing or preparation for a briefing?

A. No, sir, it does not. It simply refreshes my recollection that Admiral Sharp was due in Saigon. . . .

Q. Do you recall now whether you discussed Admiral Sharp's visit with anybody, on or about May 17, 1967?

A. I don't recall it, sir.

Q. Do you recall whether or not you discussed it with General McChristian?

A. I don't recall it, sir, at this time. . . .

Q. Under procedures in effect in May, 1967, how would you have learned of Admiral Sharp's visit?

A. I could have learned about it in many different ways. I could have passed an officer in the hallway, and he could have said "Admiral Sharp is here in town." . . .

Q. Do you recall any discussion with General McChristian on the subject of the visit by Admiral Sharp?

A. No, sir. I do not recall that. I wish this paragraph could be read, but this is not my turf. . . .

Q. [reading] "Admiral Sharp is due in next week. General McC" —that's General McChristian, Colonel Hawkins?

A. That's correct.

Q. —"doesn't have to brief him. Think General McC is stacking arms anyway." . . . *How would you have learned,* Colonel Hawkins, as to whether or not General McChristian would have had to have briefed Admiral Sharp?

A. I stated here, sir, "I think General McChristian"—wait a minute. "General McChristian doesn't have to brief him." I don't remember how I would have found that out, sir. [Faltering blather.] I have no reason—I have no information upon which to base the statement that I made when I wrote this letter. I would have known then, but I don't remember this in 1984 [sic]. It's just a statement.

Since there were no conventional villains in these cases, the courtroom took no pleasure in the declining credibility of a once affable and disarming witness; and the demeanor of this witness was somehow turning simultaneously tentative and mulish. Dorsen asked him whether yet another document "refreshed" his recollection of the briefing of Admiral Sharp—which, it was now clear, he had in fact discussed with McChristian.

A. No, sir. It does not. The only briefing I know about is the briefing or briefings that I gave to General Westmoreland, on the 28th of May, as corroborated in letters to my wife, and on the 14th of June, as corroborated in letters to my wife. And the reason I recall these was because it was a sort of *traumatic experience.* I gave many other briefings, but I had no reason, I guess, to remember those.

The once jovial, folksy personage was using the language now of trauma, although why either of his briefings of Westmoreland (to the extent he could recall them) should have been traumatic was not clear.

Q. You have no recollection of a briefing on or about May 19, 1967, to Admiral Sharp?
A. No, sir. I have no recollection that I presented a briefing to Admiral Sharp on May 19th.

Also:

Q. Do you have any recollection of *hearing about* such a briefing, Colonel Hawkins, of Admiral Sharp or any other people, on or about May 19, 1967?

A. *I may or may not have for one of various reasons.* I do not recall
the briefing, sir. I have answered that *over and over and over
again, sir.*

MR. DORSEN: Your Honor, would this be a convenient time for the
break?

THE COURT: All right. We will adjourn for lunch. We will resume
at quarter to three.

That afternoon, however, under a special arrangement in
Westmoreland, whereby no elderly or infirm witness would
be required to testify for more than four hours in succession,
Hawkins' cross-examination was interrupted. The morning it
would have been resumed, the next court calendar day (February
19, 1985), was the Tuesday morning of the Joint Statement and the
"discontinuance." The Ellsberg matter was thus never raised in
open court. Certain other unequivocal testimony, from Hawkins'
deposition ("Q. Is it clear to you that there was no order for you
to do anything, as that term is understood in the military? A.
There was no order, no"), was never brought out. The testimony
Dorsen had objected to was never stricken. And, with his small,
confused, equivocal tirade ("I may or may not have"; "I do not
recall"; "I have answered that over and over and over again, sir"),
the second of the two fabled military witnesses who were supposed
so to have daunted Westmoreland left his hours of celebrity and
the witness stand.

The witnesses, military and civilian, from the intelligence
communities (and there were others, both for the defense
and for the plaintiff, besides the fabled two), had their odd, major
role in *Westmoreland;* but the most remarkable witnesses, in both
Sharon v. *Time* and *Westmoreland* v. *CBS,* were undoubtedly the
members of the press. As early as the first depositions in *Sharon,*

it was evident that witnesses with a claim to any sort of journalistic affiliation considered themselves a class apart, by turns lofty, combative, sullen, lame, condescending, speciously pedantic, but, above all, socially and, as it were, Constitutionally arrogant, in a surprisingly unintelligent and uneducated way. Who *are* these people? is a question that would occur almost constantly to anyone upon reading or hearing the style and substance of their testimony. And why do they consider themselves entirely above the rules? These people were, to begin with, professionals, accustomed to speak with finality, never questioned except by their bosses; otherwise (in a field that, unlike, for example, true scholarship, suppresses second thoughts and confirming, or contradictory, inquiry) accustomed, in what they said or wrote, to being believed. In addition, these people had, in recent years, the power and glamour of the byline, and the contemporary notion of journalists as, in effect, celebrities bearing facts. What they were intellectually was in some ways surprising: better educated than their predecessors, they were not remarkable for their capacity to reason, or for their sense of language and of the meaning of even ordinary words. Nonetheless, they appeared before the courts not like any ordinary citizens but as though they had condescended to appear there, with their own conception of truth, of legal standards, and of what were to be the rules. As for "serious doubt," it seemed at times unlikely that any of these people had ever entertained one—another indication that "serious doubt" cannot long continue as a form of "actual malice" in the law. What was true and false also seemed, at times, a matter of almost complete indifference to them. Above all, the journalists, as witnesses, looked like people whose mind it had never crossed to be ashamed.

The only rule that they did seem unequivocally to accept they used either to hide behind or to inflate their own importance. The shield law, for "confidential sources," was invoked in *Sharon* with such frequency and in such a preposterous variety of circumstances (when the source had already been named, several times and on the record; when the source was already, for other reasons, public; when the witness clearly had no notion who or what the source was; when the issue was not who the source was but what he said; when nothing that was said was "confidential"; when there was no "source") that it sometimes seemed that the witness, using, in fact, the same locution, "I decline to answer on the grounds that," had no better claim to be protecting by this means the small, worthy publications and the First Amendment than a rich racketeer who would claim, by invoking the privilege against self-incrimination, to be protecting worthy, poor defendants and the Fifth.

Of all the witnesses in both cases, Halevy, Kelly, Duncan and Crile seemed to represent, in their various capacities, the most extreme and yet characteristic claims of journalism before the courts. Also: a relatively minor figure, the fact checker (called, at *Time*, "reporter-researcher"), Helen Doyle (minor only in the sense that it was in the very nature of Halevy's story not to be subject to Doyle's or to any conventional checking, but remarkable for the proposition that even *Time*'s fact checkers assumed all of the journalist's peculiar manners on the stand); Sam Adams, the paid consultant and former member of the C.I.A., for bridging, in an extraordinary way, the special claims of journalism and "intelligence"; and Ray Cave, then *Time*'s managing editor, less for his testimony on the witness stand than for his appearances, in the corridors and on the courthouse steps, before that other jury, the press or, more precisely, *Time*'s colleagues in the press.

These were the earmarks of Halevy's testimony on the stand and at his deposition: a virtual incapacity to give a straight answer to a simple factual question, coupled with an almost complete indifference both to what is conventionally understood by "facts" and to consistency between his own factual accounts or versions from one moment to the next; remarkably frequent use of the words "clear" and "very clear," almost invariably in the course of unintelligible, unresponsive or plain absolutely implausible answers, and of the phrase "in substance, not in words" (almost nobody, in Halevy's testimony, ever *said* anything in words; people addressed each other either "in substance" or "in body language"); a highly personal idiom, which lapsed, at difficult moments, into malapropism of an almost delightful sort,

Because, as a journalist . . . you don't want to be involved, you don't want to be caught with the red herring in your hands.

Because I was described at the time . . . as a traitor, as Lord Ho Ho of Israel, as the Rose of Tokyo.

If I had that conversation with one of these prime sources, I believe that the issue of the memo was brought up, but it's an iffy;

an idiosyncratic notion of his craft, and of writing generally,

A. [It was] a matter of composing, in writing, and not of conveying information. . . .

It's a form of writing when I said "questioning": it was statements.

Q. Did you notice a difference in words?
A. Not in meaning, no.

THE COURT: You didn't notice a difference in words?
[Deposition: "A. No, it was in the exact language that we sent to New York, and it was beautifully phrased, and we had no problems with it."]

Q. [You didn't notice that] there had been a change?
A. It's the same meaning. . . . When we talk about language, I understand meaning;

an occasional, unembarrassed petulance,

Q. How do you know what he told him?
A. Sir, if you will let me finish, I will tell you.
Q. Go ahead. . . .
A. No, I will stop . . .

Q. Somebody mentioned?
A. Not somebody. Pierre Gemayel is not somebody.
Q. Pierre Gemayel?
A. Somebody.

A. Nobody of those who attacked me so viciously four years before that said "I am sorry. I am apologizing," any kind of thing, nothing.

Q. Go ahead, finish your conversations.
A. No, be my guest.
Q. I didn't hear what you said.
A. I said, "Be my guest." You stopped me.

THE COURT: . . . Is that what you mean?
A. No, because he is again taking my answer, twisting it, turning it upside down and expects me to say yes. No, I can't do it.

A. What I said in my deposition and what I am saying here. You are distorting it. What do you want me to do with it? I am the witness, and you are attacking me. So be it;

and a kind of bizarre, self-confident, but utterly misguided pedantry, which led him to insist on certain distinctions ("You used the word 'investigation.' I said 'search.' There is a big difference between the two"; "There is no intelligence officer, Mr. Gould. I said an intelligence person"), and to venture several times (Judge: "told"; Halevy: "stated." Judge: "was"; Halevy: "were") to correct the grammar of the judge. Kelly, too, was inclined to this sort of thing ("I said 'military *dash* intelligence' "), and so were virtually all *Time* witnesses, from Duncan to the fact checker. Despite a considerable facility in English, Halevy had a tendency to characterize as "trivial" or "totally irrelevant" certain key elements of the case. Thus, whether or not he had written the words "for Revenge" in the headline "Green Light for Revenge?" became, between his deposition and his testimony at trial, "totally irrelevant"; so did whether or not he himself had *seen* (and told Kelly he had seen) the "newly discovered notes," or "minutes," of the meeting at Bikfaya at which "revenge" was allegedly discussed. What was said to him by Duncan in Athens, when Duncan put him on "probation," became "irrelevant," in the light of the letter that confirmed that conversation. Indeed, the article "The Verdict Is Guilty" itself became, according to Halevy, "totally irrelevant" (and, in effect, understated) in view of his own post-publication research. And yet, fairly late in Halevy's trial testimony:

Q. Do you know what "irrelevant" means?
A. I think I do.

Q. Tell us what you think it means.
A. Insignificant, not important.

Nor was this sort of difficulty confined just to Halevy. Four days later, on the witness stand, Kelly, the Jerusalem bureau chief, repeatedly characterized the whole paragraph at issue in the lawsuit, as he had once characterized it in a telex to Duncan, as "innocuous."

Q. You characterized that as innocuous, did you not?
A. Yes, sir. I did.

A. I still think it is innocuous, sir.
Q. "Innocuous" means what to you?
A. Without great drama.
Q. What? I am sorry. I didn't hear you.
A. Without drama, without great importance.

And, of course, these bits of testimony would themselves be, by any definition, irrelevant and innocuous were it not for the fact that these witnesses had, in their professional capacity, made substantial contributions to the paragraph, which the world's largest and most respected news magazine was engaged in this major litigation to stand behind.

It was not difficult, when all the testimony was in, to reconstruct what must have happened in *Sharon*. Halevy, having been severely censured at least once for a story *Time* printed and had subsequently to retract (and having been warned, as a condition of his probation, to produce "multiple sourcing," where possible, on all stories), heard or read in early December of 1982 that there existed previously undisclosed notes of Sharon's condolence call of September 15, 1982, on the Gemayels. In all probability, his "source" was Lebanese; more specifically, Phalangist; most specifically, one Fadi Frem (a son-in-law of Pierre and brother-in-law of Bashir and Amin Gemayel), whom Halevy alone, and with great insistence, placed at the Bikfaya meeting. By all other accounts, Frem was outside. In any event, this Phalangist, for perhaps obvious reasons (the Lebanese had conducted no inquiry of their own into responsibility for the massacres at Sabra and Shatila; no Lebanese consented to appear publicly before the Kahan Commission), told Halevy that newly discovered *Phalangist* "notes," or "minutes," of the meeting showed that Sharon "gave them the feeling . . . that he understood the need to take revenge." Indeed, the very wording of Halevy's Memo Item of December 6, 1982, on slightly closer scrutiny, made no sense *unless* the source was Phalangist, since no one else was placed to know what "feeling" Sharon gave "them"—and no one else, of course, had quite so immediate an interest in shifting blame for the massacres from the Phalangists to Sharon. No doubt the "source" portrayed Sharon's role at the meeting in stronger terms than these. But a story reading "According to Fadi Frem" (or "a highly placed Phalangist"), "who made notes of the meeting, Sharon ordered the Phalange to massacre the Palestinians" was not a story *Time* would print. In fact, to its considerable credit and at the editor-in-chief's insistence, *Time* ran, in the same issue as "The Verdict Is Guilty," a brief story pointing out that Lebanon had never conducted a real inquiry of its own. So Halevy, perhaps judiciously rephrasing ("gave them the feeling," for "ordered them"), filed his Memo Item of December 6th, attributing his information to "a highly reliable source." When the New York office asked, two days later by telex for "clearance" (that is, whether the item was sufficiently reliable to run not just in the Worldwide Memo but in the magazine itself), Halevy, without hesitation and without, by his own admission, checking further (claiming, at his deposition, to have been caught that week in the rush of his departure from Israel for Central America; though, virtually unperceived by any of the lawyers, he revealed at trial that his departure had really occurred the following month), simply cleared it.

Now, Duncan, as can be pieced together from other testimony, had warned Kelly, when Kelly became Jerusalem bureau chief, that Halevy was rather "a special blessing" and that, on the basis of Halevy's history at *Time*, Kelly should be especially careful about Halevy's sources. Halevy, it is quite clear from Kelly's testimony (and Halevy not only did not deny it; he could not in fact bring himself, till the bitter end, to admit that he had *not* read the "newly discovered notes"), assured Kelly that he himself had seen, by way of an *Israeli* source, the "notes" to which his Memo Item referred. (It was widely known in Israel that General Rafael Eitan was looking for such notes.) Bearing in mind, no doubt, the admonition about "multiple sourcing," Halevy also said or implied to Kelly that he had several "sources" for his story, mainly, however (it is clear from Kelly's testimony, somewhat enshrouded by claims of the shield), the best "source" of all: a man undeniably present at Bikfaya, the "official notetaker" from the Israeli intelligence service, the Mossad. Something about the Memo Item, however, caused Duncan (according to Duncan's testimony) to ask Kelly whether he was "comfortable" with the story and its sources; Kelly replied that Halevy had both actually seen the "notes" themselves and learned about them (and here Duncan, too, somewhat veiled his testimony in claims of the shield) from the "notetaker" of the Mossad. Even so, something about the whole matter caused Duncan to hesitate. Though Halevy had "cleared" the story, and Kelly had conveyed Halevy's assurances about it, the story did not run that week in *Time*. Duncan and Kelly agreed that it should be subject to an "ongoing investigation." And there the matter rested for five weeks, until Halevy, surely exasperated that the "scoop," for which he thought he had provided such an impeccable provenance from "sources," had not been published in the magazine, finally left for Nicaragua, and a very minor story about Israeli arms shipments abroad, which did not run until months after Halevy wrote it—and weeks after the Sharon lawsuit had begun.

On February 8, 1983, Halevy returned to Israel to help with *Time*'s cover story on the Kahan Report. Kelly, who had been in Israel only three months, and who did not know even the alphabet in Hebrew (in his deposition and at trial, he claimed that one reason he had not checked the story directly with Sharon was that he was incapable of looking up Sharon's number in an Israeli phone book), asked Halevy whether he knew what was in the Kahan Report's secret section, to which the published document referred at least nine times within brackets, Appendix B. And Halevy, perhaps understandably eager to see his story of two months before finally published, said, according to Kelly (and

Halevy testified, "His recollection" of the conversation "is ten times better than mine"), "I know one thing that is in it: my Memo Item from December." Kelly asked him to check it. Halevy went to an adjoining office, where, he said, he phoned his "sources." A short time later he returned to Kelly's office and (according to Kelly) said, "It's confirmed. It's in there," or (according to Halevy) communicated, in body language, "a sort of thumbs up," "in substance, not in words, that the information which we discussed earlier previously is confirmed." Kelly duly filed his story, including, in what became known as Take Nine, the sentence "And some of [Appendix B], we understand, was published in *Time*'s Worldwide Memo, an item by Halevy, Dec. 6, for which we gave clearance . . ."

In New York, *Time*'s writer William Smith rewrote the Memo Item, as is the magazine's institutional practice, making substantial changes. (Halevy: "No, it was in the exact language that we sent to New York, and it was beautifully phrased.") The changes, however, were easily explicable: "discussed with the Gemayels the need for the Phalangists to take revenge" for "gave them the feeling, after the Gemayels' questioning, that he understood their need to take revenge . . . and assured them that the Israeli army would neither hinder them nor try to stop them." And, also in accordance with *Time*'s routine procedures, Smith's completed story was anyway telexed to the Jerusalem bureau, for "C & C"; that is, "Comments and Corrections." The staff members of the Jerusalem bureau, to their credit, did find and correct two minor factual errors—both of which, as it happened, were anti-Israel in their implications. And one of the reasons all of *Time*'s personnel who were involved directly in the reporting, writing, and editing of the paragraph accepted so readily its allegations concerning Sharon, it emerged from all their testimony, was paradoxical: the Kahan Report, as published, did not seem to them to contain a case against Sharon strong enough to support the commission's recommendation that he be fired, or resign, from his position as Minister of Defense. That is, in a kind of failure to comprehend the commission's finding of what it called "indirect responsibility" (namely, a degree of moral responsibility imputed to one who, though he did not know that disastrous consequences would follow his actions, or failures to act, should have known, or, more important, should have acted as if he knew), the magazine's employees searched the published report in vain for evidence that Sharon *did* know, and even intended, that massacres would follow from his actions; and, finding no evidence for such knowledge, concluded (as every *Time* witness put it) that the real case against Sharon lay "between the lines." From "between the lines" of a published report to its unpublished, "secret" appendix is a short intellectual jump—even though the published report, in this case, specifically called attention, by mentioning Appendix B in brackets, to each instance of reference to its secret section, and though the evidence *Time*'s employees thought they found (a one-sentence account of Sharon's condolence call on the Gemayels) had no such brackets or reference of any other kind. With this profound but understandable intellectual failure (the kind of "indirect responsibility" the Kahan Commission defined had no precedent in law); and under deadline pressure; and with Halevy's word for his assurances from his proliferating "sources" (which included, by now, the "notes" themselves; the Mossad "note-taker"; an "Israeli general"; an "intelligence person"; and Appendix B), *Time* published its paragraph, containing the allegation, regarded universally and within *Time* itself as a reporting coup, that a secret section of the Kahan Commission's findings contained "details" of a conversation in which, on the day after the assassination of Bashir Gemayel and on the eve of the massacres at Sabra and Shatila, Sharon had discussed with the Gemayels "the need . . . to take revenge."

All this was explicable, defensible, and human; and, with the arguably minor exception of Halevy (in misrepresenting the number, the reliability and the nature of his "sources"), all *Time* personnel conducted themselves professionally, and even honorably, up to and including the moment when the cover story reached the stands. Duncan, for example, showed an admirable instinct in hesitating to publish, at the time and without "ongoing investigation," Halevy's Memo Item of December 6th. Of course, to an outsider, or perhaps only in retrospect, every element of the story is totally and self-evidently preposterous. At least from the moment Halevy claimed to have "confirmed," *by phone, from the*

Jerusalem offices of a major publication, information that any Israeli "source" could have given or confirmed to him only in serious violation of Israeli secrecy and national-security law, these journalists, so preoccupied with "secrets," and "confidential sources," and "investigative reporting," and invoking the shield law to protect the identity of "sources," should have suspected that something, in fact everything, was amiss. Even Duncan, at his deposition, in explaining, in a fairly condescending way, why he did not ask Kelly, on one occasion, who certain "sources" were, said, apparently without realizing at all the implications, "I would never use names on the telephone in Israel." Israel has a censor. Israel has a secret service. Israel is, technically and legally, in a state of war with all its Arab neighbors except Egypt. It seems axiomatic that in most countries, but particularly in Israel, not one "source" (and particularly not, as Halevy would have it, several "sources," and those highly placed in civilian and military intelligence) will violate, seriously and at a moment's notice, by telephone, on a line with the offices of a major, internationally circulated publication, the highest secrecy and security laws of his country, to oblige even an "investigative reporter," who wants to confirm a story, to the satisfaction of his immediate boss, who is in the process of sending the ninth "take" of a telex, in the adjoining room. Still, Kelly was inexperienced in Israeli matters. Duncan was not in direct communication with Halevy. Mistakes will happen, in any enterprise, including publication, and especially, by its very nature, publication of the news. And there was still the possibility that, except for the "confirmation," the story was not a mistake. Up to and through the moment of publication, in other words, *Time*'s position and its paragraph were well within the rules.

It was, of course, *after* publication that difficulties arose. Because when the person most obviously and directly implicated in the paragraph, and others in a position to have knowledge of the matter, vociferously and unequivocally denied it, *Time* refused both to investigate the matter further and to consider a retraction. The bureau chief congratulated the chief of correspondents for having created such a stir; and the institution refused to doubt. And neither the facts of the matter itself nor the journalistic processes that led to publication could have been reconstructed by anyone outside of *Time* unless Sharon had brought suit. Once suit was filed, the difficulties were compounded: still without further investigation of any kind, *Time* stood by its paragraph and spared no money, time or moral effort to defend it, on no firmer basis than a kind of institutional solidarity; a relatively unexamined conception of the interests of journalism and the Constitution; and Halevy's already, well before the first day of his deposition, compromised and somewhat tarnished word.

To the question Why publish the story? the answer was easy: *Time* believed it to be true. To the question Why defend it, with the most aggressive strategies of well-funded major litigation (and beyond: in contradiction to a complete concession made last January as part of a settlement before an Israeli court, *Time* defends the substance of the paragraph to this day)? the answer *Time* still believes it to be true is not sufficient. Why not? For one thing, older than the First Amendment safeguards of freedom of speech and of the press was Western civilization's interest in the Ninth Commandment. "False witness," by any definition, has always included libel and slander, and certain forms of perjury. The two former generals seemed particularly robust "neighbors" under the commandment. (And it is no more difficult to reconstruct, on the basis of testimony, the processes that led to *Westmoreland;* the simplest explanation, however, is that if Crile, or anyone, had gone to CBS News with a proposal for a program based on the thesis that five years ago, and eight years after the events in question, we lost a war as a result in part of having underestimated enemy troop strength, and devoted to ninety minutes of balanced exposition, from one viewpoint and another, of who might have been responsible for those underestimates, if they were in fact underestimates, CBS News would have said, at best, "What else is new?" and "Are you crazy, ninety minutes?" and sent him on his way.) It can also be said that no person or institution, in all the years before broadcasting and the other forms of mass publication, was placed to bear false witness into nearly every household, on anything like the modern scale. Moreover, Professor Owen M. Fiss, of the Yale Law School, has argued that the scale of the contemporary media has created a condition, never contemplated in the Constitution, in which the two freedoms, of speech and of the press, may actually be at odds. When journalism brings to bear the whole technology of dissemination, backed at every point by the whole arsenal of litigating strategies, the speech of all but the most powerful is, to all intents and purposes, suppressed. Sharon and Westmoreland were "neighbors" powerful enough to make themselves heard, in press conferences, against what they regarded as false witness, and, when the press, in each instance, stood by, and even reiterated, its position, to pursue the matter, under oath, and through the courts. Both would, as a result precisely of that power, if not immediately then at some appellate level, have lost their cases; but, along the way, they had the means and the opportunity, under the legal system's toughest standard, to prove, to the satisfaction of a jury, that the witness borne against them was false. But few citizens are placed as powerfully as former generals. And though the First Amendment has been held, since *Sullivan*, to tolerate a certain category of inadvertently false statements, in the name of freedom of debate and of expression, it cannot be held to license wholesale violations of the Ninth Commandment, or to abrogate a profound system of values, which holds that words themselves are powerful, that false words leave the world diminished, and that false defamatory words have an actual power to do harm. Nor can it be that any Constitutional or journalistic interest is served by these stages of resolute insistence (first, in the world, after the moment of publication; then, under oath, in the courts) that the story, the "witness," as published, is true; and of resolute refusal to inquire (first, for reasons largely of public relations; then, when suit is brought, on the advice of lawyers), all for the sake of "winning," and without care, at any point after publication, whether the story, the witness (now even in the literal, legal sense), is, quite simply, false.

But *Time* and CBS, aggressive as they were, with and through Cravath, in the conduct of their cases, were not, at least not entirely, knaves, or fools or villains. Both cases, in fact, were very nearly settled at various points along the way. CBS, fairly early in the trial, offered to pay Westmoreland's legal costs, plus a nominal sum, and to issue a judiciously worded retraction. Burt, however, having fared better than Boies in discovery and the, arguably improper, battle of leaking evidence to the press in the months before trial, became overconfident in his ability to handle the trial itself, and turned the offer down. During the trial, while Boies found time to make himself available to reporters on many evenings, Burt became alternately introverted and short-tempered with the press and, to a degree that even the jurors observed, with his own staff. His performance in court was not being well reviewed. What praise, and even advice, Burt received, and seemed to value, came increasingly from Boies—who frequently assured him, in the presence of others, at the end of the courtroom day, that he had handled a witness or a line of questioning extremely well. Boies also told Burt, several times, that Dorsen was ineffective and not a team player, and actually advised Burt to take Dorsen off the case. Asked, after the trial, by a reporter *when* he had given Burt this advice, Boies said "six or eight times," three times pretrial and the rest while the trial was actually going on. Meanwhile, Burt and his own few associates were becoming, as one young associate subsequently put it, "estranged."

In *Sharon,* it was *Time* that turned away: once, before the trial began, from a settlement that *Time*'s attorneys assured opposing counsel they would recommend to their client (and that the client then turned down); again, in December, near the end of trial, when *Time*'s attorneys assured opposing counsel that their client had accepted a proposed settlement, and the client, before signing, changed its mind. This second failure to settle marked a turning point in *Sharon. Time*'s reconsideration, and rejection, of the settlement it had just agreed to has never been satisfactorily explained. Indeed, it has never been explained at all; there is only the court record to show that it occurred. What might possibly have prompted the reconsideration was, of all things, an article on the Op-Ed page of *The New York Times.* In the article, Ira Glasser, executive director of the American Civil Liberties Union, praised CBS and *Time,* by implication, for withstanding the grave threats posed by the lawsuits to First Amendment rights. Neither Glasser nor the *Times,* of course, could know that, on the very day the piece was published, an accord between the plaintiff and the defendant in *Sharon* would have been (and, possibly because of the piece, was not) signed. All courts and all judges advocate settlement, wherever possible, in civil cases. It is a matter of principle, and of public policy, to encourage settlement instead of litigation to the bitter end. And Judge Sofaer, in an Opinion and Order signed on November 26, 1984 (but sealed until late January, when the case was over), put it very firmly:

> The favorable treatment accorded to the judgments of reporters, in their reportorial function, provides no support for deferring to an excessively aggressive and hence unnecessarily costly litigation strategy adopted by the press at trial. The press, in short, has no more right than any other litigant—and far less reason in light of its Constitutional defenses—to turn a libel litigation into an unlimited war. . . . [The] remedy lies in adjusting the law to enhance conciliation [rather than persisting in] their increasingly inflamed views of each other in a drama whose conclusion could be a major disaster for at least one of them.

And by December 20, 1984, in the courtroom (jury not present):

> And so the issue is posed very starkly. Mr. Halevy is at risk in this litigation. Mr. Sharon is at risk in this litigation. I have said that to the parties from the outset. I have tried to tell you both that you are putting yourselves in the hands of the jury, not only yourselves as *institutions,* or as *law firms,* or as *magazines,* but as two people, Ariel Sharon and David Halevy.

It is very unusual for a judge to include "law firms" among the parties at risk in litigation. December 20th was also the day the defense, at the conclusion of the plaintiff's case, without calling a single witness, rested. All *Time*'s witnesses had, of course, appeared, and been questioned by their own counsel, when they were called by Sharon's attorneys, as "hostile" witnesses, to the stand.

MR. SAUNDERS: Yes, your Honor. We will rest.
MR. GOULD: I need hardly explain to your Honor that we are astonished, in view of the colloquy that we had this morning.
THE COURT: I am not astonished. Just for the record. . . .
MR. GOULD: You know, it is one of the peculiarities of this case that

they did put in a case, through the witnesses that we called, while technically they were our witnesses, obviously.

On January 2, 1985, when there was no longer any doubt, in anybody's mind, that there were no "details," or even any mention, either of a discussion of "revenge," or even of Bikfaya, in Appendix B; but when it was still unclear whether Israel would or would not provide access to all other evidence relevant to the case (both attorneys said they had prepared their summations to the jury on the assumption that Israel would not provide such access; the judge said that he had made the same assumption in drafting his charge), Judge Sofaer made one last, wistful effort to encourage settlement. This was the day he expressed his intention "to put this case to rest forever"; but he also said:

> I haven't given up on constructive talking. It seems like the atmosphere has gotten less and less conducive to that, whereas it should be getting more and more so.

But there was no settlement. And the reason *Time*'s repudiation of the second agreement marked a turning point was that Cravath, in what Judge Sofaer had already characterized, in his Opinion and Order of November 12, 1984, as "*Time*'s all-out litigation strategy," thereafter set out on *so* broad and aggressive a course of litigation that it attacked not only Sharon, for alleged acts of brutality and dishonesty ranging back to his earliest youth (including an incident, in 1953, at Kibye, which was covered, in a particularly lurid piece of misreporting, in *Time,* under Henry Luce), and for alleged perjury before the Kahan Commission (in testifying that he did not know or intend that the massacres at Sabra and Shatila would occur), and for alleged perjury in *Sharon v. Time* itself (for denying that the discussion at Bikfaya of "the need to take revenge" occurred), but, inescapably and by implication, the integrity of the Kahan Commission. Because, in imputing to Sharon only "indirect responsibility" for the massacres; and in not mentioning the "revenge" discussion in the published report; and in not attaching to its one-sentence, uninflected account of the "condolence call" at Bikfaya a mention in brackets, or any other sort of reference to Appendix B, the commission became, inescapably, not an honest (and legally unprecedented) inquiry into national responsibility but a whitewash and a coverup. And the attack, of course, implicated the whole State of Israel. Because certain acts of alleged brutality ascribed to Sharon were incidents in Israel's early history, which Israel regarded as acts committed, as humanely as possible in the circumstances of war, in its own defense; and because if the Kahan Commission was not an honest inquiry then the State of Israel, which had appointed the commission, and accepted its report and recommendations, was, initially and finally, but at all times directly, responsible, probably for the massacres themselves but in any event for the coverup. And it is likely that, in so broadening its attack and its theory of the case, Cravath inadvertently caused the government of Israel to reconsider its reluctance to permit unprecedented access, in private litigation, to its most secret documents. It may be that the defense, in this broad view of the case, for some time believed that Israel *could* not permit such access, under rules agreed to by the court and both parties, because the documents themselves would prove so compromising, and thereby confirm the defense's theory of the case; or that Israel would not permit such access, simply because it had not already done so, and certainly had shown no eagerness to help the plaintiff, whom many Israelis, including members of the government, considered, for reasons quite outside the litigation, dangerous. Certainly the government of Israel could not so precisely have calculated the time of its decision as to coincide quite literally with *Sharon* v. *Time*'s last minute; and certainly Cravath so abruptly rested its case when it realized that Israel's decision was imminent, and in the hope that it would come too late. For some time, American judicial process and Israeli parliamentary process were in suspension. In all likelihood, it was the breadth and harshness of Cravath's attack that triggered the result. But what set these forces in motion had been, after all, a paragraph; and the very narrowness of the initial issue brought not so much *Time*'s journalistic procedures as its participation in the judicial process into particularly sharp relief.

"And so the issue is posed very starkly" had been, for a particularly precise and eloquent judge, an odd thing to have to say. "Mr.

Halevy is at risk in this litigation. Mr. Sharon is at risk in this litigation." But Sharon, though "at risk" in the obvious ways, was a relatively minor figure in the case; and the judge also, at one point, suggested mildly, to *Time* to check whether its paragraph might have been wrong, and, if it was, to say so, and leave "the ultimate issue of Minister Sharon's morality to the arena of public debate, where it belongs." And the case was not, after all, *Sharon v. Halevy;* it was *Sharon v. Time;* and *Time* somehow chose to *make it the same thing.* There are several reasons a publication might choose to do this: that the reporter is an admirable, oppressed and courageous figure (a sort of John Peter Zenger reason); or that the reporter is an ordinary, competent, representative member of the staff, in the sound exercise of his profession (a reason of professional principle and staff morale). But there was something about Halevy that seemed to turn all such reasons upside down, and to bemuse and inspire *Time*'s attorneys to the outer edge of their litigating style, as it transformed the magazine's hierarchy of veteran, seasoned journalists into complacent, credulous, patronizing figures, each one incapable of giving a straight answer to a factual question, in his own individual way. It must be admitted that there *was* something disorienting about Halevy. *Lord Haw-Haw* and *Tokyo Rose* were easy enough; but any number of things he said gave one a little jolt, or double take, of, Wait a minute, just too late to catch up with whatever he might say next. It always seems surprising that as witnesses before even the most august or crowded courtrooms, in even the most difficult cases, people, even normally timid people, do not seem nervous. By and large, witnesses are calm. The most common explanation for this is that they have so often been through the same material, with the same opposing counsel, under such "hostile" circumstances, at their depositions, that being questioned in the presence of the judge by their own counsel, or even by opposing counsel, seems relatively benign. Still, Halevy's frequent "Be my guest"; or "It's not my writing. I did not carry out the massacre; the Phalangists did. So, sir, what are we talking?"; or "I don't want to argue with you, Mr. Gould"; or "It's not my duty to judge you here, Mr. Gould" seemed the answers of a man inordinately at ease, in his own courtroom.

Q. Did he come to you or did you go to him?
A. Does it make any difference?
MR. BARR: *Answer.*
A. I am sorry. I came to him.

This exasperated *"Answer,"* from *Time*'s chief counsel in the case, was the only indication that the attorneys were ever anything other than enchanted by this correspondent. (It may even be that there is something both amusing and especially challenging to a lawyer in a witness who will, or might, from one moment to the next, say *anything.*) And, from at least the first day of his deposition, counsel and client must have realized they had something of a rogue witness on their hands. Here is how his deposition, and Kelly's and Duncan's, looked.

David Halevy's deposition occupied four full days, beginning on Wednesday, September 19, 1984, and ending with a brief session on Tuesday, September 25th, the fifth day, with testimony that lasted only an hour and forty minutes. His testimony at the trial occupied six full days, beginning on the afternoon of Tuesday, November 27th, and continuing through the morning of Thursday, December 6th. In the afternoon, he was succeeded on the stand by Harry Kelly, whose deposition had taken four days, from September 17th through September 20th, and had included altercations between counsel, Richard Goldstein, of Shea & Gould ("I think that is done in utter bad faith and I say so on this record, . . . I think it's an outrage that you want to practice like this"), and Stuart Gold, of Cravath ("I think, Mr. Goldstein, that your statement is so outrageous, I don't even want to grace it with an answer"), and ended with a walkout, by Kelly and Gold. Kelly spent three days on the stand, from December 6th to December 10th. He was succeeded by William Smith, the writer; Helen Doyle, the fact checker; the deposition testimony of two minor witnesses; and then Duncan, whose deposition had lasted three days, from September 11th through September 14th, and who spent three days, from December 13th through December 18th, on the stand. Duncan had been the first major *Time* witness to testify on deposition, Halevy the last. In other words, Halevy, Kelly and Duncan were called to the stand in the reverse order of their depositions; and they spent altogether twenty-four days under oath.

It may be that, in the contemporary notion, or fable, of what an "investigative reporter" is, in contrast, for instance, with any earlier type, the contemporary "investigative reporter," in contemporary myth, and even by his own account, is inevitably not just a rascal but a sort of scoundrel. That is, even though he may emerge from time to time with what the world (or, at least, his editors and colleagues) regards as valuable information, amounting to a reporting coup, at other times he is bound, by his techniques of mystification, which include the "confidential source," not only to misunderstand, distort and exaggerate what he does know (or has heard somewhere and claims to know) but to fabricate, or at least be tempted to fabricate, what he doesn't. For the editors of an otherwise responsible publication, such a fellow must present a sort of quandary. He purports to know a story still unknown to any of his rivals. In the past, he has occasionally been right with stories of that kind. On other occasions, he hasn't. In any case, he is the publication's employee. His employers obviously believe, at least initially, that they have grounds to trust him. And if they do not accept and print the story he claims to know, they run what they have come to regard as the awful threat that some rival publication is going to scoop them. The pressure to publish the story, moreover, is increased by what the editors see as the charm and persuasiveness of this fellow, who *has* after all (the same quality) managed to ingratiate himself from time to time with a "confidential source." And since contemporary journalists so rarely contradict *whatever* story a colleague, albeit a rival, may have published, but rush, rather, to pursue the same, perhaps erroneous story further, the editor is under almost no countervailing pressure not to publish. At worst, he risks an outraged letter from someone, somewhere, which, no matter how thoroughly it may demolish every factual assertion in a given piece, never carries, and, of course, can never carry, the weight of the initial and erroneous story. A thorough study of letters columns in publications ostensibly concerned with news can be a revelation, and a case history in disproportion and injustice, compounded when the editors follow the letter either with a scathing answer from the writer of the original story or with some statement to the effect that the publication stands by its story. The *Times,* almost alone among major news publications, has made an effort to rectify this situation: with both a prominently featured Corrections column and an Editors' Note. But this very policy required a kind of courage—in the face not only of the glee of rivals when such a note or correction appears (as it does now almost every day) but of the criticism of employees and colleagues (who feel that some standard of loyalty is at stake, or that such notes make the paper look ridiculous), and even of readers, who, remarking the frequency of the notes (and the fact that almost no other newspaper has them), tend to think that the *Times* makes an inordinate number of mistakes. And, though both these correction columns may, from day to day, be far from perfect, they express at least an institutional acknowledgment not only of the power of journalism, and the relative helplessness of those whom it misrepresents, but of an obligation to what is, after all, journalism's first and fundamental purpose: accurately to report, and not, out of some atavistic institutional reflex, actively to mislead, to compound an initial error by either leaving it unchallenged or insisting it is true.

In any event, the first day of David Halevy's deposition, September 19, 1984, began slowly and, it seemed, undramatically enough, with only the slightest indication that there would be any difficulty, for example, between opposing counsel (for plaintiff, the young attorney at Shea & Gould, Adam Gilbert; for defendant, Cravath's Barr), and, on the part of Halevy, just a few intimations of his personal style and idiom. "I think Mapai," he said, for example, of a political party to which he once belonged, "was in the center, with a little pinky color there, that's all. . . . There was a tint of pink, of red, of leftish." Within minutes, however, in response to a series of questions which began "After 1969, were you affiliated in any way with any political party in the State of Israel?" and which included "Have you

ever performed any services to the benefit of the Labor Party?,"
Halevy (having already volunteered that in 1969 "I gave a bye-
bye kiss to party affiliation") answered, five times, "No." Soon
after that, having responded negatively, and even expansively, to
a series of questions as to whether he had ever "been sued," or
even "been party to a litigation," Halevy, in response to the
rather startling question "Have you ever been involved as a defendant in any criminal proceeding brought in any jurisdiction?," also answered, "No." The very next question, however,
"Do you recall, sir, whether or not a charge was ever filed
against you in Magistrate's Court in Tel Aviv?," elicited from
Halevy, "Sure. I knew that you will come to it, Mr. Gilbert."
And, within less than four paragraphs, it developed that, in a
complicated episode that included Halevy's holding his maid at
gunpoint, "I was charged with an illegal arrest." There followed
a long exchange, which included:

Q. Was a criminal proceeding commenced against you . . . ?
A. I don't know. . . . I had a lawyer. You can ask him.
Q. To your recollection, did the charge involve improper use of a
revolver?
A. If you want—
MR. BARR: Objection.
A. If you want to take what—
MR. BARR: Yes or no. Answer yes or no.
MR. GILBERT: He can answer it in as many words as he likes.
MR. BARR: Yes, he can, but I am telling him to answer it yes or no.

And the answer was "Yes."

From there, it became clear that the deposition was going to be
neither as undramatic nor as quotidian, and even tedious, as it at
first appeared. The episode with the maid held at gunpoint became
increasingly exotic, but, in spite of the effect Halevy's initial series
of "No"s might have had on his credibility, never came out at
trial. The denial of any affiliation after 1969 with any Israeli political party did surface, however, within the first ten minutes of
Halevy's appearance on the stand. "In 1969, I quit all my involvement in politics," he testified serenely. Then:

Q. At no time were you a member of the Labor Party?
A. At no time at all.
Q. Now, sir, I would like to direct your attention to a deposition that you gave on May 28, 1982, and I am referring to page 10.

And it turned out that, according to Halevy's sworn testimony, in 1982, in a lawsuit called *Sharoni* v. *Media International,* he *had* been a member of the Labor Party; in fact, "I joined the Labor Party and served as editor-in-chief of the Labor Party." Halevy's attempts to account for this transparently flat contradiction included: "The matter . . . during that deposition was not the interest of anybody"; and "It was not the issue. It was not a political deposition"; and "Nobody understood there anything about the Israeli politics . . . I didn't want to confuse them." Furthermore, somewhat later in the trial, Halevy's testimony that he quit all political affiliation (gave, in his words, "a bye-bye kiss" to politics, in 1969) faced what might have seemed, to another sort of witness, another flat and awkward contradiction. Duncan, according to his own testimony under oath, had specifically demanded in 1978 that Halevy desist from his "involvement in Israeli politics," which had included his work for Shimon Peres and the Labor Party in the campaign of 1977.

The maid at gunpoint, and Halevy's sworn testimony, on every side of the question, when, how and whether he had been involved in Israeli politics were, of course, minor, almost inconsequential episodes in the course of litigation, entirely unrelated to the central issues of the trial. But even these first moments of Halevy's testimony, at his deposition and at trial, contained certain key elements of everything that was to follow. First, and most technically, there was the fact that although plaintiff's counsel led the witness almost immediately, in his deposition, into a demonstrably untrue answer (more precisely, an entire sequence of such answers), counsel did not press him too hard. Once Halevy had stated, under oath, unequivocally and for the record, that he had never worked for the Labor Party, and that he had ceased all involvement in Israeli politics in 1969, there was no need (in fact it would have been an act of unprofessional folly) to confront him immediately with his sworn contradictory testimony from that earlier trial. Better by far to let him take the stand and testify, serenely and complacently, in the courtroom, believing, or having every reason to believe, that the earlier testimony, in *Sharoni* v. *Media International,* was safely forgotten; and let the jury (and, for that matter, his own counsel, Barr, to whom the earlier testimony evidently came as a surprise) see how he reacts when he learns that opposing counsel has the information now. What is no news about this is that "discovery" (including, especially, depositions), and perhaps even the entire process of civil litigation, is a kind of game. A less competent attorney than Gilbert might have sprung the earlier testimony right there at Halevy's deposition, thereby alerting both the witness and his counsel, and giving them ample time to prepare a perhaps less lame explanation ("It was not the issue. . . . I didn't want to confuse them") for what the witness now testified, on the stand, was his own false prior testimony under oath.

A more surprising element, reflected not only in this minor incident but pervading nearly all subsequent depositions and the trial itself, was the rather cavalier attitude, even the insouciance, with which all defense witnesses, and their counsel, seemed to face every instance, and there were many, of violations of what is supposed to be the game's most fundamental rule. Tell the truth, every responsible lawyer tells his witnesses in preparing them for their testimony under oath. Yet witnesses on the stand testified so often and so demonstrably in flat contradiction to their own earlier sworn testimony, or to any conceivable version of the truth, that the judge, as though embarrassed (and this is the custom in modern civil litigation), would restrain plaintiff's counsel from stressing or calling too much attention to it. "The record speaks for itself," Judge Sofaer (and, in the other case, Judge Leval) would say, from time to time, when counsel pursued such statements to the verge of demolishing too thoroughly the credibility of any witness; or "The jury will evaluate it"; or "Counsel, you can argue that to the jury." The press witnesses in both trials, on the other hand, seemed so perfectly unfazed at being caught (any ordinary citizen would consider himself "caught") in two flatly incompatible sworn statements that, quite apart from any implications this might have for their sense of fact as journalists, their impression, as witnesses, of what consequences follow in a court of law from less than truthful testimony under oath was clearly not grave.

The first day of Halevy's deposition yielded, in addition to the instances of the witness's personal style and idiom and the two immediate instances of the witness's willingness, indeed, near-imperturbability, about testifying falsely under oath (never having been sued before, when there had been the incident of the maid at gunpoint; and the "bye-bye kiss" to politics in 1969), several instances of the witness's making statements that were inherently implausible (that he learned the story, for example, of the "revenge" discussion two or three weeks before he filed the Memo Item of December 6, 1982; that to the Memo's headline "Green Light for Revenge?" he had contributed only the words "Green Light" and the question mark, and that someone else, perhaps in London or in Paris, had added "for Revenge"); that he had a notion of the protections offered by the New York Shield Law, which adopted the language ("I decline to answer," etc.) but vastly exceeded the protections of the Fifth Amendment; that his memory of certain events of vital importance to the central issues of the case differed radically from the memory of both Kelly, his Jerusalem bureau chief, and Duncan, *Time*'s chief of correspondents (but that, in a rather coy and guarded way, he deferred to their versions). He had, by the first day of his own deposition, read the first two days of Kelly's deposition and all three days of Duncan's. In response to the question whether Kelly was accurate in his testimony that Halevy told him that he himself had read the notes, Halevy said, for instance, "Mr. Kelly is entitled to his answer; I'm entitled to my answer"; "I recall that I thought Mr. Kelly gave you too much information"; and even "I don't recall what was said there, because [whether I saw the notes or not] is a trivial issue, and I think"—at which point his own counsel spoke up with an interruption. The first day revealed, as well, the witness's idiosyncratic notion of what journalistic writing, or any writing, is (when he wrote, for example, in his Memo Item, "a highly reliable source," in the singular, he meant several sources: "[It was] a matter of composing, in writing, and not of conveying information"); and an altogether remarkable indifference to consistency (asked how many were the sources for his Memo Item, he gave, in the course of this day, for example, the answers "between eight and fifteen"; "I will say many"; "not less than eight and not more than fifteen"; "Yes, two prime sources. I don't recall if there were any more"; "But to be exact with you, I will say there were three prime sources"); etc.

The relation between counsel on this day also provided a continuation of what happened in the deposition of Sharon (and Duncan and Kelly), and all subsequent Cravath depositions. "Mr. Gilbert: Tom, could I ask you not to rap your fingers on the table" was an early note: later, "Mr. Barr: Once in the record makes it clear. We don't have to triple check. That is not the way we take a deposition"; then, in answer to Gilbert's question "When may I expect an answer from you?," "When you get it." Nearer the end:

MR. GILBERT: Tom—
MR. BARR: Let me finish.
MR. GILBERT: This isn't the kind of thing we need on this record. You can tell it to me—
MR. BARR: You started it.
MR. GILBERT: I asked you whether I could have some documents to examine this witness about it.
MR. BARR: You started it.
MR. GILBERT: You said I could.
MR. BARR: You started it by saying that isn't very helpful.

Until, at the end of the day:

MR. GILBERT: Tom—
MR. BARR: Let me finish. If you won't, I'm not interested. . . .
MR. GILBERT: Wait a second. Don't run off.
MR. BARR: Go ahead. You can say it as many times as you want. The deposition is adjourned.
MR. GILBERT: Do you want to stay here while I call the judge? I am going to call him right now. . . .
MR. BARR: You do anything you feel like doing.

Whereupon, at 5:05 p.m., Barr departed, taking the witness with him. The following morning, the second of Halevy's deposition, began with the conference call to the judge, which Gilbert had attempted the preceding afternoon. (Calls to the judge in the middle of depositions are extremely rare; in *Sharon,* they averaged more than one per witness.) The colloquy included this exchange:

MR. GILBERT: I want to finish this deposition now. . . . Are you prepared to keep Mr. Halevy past four o'clock today?

MR. BARR: I want you to call the judge, and talk to the judge, Sonny.

MR. GILBERT: What did you call me?

MR. BARR: Sonny. That's what you are acting like.

MR. GILBERT: You are the most boorish adult—

MR. BARR: Call him.

MR. GILBERT: —that I think I have met in a long time.

MR. BARR: Are you going to call him or am I?

MR. GILBERT: I am going to call him.

MR. BARR: Do it.

MR. GILBERT: Before I do, Mr. Barr—

MR. BARR: Jesus Christ.

It is not altogether unusual (in fact, it seems to be one distinct style in the contemporary practice of law) to proceed as rudely and ferociously as possible. It may even be a standard technique for lawyers in that style to interrupt (particularly when opposing counsel is a young, relatively inexperienced attorney) by every possible means (including the use of speeches, hints to the witness and every variant of bellicose incivility, interspersed with utterly frivolous objections) the whole rhythm of a deposition—especially when there are certain substantial matters, embarrassing to the client and the client's witness, that might, in an ordinary, courteous, orderly deposition, come to light. Opposing counsel, whose line of questioning is thus disrupted, cannot, of course, be constantly calling up the judge. By afternoon, the lawyers' relationship had deteriorated further. Barr had just expressed himself to the effect that Shea & Gould's inability to take depositions on the Jewish holiday Rosh Hashanah "is inherently incredible to me" and "a dodge."

MR. GILBERT: Mr. Levy—

MR. BARR: After two days, can you remember the witness' name, counsel? Normally, when I fail to call someone by his right name, I apologize. Don't you?

MR. GILBERT: Mr. Halevy knows that it was an unintentional error.

MR. BARR: All I'm asking is common courtesy.

MR. GILBERT: I am prepared to extend as much courtesy as I can, more so than you, who seems to want to use words like "Sonny," "horseshit," etc.

MR. BARR: Let me tell you something, counsel. One more time, I warn you, one more time of that kind of uncalled-for, unjustified conduct on your part, and we will terminate the deposition, and you will go and explain to the judge why you should say things like that.

MR. GILBERT: Is anything that I quoted of yours inaccurate?

And this style of professional conduct was by no means confined to the Halevy deposition. On September 11th, 12th and 14th, when Duncan was the witness, the attorneys (Saunders and Goldstein) had been more restrained. But Saunders objected so frequently, and at such length, and for such unconventional reasons, to Goldstein's questions that Goldstein, remarking that these objections both disrupted the deposition and gave clues to the witness how to answer, made two phone calls to the judge. At one particularly delicate moment, when the questioning was approaching the matter of whether or not Duncan had been told that one of Halevy's "sources" had been present at the condolence call, Duncan became confused and decided, literally at Saunders' prompting, to ask for a break to go to the men's room. Goldstein, alluding all but explicitly to the possibility of coaching such a break would provide, asked Duncan just to stay long enough to answer yes or no to the pending question:

MR. SAUNDERS: . . . The witness wants to go to the men's room. *This is not a rubber hose interrogation.* Let the witness go to the men's room.

Q. Is it inconveniencing you to take another twenty seconds and answer a question of mine?

MR. SAUNDERS: Mr. Goldstein, that's not proper. *Let the witness go to the men's room.* What is this? *Go to the men's room.*

When Duncan returned from the break, Goldstein said, as he rephrased his question, "Let us try to clear this up, Mr. Duncan. . . . Your answer is yes, no, or I don't recall, or anything else you want to say"; and Saunders, by no means a humorless man, said, "I hope you won't try and limit the witness." By the next day, Goldstein had his ruling from Judge Sofaer (that counsel were to confine their objections to the words "objection" and "objection to form," and let the witness answer). But the ruling was ignored absolutely throughout the depositions; and counsel could not, after every other question, keep calling up the judge.

MR. GILBERT: This is a conference call being placed to Judge Sofaer, Adam Gilbert . . . with Tom Barr, regarding the Sharon matter.
VOICE: Who did you wish to speak with?
MR. GILBERT: Judge Sofaer.
VOICE: Is this another dispute on the deposition? . . .
MR. GILBERT: Yes it is. . . .
[Pause]
THE COURT: Hello.
[Some time later]
MR. BARR: Thank you, your Honor.
THE COURT: Thank you. I think that you should stay calm, gentlemen. You are all wonderful people.

In the Kelly deposition, it was attorneys Gold and Goldstein; and on the first day:

MR. GOLD: . . . And if you do not avail yourself of that opportunity, we will feel free to tell Mr. Halevy he may go about his other business.
MR. GOLDSTEIN: And we will feel free, unless we consent to that, to move to have your answer stricken. So we will both feel free as birds, and we will let the judge decide which one of us did the right thing. . . .
MR. GOLD: Mr. Goldstein, I know you know the history of the Doyle deposition and *your firm's very poor showing* at the way you handled it in terms of its scheduling.

MR. GOLDSTEIN: I would honestly say I have no idea what you are talking about. I also say, I don't want to waste any more of this page, and I think that—do you want me to wait until you are done? I don't like to talk when somebody is not listening, Mr. Gold.

MR. GOLD: Does that require a response by me?

MR. GOLDSTEIN: I think that required a little courtesy for you to be listening to me when I am talking. I think the whole thing is childish. . . . I think the judge is understandably tired of hearing it, so I am going to ask the reporter to stop. . . . I will tell you that I won't pay for anything from this point on that relates to this subject.

By the second afternoon:

MR. GOLD: If you stop— . . . In response to your statement, all you have to do is stop the little tricks.

MR. GOLDSTEIN: Don't ever accuse me of a trick. I will leave it at that. Don't you dare accuse me of a trick on the record.

Two days later, in the Halevy deposition (whose first two days ran concurrently with Kelly's last two):

MR. BARR: No tricky questions.

MR. GILBERT: There is no trick here, Tom. . . .

MR. BARR: Counsel, I pay acute attention to everything you do, for the purpose of catching the little tricks like that. . . .

MR. GILBERT: Are you going to withdraw your statement that it is a trick?

MR. BARR: Do you want to withdraw the question? . . . Otherwise, leave it all in.

MR. GILBERT: We will leave it all in. It is an insult.

MR. BARR: You have very thin skin. You ought to get over that if you are going to be a trial lawyer.

MR. GILBERT: Mr. Barr—

MR. BARR: You get insulted too easy.

MR. GILBERT: I don't think so.

MR. BARR: You have too many problems of that sort.

And in the last minutes, of the last day, of the Kelly deposition:

MR. GOLDSTEIN: . . . What is your position with respect to the personnel files and my ability to examine Mr. Kelly with respect to any information gleaned from those files, which you are presently producing at your offices downtown?

MR. GOLD: . . . Mr. Kelly will not reappear here after 3:45 today.

MR. GOLDSTEIN: Are you finished?

MR. GOLD: Yes.

MR. GOLDSTEIN: I will telephone the judge at 3:45 or at such time as you tell me that you are closing this deposition. I think you could have told me earlier today, just as a courtesy, of your intention to leave at 3:45. But that aside, if you are going to pull this witness, in what I consider to be a complete violation of the very clear order of his Honor, which said we were to have access to the files "prior to scheduled depositions," in quotes, underlined, exclamation point, I consider that a contempt of that order. I think that this effort to construct a way to impede our ability to look at those files is abhorrent. . . . I think that is done in utter bad faith, and I say so on this record . . . I think it's an outrage that you want to practice like this.

MR. GOLD: I think, Mr. Goldstein, that your statement is so outrageous, I don't even want to grace it with an answer. . . . You have had more than your fair share of this witness' patience. You have already exhausted mine.

MR. GOLD: Mr. Goldstein, do you have any further questions?

MR. GOLDSTEIN: Yes.

MR. GOLD: Are you willing to tell me the subject matter of those questions?

MR. GOLDSTEIN: No, I don't believe I am under any obligation to.

MR. GOLD: It is now four o'clock. I have a meeting. . . . If he feels he needs more time with him, I remain willing to listen to his reasons when I come back for the completion of the Halevy deposition. . . . I thank the witness for his patience and time. Let's go.

And Goldstein was left, somewhat forlorn and speaking for the stenographer and for the record: "Since Mr. Gold has chosen to leave and take the witness, I am making this statement outside his presence. . . . Thank you, Mr. Reporter."

Although all this is on file, and a matter of official public record, none of it took place in the presence of the jury or the court. Nor, obviously, are depositions part of the transcript of the trial itself. And the ventilation of all this high-handedness ("I remain willing to listen to his reasons"), rudeness and antagonism is by no means part of every litigating style. But Cravath is not the only highly respected law firm (though it is perhaps the best known) to pride itself on the almost unremitting combativeness of its attorneys— who may be mild, kind, even poetic creatures outside their working lives. ("It's like having a pack of Dobermans, who are clamoring to be unleashed," a major client of the firm's real-estate department once said admiringly. "I happen to prefer to avoid conflict, but it's reassuring to know I have this pack I can unleash.") Throughout these depositions, however, one cannot escape, as Halevy might have put it, in his Memo Item, "the feeling" that the Cravath depositions were conducted, in part, to reflect the bullying standard, and to be read each night by other attorneys from Cravath. (Indeed, when a less important attorney from the firm, Ellen Oran, spent a relatively civil day at a deposition with her counterpart, Andrea Feller, from Shea & Gould, one could not help noticing the contrast between that day's conduct and Ms. Oran's participation in depositions when male attorneys were present, which was as rude as any of the others had been. It was as though someone at the office, in the evening, might accuse such an attorney of having failed the standard, a failure that would be quickly compensated for the following day.) Later in the case, on the other hand, one could not escape the feeling that Shea & Gould's case, as it was waged *in court,* was conducted in part to be read by, and to please, General Sharon. These feelings would be of almost no importance were it not that both tactics, both audiences, both styles of legal conduct literally produced the outcome of the case: Cravath's almost mindless aggressiveness triggered a reaction from the government of Israel (which was clearly disinclined at the outset to help this private plaintiff, who had well-known political aspirations of his own); and Shea & Gould's perhaps equally unconscious playing to its client led it to make certain arguments in his praise and his defense, and to neglect several of its strongest arguments, probative of actual malice—in particular, concerning two unusually audacious last-minute claims by Halevy about his putative "notes" and "sources," and such early discrepancies as the one about departure dates. Evidence of "recent fabrication" is considered probative of actual malice. On the other hand, Gould's sole purpose in taking on the case had always been just to prove falsehood. And "clearly and convincingly" is the highest standard of proof in civil law. "It never lay within our horizon, within our vision of the case," he once said to a reporter, "that we could leap the last hurdle. I can't prove everything that is." In any event, the mini-trial, which is the set of all completed depositions, showed a pattern of tensions of another kind.

For Duncan and for Kelly and, in another way, for Halevy, the tension was fundamentally internal, intra-office, intra-collegial— between being witnesses who best served the interests of the case and being good at, or even having done, their jobs. If Halevy *had* seen the "notes," or "minutes," of the Bikfaya meeting; and if he *had* been shown them by the "official notetaker" from the Mossad; if, among the other "sources" for his story, there *had* been an "Israeli general"; and if he *had* confirmed with reliable "sources" that his original story was contained in Appendix B; and, finally, if the only impediment to his naming the "notetaker," and the "general," and the others (and the only justification for his invocation of the shield law) *had* been the understandable need to protect their identities, then Halevy's conduct as a reporter would, of course, have been exemplary. The difficulty, one difficulty, anyway, was that all these characterizations were specific enough to constitute, in effect, a waiver of the shield. The government of Israel, from whom it was theoretically necessary to conceal these "identities," would surely be capable of ascertaining, for example, who the "official notetaker" of Bikfaya (or, for that matter, the "Israeli general" who so readily disclosed national secrets to someone as conspicuous as *Time*'s correspondent in Jerusalem) actually was. And if Kelly, as bureau chief, had not simply trusted Halevy's characterization of his "sources" (if Kelly, that is, had not been only a relatively helpless foreigner, unfamiliar with the language or the country, and dependent on Halevy's word), if he had had some independent knowledge, or some inkling of who these alleged "sources" were, he might have been an exemplary Jerusalem bureau chief. And Duncan, in inquiring of Kelly about the "sources," and in asking for an "ongoing investigation" (which, of course, never took place), was, at the time, all one could ask of a chief of correspondents. The difficulty is that if Duncan had *not* inquired of Kelly he would have been derelict, in his own mind and in the minds of colleagues; so, beginning at his deposition, he had to testify that he did inquire, and give some indication of what Kelly said Halevy's sources were. And in the course of his testimony about this exercise of his professional responsibility he had to make admissions detrimental to *Time*'s version of the case: Why did he not "follow up," to find out the identity of sources? "In the first place, it is quite difficult, given the degree of censorship, not to say various kinds of snooping, that take place on communications inside and outside Israel. I would never ask nor expect to be answered a question like that either on the telex, or computer communications, nor on the telephone." Also, ". . . Mr. Kelly is . . . a very experienced news executive who was well aware of my concerns, well aware of his own concerns on this. We had discussed these matters before." Also, "I also recall that there was discussion of someone who was at the meeting. I do not recall whether the someone who was at the meeting was the first source who was characterized to me or not to me, that is not ruled out in my mind. That first source might have been at the meeting. Then there was also discussion of other corroborating sources. . . ."

> Q. Do you recall that Mr. Kelly was telling you that, as an additional source for the information, Mr. Halevy had spoken with someone who claimed to have been at the meeting and who corroborated the information in the item?
> A. I have that general recollection, but I believe that to be true. . . .

That is, when Duncan was at his most professional, and apparently most truthful, he said (1) that no one in his right mind could be expected to discuss secret matters on the phone with or within Israel, and (2) that he relied on Kelly's accounts of Halevy's characterizations of the "sources" for the story—including those which proved at trial, by Halevy's own account, to be unfounded. (Even Halevy never claimed, for example, at the trial that any of his "sources" had been, or "claimed to have been," at the Bikfaya meeting.) Thus, in truthfully confirming Kelly's account of Halevy's characterization of his "sources," Duncan had, inescapably, to imply that, at the time, Kelly had been misled. When he was being less than truthful (about, for example, the personnel file, and the history of the Begin health story, which *Time* had subsequently to retract), that is, when he was trying, as a witness, actively to protect or to advance *Time*'s legal case, his testimony was even more detrimental to it, in that his deposition testimony, and the personnel file, and the Begin health story came back to impeach his credibility at trial. In his efforts, against all the sounder journalistic instincts, to oblige *as a witness,* Duncan made, midway through his deposition, what was, in the peculiar circumstances of the case, a strange, sophistical argument:

Q. . . . I would like you to look at the last sentence, which reads "Sharon also reportedly discussed with the Gemayels the need for the Phalangists to take revenge for the assassination of Bashir, but the details of the conversation are not known." Does that sentence reasonably allow for the interpretation that General Sharon encouraged the massacre?

A. No, it doesn't say that.

Q. I have not asked you if that's what it says. My question, sir, is whether one can reasonably interpret that to mean that General Sharon encouraged the massacre?

A. No.

Q. Might not a reader construe it to mean that General Sharon approved or encouraged the massacre in the course of this discussion?

MR. SAUNDERS: I object to that question on the ground that it is wholly hypothetical. You have not described what you mean by "a reader." You may answer the question. . . .

A. I don't believe so. . . . I believe that a reader has no more reason to believe that than the reader has to believe that Minister Sharon attempted to dissuade the Gemayels from taking revenge. . . .

The objection, of course, was frivolous (and in violation of the judge's order); but it gave the witness time to think. And Duncan went on to say that he was sure that all the other people who worked on the paragraph, and every reader of it, would agree with him: that "discussed the need to take" could, in this instance, mean "attempted to dissuade from taking." This was an argument that not even the lawyers tried to make.

Kelly's deposition, however, was the next in sequence; and Kelly, in accordance with Cravath practice, had read Duncan's deposition. (Another litigating style assumes that witnesses testify more freshly and honestly when they have not read one another's depositions.) And, sure enough:

Q. Do you understand [the sentence] to mean that Ariel Sharon approved the taking of revenge by the Phalangists for the assassination of Bashir?

A. No . . . On the contrary, I think you could also read it that it was discussed with him and he may have tried to dissuade them from taking revenge.

It is an illustration of the contortions through which a lawsuit can put its witnesses that a sentence in a paragraph explicitly and demonstrably based on a telex that bore the headline "Green Light for Revenge?" (and that included the sentence "He also gave them the feeling, after the Gemayels' questioning, that he understood their need to take revenge . . . and assured them that the Israeli army would neither hinder them nor try to stop them") should be interpreted by two witnesses, in the profession of journalism and under oath, as possibly describing, to a reasonable reader, an attempt to dissuade. For Kelly, at his deposition and at trial, the tension between having been, within certain limits, an effective bureau chief and trying actively, as a witness, to advance *Time*'s interest in the case, the tension, in other words, between his professional and his legal person, was most acute. Also, of all the *Time* witnesses he showed the most pronounced inclination toward a certain honesty, humility and even capacity for doubt. "I think you always or occasionally look back at stories," he said, to his eternal credit, in answer to a fairly general question, "and wonder, you know, 'Is this really right?' " It is surprising, in reviewing the testimony in these cases, how something, anything, with the ring of the *authentic* seems to leap out of the page. Halevy, for example, testified that at the funeral of Bashir Gemayel, the Phalangists, beside themselves and half refusing to believe that he was dead, were chanting, "Allah, Lubnan, Bashir, Was bas" (God, Lebanon, Bashir, that's all); and for one moment, a brief, perhaps, for all one knew, misguided moment, something *rang true,* something electrifying, as though someone had walked over the grave of Bashir Gemayel or of a certain kind of "investigative journalism" in our time. Kelly had to support Duncan's account of their phone calls and of what Kelly had said about Halevy's sources. If Kelly had made no inquiry of Halevy about the "sources," Kelly would have been derelict in his professional duty, so he had to testify honestly about at least these things: ". . . Mr. Halevy said he had seen the notes"; "As I recall, Mr. Halevy said he had been shown the notes."

> Q. Did Mr. Halevy tell you whether the notes had been prepared by someone who had been at the condolence call?
> A. My understanding is that he did.

> A. . . . I said, "We really have to find out what is in Section B, Appendix B." Mr. Halevy replied, "I know one thing that is in it: my Memo Item from December."

And:

> Q. Do you know whether the notes that Mr. Halevy told you that he saw of the condolence call were Mossad notes?
> MR. GOLD: Answer "yes" or "no."
> A. I assume they were Mossad notes. . . .

The reason Gold interposed the instruction "Answer 'yes' or 'no' " was to coach the witness to confine his answer to the narrow question, whether he *knew* whether the notes Halevy said he saw were Mossad notes (and then, in response to the question whether Halevy had told him that they were, to invoke the shield). But Kelly ignored the instruction (which was, in any event, another

violation of the judge's ruling), and answered the question forthrightly. Kelly's was the most overtly "coached" of all the depositions, so much so that Goldstein was constantly on the verge of
calling the judge to complain of "improper consulting." But Kelly
frequently ignored even the most direct hints to him by counsel.
As for the rote, or catechism, of previously published "sources"
(Sharon's public testimony in October of 1982; the Kahan Report,
as published; prior articles in other publications), he was either too
honest or he simply couldn't get it right. At the same time, Kelly
wanted to convey the impression that, as bureau chief, he had not
had to rely *only* on Halevy's word about his "sources," that he had
some independent knowledge of his own. Thus, Kelly's were
among the most frequent invocations of the shield.

> I am a little fearful if I give you an answer one way or the other,
> it could jeopardize the identity of the source.

> I think there we get into a problem of disclosing the identity of
> the source.

> I did discover one more piece of information, but to explain it any
> further would jeopardize the identity of the source.

> I am unwilling because it would jeopardize the identity of the
> source.

> I am afraid to explain or to tell you; that would jeopardize the
> identity of the source.

And the reason for this ritual invocation was an odd one. Kelly,
as is apparent from his other testimony, simply did not *know* who
the sources were:

> A. No, I didn't. I figured I wouldn't know who it was anyway, by
> name.

> Q. You mean you are unwilling to tell me the source?
> A. I am not only unwilling, but I can't remember the man's name.

> A. I never heard of the man in my life.

The apparent reason for the inconsistency was that Kelly wanted people (colleagues, perhaps even himself) to believe that he *knew enough* to invoke the protections of the shield. There was also the matter of support and deference, within the magazine's own hierarchy. Thus, at trial, Kelly said, several times, that he himself "may" have added the words "for Revenge" to Halevy's "Green Light"—when Halevy had already admitted, in contradiction to his deposition testimony, that he had written them himself.

Something more difficult to understand seems to have made Kelly incapable of even the most elementary consistency regarding his professional obligations, Israeli secrecy law, and Appendix B. "I don't know all the contents of Appendix B," he said (in what may have been the understatement of the entire case); and he also repeatedly insisted that Ehud Olmert, a member of the Knesset Defense and Foreign Relations Committee (who had told Kelly that *Time*'s paragraph was wrong), had not claimed to have read "all" of Appendix B when he told Kelly there was no "revenge" discussion in it. But apart from the inherent implausibility of this (how could Olmert have claimed something was not "in" something he had not read "all" of?), Appendix B turned out to consist, it was revealed in the trial's last days, of just twelve pages. And the fundamental inconsistency in Kelly's whole testimony about it was this: when people attempted to tell him what was (or, more precisely, what was not) in Appendix B, he claimed he could not trust them, because "the findings were secret, and it was illegal for them to describe to me what was in Appendix B." It would, of course, have been more than equally "illegal" for them to "describe" what was in the appendix to Halevy. Kelly seemed incapable of grasping that, while it may be illegal to describe what is "in" a secret document, it can scarcely be illegal to describe what is not "secret"; namely, what is not "in" the document at all. But:

Q. Did you understand at the time you wrote Take 9 that Appendix B was a secret document under the laws of the State of Israel?

A. Yes, I did.

Q. Were you concerned that by sending Take 9 to New York, you were violating laws of the State of Israel . . . ?

A. No, I wasn't concerned . . . [it] was available to the censor. They saw it and if they wanted to eliminate it, it was in front of them.

And yet:

Q. Did you consider whether or not your Take 9 should be submitted to the military censor for his review prior to its being sent from the Jerusalem bureau?

A. No. Because this take was plainly written from public information, the Kahan Commission Report, and the censor doesn't require you to submit that kind of news material.

This last was obviously the lawyers' answer (that the paragraph was merely a reprint of other documents already published), and it made the position of Kelly essentially this: that Halevy had obtained the information from "sources" so secret that Kelly, who did not know them, nonetheless invoked the shield law to protect them, in other words refused, on shield-law grounds, to tell what, as it happened, he did not even know; that, since disclosing the "secret" information was illegal, Kelly could not trust any "sources" who would disclose similar (or, as it happened, conflicting) information to him; that telexing the "secrets" for publication was not, however, illegal, because otherwise the censor would have stopped it; but that there was no need to submit it to the censor, because the "secrets" it would have been illegal to disclose to Kelly were already "plainly" public information anyway. The chimerical, also real, Israeli censor was to play an important role both in Halevy's deposition testimony and at the trial. The one thing that seemed never to have occurred to Kelly, or to any other defense witness, was that the censor might have, in Kelly's word, "eliminated" the material if it really were a national secret, but that it was not a national secret (and was therefore not eliminated by the censor), *because it was not true.* Another thing is striking about Kelly's deposition, with its extraordinary density of "I don't recall": his recollection of the phone call, or calls, with Duncan concerning whether he was "comfortable" with the sources, and of agreeing to an "ongoing investigation," differs significantly from Duncan's as to when the call, or calls, occurred. Kelly was, from every indication, the defense's most honest witness. It rang true, for example, when he testified that, on the long flight from Tel Aviv to New York, he and Halevy had not discussed the case (or, rather, that Halevy had broached the subject and Kelly had said, "We don't talk about it, buddy"). Yet, as to the timing and the content of what transpired with Duncan, his memory is at its most vague. And, from the record, in its entirety, it is by no means clear that whatever conversation about "sources" and an "ongoing investigation" occurred, occurred at the time of the Memo Item, or any time before publication. The uneasy likelihood, on the basis of the record, is that no such conversation occurred at all—until after Sharon filed suit.

The deposition of David Halevy was remarkable in so many ways and differed so radically from his testimony at trial that plaintiff's attorneys, clearly unable to keep up, or to select, or to compress, tried, unsuccessfully, to enter all eight hundred pages of it, intact, into the transcript of the trial. Down to the minutest detail—

Q. Do you recall the first time that you saw the headline "Green Light for Revenge?"
A. . . . The first time I saw that was after the lawsuit. . . .

Q. Subsequent to the publication of the article entitled "The Verdict Is Guilty"—
A. I don't know of any article by that name. . . .
Q. Would you take a look at 0618 of Halevy's Exhibit 16.
A. Yes.
Q. Do you know what this article is?
A. Yes. It is part of the cover story "Verdict on the Massacre."
Q. Do you know whether or not the article has a headline?
A. I see a headline.
Q. What is that headline?
A. It says "The Verdict Is Guilty."
Q. Have you ever seen that headline before?

A. Not to the best— I mean, I probably saw that, but I don't remember that headline.

(One thing that readers of most newspapers, and many other publications, have no way of knowing is that the writer whose name appears in the byline was in no way responsible for, was not even consulted about, the headline that appears above his piece. But that is not the sort of disclaimer Halevy was making here.)

A. . . . Here comes the commission report. And, in essence, it says, in a very ego-minded, very ego-sided, pointed side of view: "Whatever information you learned, Mr. Halevy, is true, but there is more, much more."
Q. That "more" is contained in Appendix B?
A. Yes, some of the "more" is contained in Appendix B.

Halevy's deposition testimony showed not so much a breathtaking disregard for what was and what was not "exact" or "accurate" or "true" as a genuine inability to tell the difference. By the time of the trial, of course, he testified that the headline "Green Light for Revenge?" had been his own. The headline "The Verdict Is Guilty," at his deposition, was right there before him, in the magazine. And no "more," and no Memo Item, was contained in Appendix B. But by the time of the trial Halevy's testimony presented a whole new set of "facts": an entirely new, vitally important "source," for instance (Israeli "General No. 2"), who both gave him the information in his Memo Item of December 6th and "confirmed" to him that the substance of the Memo Item (the "revenge" discussion at Bikfaya) was in Appendix B; and also an entirely new set of official "notes," or "minutes" (of a meeting, apparently on September 12, 1982, between Sharon and Bashir Gemayel), which Halevy actually claimed, at trial, *to have in his possession*, and offered to produce. Both claims, but particularly the second, came as an enormous surprise, even (as the defense in Westmoreland would have put it) a bombshell, to the courtroom, the judge and Halevy's and *Time*'s own counsel. The meeting between Sharon and Bashir Gemayel on September 12th was in a sense irrelevant (since Sharon could hardly have discussed the "need to take revenge for the assassination of Bashir" *with* Bashir, two days before the assassination, and three days before the meeting described in *Time*'s paragraph, took place); but that meeting was, for other reasons, of considerable historical interest and importance. And if Halevy had even seen the "notes," let alone possessed a copy of them, it would have been an immense reporting coup. Within days, however, it emerged that the "notes" to which Halevy had referred so cavalierly and yet stunningly in court were notes of another meeting, at an earlier time, between other people entirely; and, also, that Halevy did not have them, or copies of them, either. But the initial claim, under oath, in court, was, if false, of such astonishing audacity that the court, Judge Sofaer, both counsel, in fact everyone, believed it. And when it turned out to *be* false, Sharon's attorneys (in what turned out to be one of Shea & Gould's infrequent lapses) actually *forgot to mention it in their summation to the jury.* (Or perhaps chose not to. The summation, which was in other ways funny and even brilliant, had to focus the jury's attention on the overriding question of the paragraph's "clear and convincing" falsity.) It was almost inconceivable that a witness would risk, in such a trial, in federal court, a false claim to possess important "notes." That he should be believed, and then, when it emerged that the "notes" did not exist, that opposing counsel should fail to call their nonexistence (with the clear inference of recent fabrication) to the attention of the jury, gave one some indication of the measure of the witness's ability to disorient, and even to derail, judgment—and, perhaps, of the reporter's capacity, in that earlier episode of "notes," with which the Memo Item and the case began, to disorient, *in precisely the same way,* his bureau chief and all the other folks at *Time.*

In any event, in all four and a half days of his deposition, Halevy alternated between refusals, under his own interpretation of the shield law, to answer questions and the improvisation of answers, often of great length, which were or as often were not responsive to any question he was asked. (When Gilbert, conscious, on a particular afternoon, of Barr's intention to withdraw his witness at four o'clock, said, "I am simply trying to ask the witness to help me along in the sense of limiting his answer to 'I don't know' if the answer is he doesn't know," Barr said, "I am going to tell the witness he should answer the question as he sees fit." Gilbert: "To the extent you can do it with brevity, it would be appreciated." Barr, with obvious amusement: "I agree with that, too. But he is a very brief and concise man, and we ought to let him continue to do so.") In his most expansive and loquacious mode, however, Halevy, seeming to elude even Barr's control, ran, in at least three ways that were to recur to *Time*'s detriment at trial, amok. First, in that fundamental and persistent question of the Bikfaya "notes": Halevy simply could not bring himself, at his deposition, to admit that he had not read them. To any variant of the question whether or not he had seen or read the Bikfaya "notes," or "minutes," his replies became senseless, or even idiotic: "Any answer on my behalf to your question will already bring you into the area of the very limited number of people who read and dealt with the minutes of that meeting"; "Any answer I'll give you now will be a breach of my previous answer"; and so forth. Halevy, in other words, meant to imply by these answers that he *had* read the "notes," or "minutes." An answer to the effect that he had *not* would not bring anyone into "the area of the very limited number" of people who had access to them but, rather, into the limitless number of people who had none. Since the remote possibility existed that, sometime in the course of the trial, the "notes," if any existed, might actually be published, Halevy's, and *Time*'s, lawyers had obviously instructed him, very firmly, to say that he had not seen them; but in this he could not quite accommodate the lawyers; his pride or his vanity was at stake. In that same tension between being an exemplary reporter, who would have the fullest possible knowledge of the "notes" before rushing into print about them, and being a forthright witness, who would admit that he had not the slightest knowledge of the "notes," he could not bring himself to make the sounder choice. Even fairly late in the trial, his admission was not unreluctant:

Q. Mr. Halevy, did you ever actually see the notes of the Bikfaya meeting?
A. You are asking if I ever saw the notes of the Bikfaya meeting prior to my composition of the Worldwide Memo, at what time, at all?

Q. At any time.
A. No, sir.

Second, in the matter of *how* Sharon "gave [the Gemayels] ... the feeling ... that he understood their need to take revenge ... and assured them that the Israeli army would neither hinder them nor try to stop them," Halevy gave incompatible answers, to the effect that Sharon did so in words ("Mr. Sharon made a statement to the Gemayel clan. ... I think it was more in the sense of a sentence, of a statement. I can't recall it"), and not in words (" 'Gave them the feeling' could be a body movement, could be silence, could be a non-outspoken rejection of their raising the issue, and could also be indifference to the fact"). This second answer provided such a novel interpretation of how a Minister of Defense "gave" the surviving members of a foreign leader's family "the feeling" of all the things it was meant to impart the feeling of (and such an extraordinary basis for a paragraph that read "discussed ... the need for the Phalangists to take revenge") that it caused Gilbert to emphasize, for the record ("Can I have that read, please"), what had just been said, and Barr to interrupt. But the exchange continued:

Q. At the time that you wrote the words "gave them the feeling," did you have an understanding that those words could also be read as meaning a verbal communication between Sharon and the Gemayels?
MR. BARR: I object to the form. Go ahead.
THE WITNESS: A verbal communication, no. . . .
A. . . . Mr. Gilbert, if I will look at you now—
Q. I understand.
MR. BARR: Let him answer the question.
A. —with flying eyes and an angry face, and won't say one insult, you will definitely understand that I am angry like hell. This is giving a feeling that I am angry at your form of questions.

It was, of course, inherently absurd that the "official notes" (or any "notes") would record not one word of what was said but what "feeling" was "given" at a meeting. So was Halevy's contention that the whole passage, no matter how it was read, was not "of and concerning" Sharon at all but "puts the direct blame on—especially on Lebanon's President, Amin Gemayel." ("I think this Memo is rather clear, as far as I'm concerned, and the heading is rather clear.") The chimerical "censor" made several appearances in Halevy's testimony, exercising an "extraterritorial" authority, which permitted the witness to characterize as "secret" (and to decline to answer) certain questions for which he did not feel inclined to invoke the shield. Halevy's other contention, that the Hebrew word for "among us," in Sharon's public testimony in October of 1982 ("The word 'revenge' also appeared, I would say, also in discussions among us"), could not mean "among Israelis" but must mean "with the Phalange or with Lebanese officials," led to the most dramatic, in fact the pivotal and final, testimony at the trial. But the third major issue in Halevy's deposition, which was to reverberate, like the "gave them the feeling" definition ("could be a body movement, could be silence, could be a non-outspoken rejection of their raising the issue, and could also be indifference to the fact"), throughout the trial itself, had to do with Halevy's own handwritten "notes," the very "notes" he claimed to have taken about his communications with his "prime sources," and on which he based the Memo Item, which in turn led to *Time*'s paragraph. Fairly late in his deposition, he embarked on what turned out to be a fateful exchange concerning the circumstances under which he took those "notes."

Q. Do you recall the circumstances under which you wrote these notes?

A. No.

Q. Do you recall where you were at the time you wrote them?

A. No.

Q. Do you recall if you were having a conversation with any of your sources at the time you wrote them?

A. From the ample fact that the name of source A . . . and another source appear here, it's probably notes I took after I finished two meetings with these two sources.

Q. Do you recall whether you made these notes at the time of the meeting with them or after?

A. I believe, after.

Q. Did these contain notes from one meeting or more than one meeting?

A. No. The fact that there are two names attached to the notes indicates, as far as I'm concerned, that I had two meetings with two people, and I quickly after the two meetings took notes; wrote them probably *in the car* and carried on.

Halevy went on about how the car had affected his handwriting, and about the important sections deleted by the censor. Which? "No idea." Then:

Q. Do you recall when the meetings occurred in relation to each other?

A. No. I would say they happened one after the other, but this is my best guess.

It does not require a professional journalist to detect that what Halevy was describing (or not describing) was not a genuine recollection of any known journalistic experience or method—and Barr interrupted, with some distracting remarks about a minor difference between Cravath's and Shea & Gould's calculation of the witness's per-diem and travel expenses. The above colloquy was, however, to recur at the trial, to somewhat devastating effect, in that Halevy never again claimed to have received information from these "sources" at meetings of any kind—or to have taken notes, for that matter, in a car. Deposition: "Q. Was it a telephone conversation? A. No." At the trial, he said that he had received all the information, from "confidential sources," on which he based those notes by telephone.

A. Yes. I think Minister Sharon had between eight to twelve meetings with Bashir Gemayel and his staff and the military and political council of the Phalangists.

MR. BARR: How did you know that? What is the basis of your knowledge?

A. Basically confidential sources, basically notes and minutes . . . which *were given to me* by the people who participated or took the minutes.

Q. You actually saw minutes of those . . .

A. Yes, in some cases I did.

It would seem that chief counsel for *Time* had become as credulous as *Time*'s bureau chief Kelly had been, in composing the telex that became the basis for the paragraph in the lawsuit. The claim, on Halevy's part, of having *seen* notes, or minutes, seemed after all not unfamiliar. But this time Halevy was ready to go further:

MR. BARR: We are now at the point where the witness is about to say what his point is, your Honor. Go ahead, Mr. Halevy.

A. And I *had in my possession* a document in those days which were the minutes of a secret meeting, or the notes of a secret meeting, between General Sharon and Bashir Gemayel . . . at the house of a high-ranking Lebanese intelligence official. . . .

THE COURT: Is this a source? It wasn't a source, was it? This is something he just didn't talk about at his deposition, is that right?

MR. GOULD: Nothing at all about it. . . .

MR. BARR: Your Honor, I offer to prove the witness will testify . . . that he had seen a set of notes of a meeting between the plaintiff and Bashir Gemayel, at which time the words were spoken which indicated that the plaintiff was aware that killings had taken place on those occasions and that he was discussing that subject with Bashir. Enough?

MR. GOULD: There was no mention of this meeting in the deposition.

MR. BARR: And there were no questions addressed to it either.

THE COURT: I don't think you can say that, Mr. Barr.

MR. BARR: I can't?

THE COURT: I mean, you can argue that. That will be for the jury to decide, whether he was fairly asked questions that would have led to the disclosure of something so obviously and patently relevant to what he claims he believed when he wrote his story. . . . You mean to say he had these secret notes at the time of the deposition and he doesn't have them anymore?

MR. BARR: I said I don't know whether he has them. We will ask him now.

MR. GOULD: Do you have the notes, Mr. Halevy?

THE WITNESS: I believe I do.

MR. GOULD: Where are they?

THE WITNESS: I don't know. I will have to look for them. Maybe here.

MR. BARR: Here, meaning in the United States?

THE WITNESS: Here, Manhattan.

MR. GOULD: Is there some reason why they weren't produced before?

THE WITNESS: Is Mr. Gilbert around?

THE COURT: Let's look at this matter after lunch. Mr. Halevy will look for the notes. . . .

MR. BARR: Meanwhile, my view of the world is that he has never been asked these questions about either—

MR. GOULD: I don't want to prolong the discussion, but our first request for the production of documents, August 31, 1983, Item E: "The sources employed by Time Inc., if any, in authoring, composing or publishing the article, including but not limited to any communications between Time Inc., and such sources or the identity of such sources."

MR. BARR: That doesn't make it.

This was on December 5, 1984, the second day of Barr's cross-examination, and the first day of what became the attorneys' and the court's pursuit of Halevy's imaginary notes. But remark what has already happened: defense counsel has elicited from the witness a statement that one of the sources he relied on in preparing the story at issue in the lawsuit was "the minutes of a secret meeting . . . I had in my possession" at the time of his deposition; plaintiff's counsel, and the judge, point out that these notes were never mentioned at the witness's deposition; defense counsel actually maintains that the witness was not obliged to mention them ("And there were no questions addressed to it either"); plaintiff's counsel reads from plaintiff's *first document request,* for "the sources employed . . . in authoring, composing, or publishing," etc.; defense counsel serenely says, "That doesn't make it." Regardless of the merits or the legal ethics of this, all parties, like Kelly, with that earlier set of notes, perhaps; like Duncan; like the whole corporate edifice of Time Inc., still *believe* the notes *exist.*

THE COURT: This is a copy of the official minutes, you say?
THE WITNESS: Yes, your Honor.

By that afternoon, in the robing room, the judge sounds the first note of skepticism.

THE COURT: I would just like to say on the record that I feel that the minutes, if there are minutes, a document, must be kept here until we resolve this matter . . .
MR. GOLD: I will pursue it with him and make sure that if he has these minutes they do not leave his possession or New York.
THE COURT: Thank you.

By the following day:

MR. GOULD: I think we ought to make some disposition about . . . Halevy's testimony that at one time he had a copy of the minutes of the meeting with Bashir Gemayel, where we stopped Mr. Barr from going forward.
THE COURT: I think we should deal with it here first, though, before we go out there in front of the jury.
MR. GOLD: Your Honor, if I can address that, a number of items. Mr. Halevy has checked. He does not have the minutes he was talking about here. He does believe, though, that they may be at his home in Israel. He was not talking about minutes of the September 12th meeting between Bashir and Sharon.
THE COURT: We could clarify that at least.
MR. GOLD: Yes.
THE COURT: He was talking about one of those meetings referred to by the commission in its report?
MR. GOLD: Perhaps. It is a July or August meeting, he says.

And the judge precisely has it. Halevy, having noticed, as anyone would notice, that the Kahan Commission Report quite openly mentioned a certain meeting between Sharon and Bashir Gemayel (and adopted Sharon's testimony on it as correct), simply invented, at some time subsequent to his deposition, that he had in his possession "minutes," or "notes," of that "secret meeting," and had relied upon them as a source. Where were these minutes? "Here, Manhattan." Later, maybe "at his home in Israel." Daring and even brazen as this was, Halevy and his attorneys kept on improvising:

> MR. GOLD: Your Honor, just for the record, I am not sure that anything such as these notes was called for by the document demand or in any of the questioning by Mr. Gilbert. The only problem I have about bringing the notes to the United States is I am certain—I am talking about Mr. Halevy—that he will want to ask the *permission of the censor* before they leave Israel.

So the thing has come almost full circle, "Here, Manhattan," to the impediment of the censor to their leaving Israel. And by the time the circle was completed, that the notes had never existed, there had been such proliferation of invention that plaintiff's counsel forgot to mention, in his summation to the jury, that the notes did not exist.

O bviously, not all reporters for major publications (or all witnesses, under oath) are alike; and the professional quality of reporters is not always or accurately reflected in their persona as witnesses. The distortion brought on by lawsuits in the conduct of people whose very profession, journalism, consists in giving factual, truthful accounts, and whose legal and civic obligation now becomes, even more solemnly and under oath, the giving of factual, truthful answers, seemed in both *Westmoreland* and *Sharon* a somehow redoubled distortion. In a sense, the major "source" in *Westmoreland* was Samuel Adams, with his "chronology" and his "list of sixty"; and the distortion was exaggerated in his person, because to the truth-telling obligations of the journalist and witness he added a third dimension, or category, the giver of factual, truthful accounts as intelligence analyst. But the originator, the most key figure in the broadcast (somewhat as Halevy, allowing for enormous differences in status and personality, was the originator and key figure in the creation of *Time*'s paragraph), was George Crile. The deposition testimony in *Westmoreland,* and the climate of the voluminous depositions themselves, was much more subdued and decorous than in *Sharon,* though it was, at many moments, equally bizarre. Mike Wallace, for instance, on his deposition, testified under oath that neither he nor anyone else who contributed to the broadcast, nor any reasonable viewer of it, could construe the "conspiracy" alleged in the broadcast to have included Westmoreland:

A. Mr. Dorsen, as of the date of the broadcast, we talked about, we used the word conspiracy. At the highest levels of American intelligence. . . . William Westmoreland was not an intelligence officer. We didn't speak about conspiracy at the highest levels of the American military command. We said, at the highest levels of American military intelligence. We said what we meant.
Q. And you meant what you said?
A. Well put.

This testimony occurred, however, at a point when Cravath's theory of the case, as expressed by Boies in interviews, was that the program was not "of and concerning" Westmoreland at all, since, as commander of all American troops in Vietnam, he was not "at the highest levels of military intelligence." Boies quietly abandoned that theory soon after Wallace's deposition was complete. And the suit was "discontinued" before what would have been particularly interesting testimony; that is, before Mike Wallace took the stand.

Though Crile spent nearly eight days on the stand, more than any other witness (Westmoreland himself spent ten half days, Adams five-and-a-half days), one almost unarguably important piece of evidence from his deposition was never brought out in court, and therefore never reached the jury before the case came to its abrupt, unanticipated end. In the initial phases of discovery, the plaintiff had routinely called for all documents, videotapes and other tape recordings related to the production of the broadcast; and Cravath had routinely (but with an objection to turning over the result of CBS's internal investigation, the Benjamin Report, until directed to do so by the judge) turned over all documents, videotapes and other tape recordings that it had received from the CBS defendants, including Crile. One witness, however, Ira Klein, a young film editor who worked on "The Uncounted Enemy: A Vietnam Deception," had testified at his own deposition that Crile's secretary had repeatedly offered to let him listen to "the McNamara tape." In response to an inquiry from Westmoreland's attorneys, Cravath reported that, according to Crile, no such tape existed, or ever had been made. Klein, however, testified that Crile's secretary had showed it to him, and spoke with such specificity of the drawer in Crile's secretary's desk in which the tape was kept that Cravath inquired of its client once again. Crile then discovered not only "the McNamara tape" (of which one side had been, he said, inadvertently erased) but tapes he had made as well, without their knowledge, of phone calls with, among others, Maxwell Taylor, Arthur Goldberg and George Ball. When asked, at his deposition, why he had not turned these tapes over in the first place, Crile testified that he had forgotten he taped those conversations. Attorneys for Westmoreland found, as they listened to the tapes (which Cravath, as was its legal obligation, had turned over), that the various recordings were linked by a sort of narrative in Crile's voice. They decided to submit them for examination to Mark R. Weiss, then a professor at Queens College, who had been a member, just ten years before, of the panel of experts who analyzed the tapes of President Richard Nixon, to explain, if possible, the eighteen-and-a-half-minute gap. In his study of Crile's tape recordings, Professor Weiss found that one of the set had been re-recorded at least once, and showed traces of at least seven distinct erasures, or gaps, of its own.

The whole matter, of course, shed no light whatever on whether or not Westmoreland had led or participated in a "conspiracy" to deceive the President and the Joint Chiefs. The issue of the defendants' credibility, however, was of critical importance in the trial. Plaintiff's attorneys found it difficult to believe that Crile could have forgotten *both* that he made the tape recordings (having assured the participants that their remarks were informal and off the record) and that he subsequently re-recorded the same conversations, deleting certain sections and linking the rest by a small narrative of his own. What the jury, with its yellow pads, would have made of this will never be known. Burt himself forgot, as Crile was running away with other questions, to ask Crile about it. And the case ended without the matter having been raised in open court. (In any event, from the moment CBS learned that Crile had secretly recorded conversations, and initially denied their existence on discovery, it "suspended" Crile, and decided that its legal interests and Crile's were no longer identical. Crile had already retained counsel of his own. Boies, however, treated the whole case as one. And Crile's attorneys, though they were paid by CBS, and participated in all defendants' briefs and motions, and though they appeared each day in court, and were admitted to all bench conferences, took no part in the actual conduct of the case. Or, rather, Victor Kovner, the chief counsel among them, took the stand and played the role of witness— reading the answers to Boies' questions, when the actual witness did not appear in court; and only the questions and answers from his deposition were thus read before the jury and into the record of the trial. From this point of view, as from so many others, the sheer waste of time, quite aside from the waste of money, in an American lawsuit can resemble something out of *Bleak House.* And in both cases it sometimes seemed that somewhat better educated and more energetic refugees from *Bleak House* were litigating on behalf of somewhat more righteous and less harried refugees from *Scoop.*)

It may be that one's impressions of the noncriminal government witnesses at the time of Watergate did those witnesses an injustice, in that unusual institutional processes and unaccustomed facets of personality are brought to light when powerful interests appear before the courts. The press, in particular, is accustomed to ask, and not to answer; to engage in and not to submit to scrutiny; to make or imply judgments, and not to be called to account. Generals, too, are used to the special prerogatives of power; but the generals in both cases not only faded, they seemed highly courteous, and even timid, in contrast to the mass-communications press. In a sense, the CBS defendants were not "press" at all: they took a thesis; found witnesses more or less to support it; interviewed those witnesses, and cut those parts of the interviews which did not support the thesis; found the arch-villain, according to the thesis (and cut to those moments when he looked angry, shifty, ill at ease), and one of his supporters, Colonel Danny Graham (whose interview they cut to twenty-one seconds); rehearsed and re-interviewed some friendly witnesses; found reasons not to interview other witnesses, who had information that would undermine the thesis; composed a script for Mike Wallace, in his adversarial style, to grill some witnesses and coddle others. In short, they were acting not as press but as producers and directors casting for a piece of theatre; and that theatre was a court. But the broadcast was created and advertised by CBS News, and claimed all the authority and authenticity that "news" (particularly television news) implies.

By the time the depositions in *Westmoreland* were completed, it could be said of Crile's decisions in creating the broadcast what Judge Leval said of one of the more egregious instances of splicing an answer onto an unasked question: "It is what it is, and it's visible to everyone. . . ." It was not, however, "visible to everyone" *until* the depositions, and even then the "everyone" was only the attorneys and the litigants. Among the program's problematic judgments were: an account of a private, critical briefing of Westmoreland, by Hawkins and McChristian, which never took place (there were in fact three and possibly four separate briefings, none with just those three participants, and none of which corresponded to the program's account); an account of a single meeting between civilian and military intelligence analysts, at which C.I.A. participants "capitulated" to the "dishonest" military estimates (when there were in fact three meetings; the C.I.A. "dictated" the estimates that were agreed to; and the military estimates were honestly arrived at, and proved fairly accurate); in the end (and most significantly), an account of enemy infiltration into South Vietnam in the five months before Tet, which explicitly accused Westmoreland of having suppressed and vastly understated the rate of infiltration, when in fact Westmoreland not only had not but *could* not have misrepresented the figures, since the rate of infiltration was being accurately monitored, by what was referred to throughout the trial as Source X (the National Security Agency), and the "estimates" thus came not from Westmoreland's command at all but from Washington, before they ever reached Saigon; an account of a meeting between President Johnson and some of his closest advisers, the Wise Men (known more formally as the Senior Advisory Group on Vietnam), which portrayed none other than Sam Adams as the hero, in that the Wise Men, having finally accepted Adams' estimates of enemy troop strength, told the President that the war, after the American defeat at Tet, was hopeless (when in fact the advisers did not consider estimates at all, and regarded Tet as an immense American military victory, but told the President that American morale at home would not support continuation of the war). And there was more: six of the eight persons, besides Adams, portrayed on the broadcast as more or less supporting the program's thesis explicitly denied, in portions of their interviews that were cut, that intelligence was suppressed, that there was a "conspiracy" of any kind, that any data base had been dishonestly "altered," or that President Johnson had not been informed of all aspects of the controversy. A seventh (Hawkins) said that he had had a "total memory block" about the events in question, until he had been "helped," over many interviews, by Crile and Adams. One (McChristian) said, in a sworn affidavit, that the editing of his views had been "improper." Another (George Allen, of the C.I.A.) was not only shown, in the editing room, other interviews before being re-interviewed himself; he was asked literally the same question seven times, before Crile found an answer he liked. And so on. "There isn't such a thing as an honest intelligence report; there's my view and somebody else's," one of the eight, Commander James Meacham, said in a part of the interview that wound up, typically, on the editing-room floor; also, "I understand perfectly well what you're trying to say. . . . I don't agree with it." Before the trial began, the litigants also had such documents as the sworn affidavit of Meacham (now the military correspondent of *The Economist*), which read, in part:

Based on my knowledge, the CBS Broadcast "The Uncounted Enemy: A Vietnam Deception" falsely portrays my actions. . . . In particular, the broadcast's version of events after the Tet Offensive does not square with my memory, and before the broadcast I told George Crile and Sam Adams that their versions of those events were untrue.

The Broadcast, as I recall, states that after Tet, the Chief of

Current Intelligence and Estimates, Daniel Graham, altered the records or memory of the computer we used in [Order of Battle] Studies. This is nonsense for several reasons, not the least of which is that Graham was *not in the chain of command* of myself or my subordinates, *and could not order us* to do anything with the computer. Moreover, OB Studies *printed out on paper a copy* of its OB holdings each month and immediately sent that to a long list of persons in Vietnam, Washington, the Pacific Command . . . and elsewhere. *These "hard copies" of the Order of Battle were always available* for comparison at any point in time. Also, the composition of the "data base" *had nothing to do with* the method by which MACV derived its enemy strength figures before or after Tet.

And so on. And Meacham was one of the eight, besides Adams, the broadcast portrayed as *supporting* its thesis. With some others of the eight (notably Hawkins and McChristian), CBS's attorneys managed to get stronger statements in court than they had made on the broadcast (and even statements in direct contradiction to those parts of their interviews which were cut); and Boies hoped to persuade the jury that, even if the program fabricated, misrepresented and misleadingly elided, the *result* was something near (or even an understatement of) the truth. But there could be no question, at least, once the sworn depositions were completed, that, quite apart from the fundamentally absurd thesis, at every stage and in every element of the making of the program, there was something wrong.

But, easy as it may be, in retrospect (and particularly with the evidence in a lawsuit of this magnitude), to find fault with a ninety-minute broadcast, these might all have been good-faith editorial decisions, based on a firm conviction of some kind. Crile had never been the sole producer of a program before. In 1980, as co-producer of a documentary, "Gay Power, Gay Politics," he had been "censured" by the National News Council (for editing applause into a soundtrack of a predominantly homosexual audience listening to a speech by San Francisco's Mayor Diane Feinstein, at a point when there had been no applause). In 1980, he got in touch with Sam Adams, whose article "Vietnam Cover-Up: Playing War with Numbers—A C.I.A. Conspiracy Against Its

Own Intelligence" Crile had edited at *Harper's* in 1975. In the five intervening years, and particularly since the hearings of the Pike Committee, at which he appeared as a witness, Adams had been working on a book, based on his theory that the willful falsification of intelligence estimates before Tet (and the rejection of Adams' own, higher estimates) had led to the loss of the war in Vietnam. Adams had been pursuing this theory obsessively, compiling his lists and chronologies and interviewing mostly lower-echelon figures, with the exception of Colonel Hawkins (whose "total memory block" he was trying, by means of the lists and chronologies, to dispel) and General Maxwell Taylor—whom Adams interviewed for two and a half hours, and whose own book *Swords and Plowshares* seemed to rebut Adams' theory in considerable detail. Among Adams' notes for the book was one that read, "I have yet to interview the four persons still living whom I believe chiefly responsible for the falsification: General Westmoreland himself, General Phillip Davidson, Mr. Robert S. McNamara, and Mr. Walt Rostow"; also, "I plan to approach them before the book goes to press, in the hope that they will shed further light on what happened, including the extent of President Johnson's involvement." There was nothing at all (the significance of this dawned only gradually) in Adams' notes about suppression of the alleged infiltration of a hundred thousand North Vietnamese into South Vietnam in the five months before Tet.

Crile based his entire proposal, or Blue Sheet, for the program on Adams' research; and, besides using him as a paid consultant, writing a script for Mike Wallace to interview him (and rehearsing Adams for that interview), and casting him, in effect, as the program's hero (whose "estimates" allegedly prevailed, at last, with the Wise Men, and even brought about Johnson's decision not to run for another term), Crile relied for his selection of people to interview on a "List of Prospects" prepared for him by Adams, and kept Adams beside him during all "friendly" interviews. But of the "four persons still living" whom Adams planned "to approach," Crile put only one, Westmoreland, on the program. He wrote the script for Mike Wallace to interview another, Rostow; and then, when the interview seemed effectively to rebut every element of the program's thesis, simply did not use any footage of

the Rostow interview. Crile himself interviewed (and surreptitiously tape-recorded) McNamara, and then ignored what
McNamara told him (and, for a time, denied the existence of the
tape). But, in all the arcana of the trial and the broadcast, Crile's
treatment of the fourth, General Phillip Davidson, was simultaneously the most telling and the most mystifying. Although the
whole broadcast ignored Davidson (who, as McChristian's successor and Westmoreland's chief of intelligence, would have been
quite literally *the* officer "at the highest levels of American military intelligence" to carry out the alleged "conspiracy"), and
although Crile claimed to believe (as Wallace, in part of the interview that was cut, told Westmoreland) that Davidson was "too
sick" to be interviewed, or even "on his deathbed," Adams knew
at least five weeks before the broadcast, and (according to the
Benjamin Report) had told Crile, that Davidson was "healthy as
a clam." Adams had even made notes ("Davidson, Gen'l Phil B.
. . . Doing fine, remarried, living down in Texas. . . . He's writing
a book on Giap"), and had even jotted down Davidson's current
address. Ira Klein, the young film editor, too, testified, at his
deposition, that Crile knew Davidson was alive and well. Crile, at
his own deposition, testified that he had believed Davidson was
too ill. All this, when the depositions were completed and before
the trial began, Crile and all the other litigants knew, before Crile
ever took the stand. And yet, at trial, after saying repeatedly, "It
was my understanding, at the time, that [General Davidson] was
on his deathbed," and after being confronted with questions based
on Crile's *own notes,* prepared for the CBS internal investigation
that led to the Benjamin Report: "Q. Let me read those into the
record, sir. 'A. General Davidson. CBS wanted very much to
interview Davidson.' That's the truth, is it not, sir?' A. That's
correct. . . ."

> Q. All right. Now, it is true, is it not, that CBS wanted very much
> to interview Davidson, correct, sir?
> A. I wanted to interview General Davidson. We all did.
> Q. [quoting from Crile's notes] "The transcripts are filled with
> accusations made against him and his intelligence operation,
> which CBS would have liked to put to him directly." And that
> refers to General Davidson, does it not, sir?

A. That does.

Q. Next paragraph. "It was our understanding, however, that Davidson was on his deathbed." . . . Did there ever come a time in 1981 when Mr. Adams told you that General Davidson was well?

A. I don't recall him ever having done that.

And so on, with answer after answer to the effect that Crile had sincerely believed in Davidson's mortal illness, and would otherwise have been sincerely eager to interview him:

Q. Mr. Crile, in your white paper you state CBS wanted very much to interview Davidson. Correct, sir?

A. Yes, that's correct.

Q. And Mike Wallace, in his interview of General Westmoreland, said that General Davidson is "a very, very sick man who we want very much to talk to," correct, sir?

A. That is correct.

And then Burt suddenly quoted from Crile's *own script* for Mike Wallace: "We want to get Westmoreland to say that McChristian was great stuff, totally reliable. *We don't give a goddam about Davidson.*"

And, of course, though Crile then embarked on one of his longer, more combative and evasive answers (for which he had been rebuked with particular severity, outside the hearing of the jury, earlier that day, by Judge Leval), there it was. What was mystifying was that, *knowing* there was all that testimony to the effect that he had been told about Davidson's robust health five weeks prior to the broadcast, *knowing* that there was, in the record, in his own script, "We don't give a goddam about Davidson," Crile should have risked all the preceding, now patently incorrect answers, and that he should have remained so unfazed, even supercilious, on the stand. No "conspiracy" at "the highest levels of American military intelligence" could have existed without Davidson: Davidson *was* "the highest levels of American military intelligence." Even if the defendants had prevailed in their early attempts to show that the program was not "of and concerning" Westmoreland, it would have had to be "of and concerning" his chief intelligence officer. Crile and, because of Crile, Mike Wallace claimed to have believed that Davidson was too ill to interview. Two people, Adams and Klein, gave testimony to the effect that Crile knew, five weeks before the broadcast, that Davidson was well. Crile, in his notes for CBS's internal investigation, and at his deposition, and on the stand, testified that he did not know; and that, had he known, he would certainly have "wanted very much" to interview Davidson. And yet the memo (one recalled that other note to Wallace: "Now all you have to do is break General Westmoreland and we have the whole thing aced") made it very clear that "we" did not "give a goddam" about Davidson. And Davidson, alive and well, was a particularly effective witness at the trial—and remains healthy, in San Antonio, Texas, to this day.

As for Sam Adams, on whom Crile relied so heavily (though, as it turned out, selectively), he remained, from well before the inception of the program until after the conclusion of the lawsuit, a complicated and ambiguous presence. When Crile first showed him the Blue Sheet, for example, with its twenty-four mentions of the word "conspiracy," Adams had said (according to his testimony for the Benjamin Report), "Oh, for Christ's sake, George, come off it." And after Westmoreland's press conference in January of 1982, at which Westmoreland and other former officials (including Davidson) denounced the broadcast, Adams had rushed into the CBS offices and said, "We have to come clean" (that the falsifications had originated in the White House), and suggested a retraction. On the other hand, it was Adams, at the climax of the broadcast itself, who claimed, in effect, to have altered history:

ADAMS: I was asked to bring together a—an estimate of how many enemy there were. And I said there were about 600,000. And I understand it was used to brief the so-called Wise Men, Lyndon Johnson's senior advisers.

WALLACE: Who are we talking about?

ADAMS: They included Dean Acheson, George Ball, Arthur Goldberg, Maxwell Taylor, and so forth.

WALLACE: What had happened is, that after Tet the C.I.A. had regained the courage of its convictions, and among other things, they told the Wise Men of the C.I.A.'s belief that we were fighting a dramatically larger enemy. That was at least one of the reasons why Lyndon Johnson's advisers concluded that, despite the military's insistence that we were winning, the enemy could not in fact be defeated at any acceptable cost. The Wise Men then stunned the President by urging him to begin pulling out of the war.

Wallace went on to say that five days after George Carver, of the C.I.A., had briefed the Wise Men, "a sobered Lyndon Johnson addressed the nation," to announce that he would not run again. Now, nearly all of this was fantasy. Adams was not "asked" to make an estimate, in late March of 1968, when the meeting in question took place. He had *made* an estimate, based on his "extrapolations," from an out-of-date monthly summary of captured enemy documents, in late 1966, and had failed to persuade even the C.I.A. that it was accurate, as, indeed, according to all knowledgeable accounts (American and even North Vietnamese) from that time to the present, it was not. Adams' figures were not "used to brief" the Wise Men. They had been repeatedly reviewed, and emphatically rejected at lower levels months before. The C.I.A., moreover, did not regain "the courage of its convictions"; and Carver, who conducted the briefing, happened to be the official who had most emphatically repudiated Adams' estimates, and did not (according to his sworn deposition) use *any* estimates of enemy troop strength in his briefing of the Wise Men. According to sworn affidavits by the Wise Men themselves, there was at the meeting in question "no discussion of any change in intelligence estimates of enemy forces." "Instead, the discussion focussed" on the attitude of the American people toward the war. The only one at the meeting of the Wise Men who was interviewed for the broadcast was Walt Rostow. He was not asked at all about the meeting. And nothing of his interview was used. Carver, as it happened, had joined Westmoreland at his press conference after the broadcast. He spent four days as a witness on the stand. As Adams' superior (and George Allen's) in the C.I.A., Carver had been one of Crile's "last-minute" contacts (Komer was another);

that is, people who were in a position to rebut the program's thesis, fundamentally and in detail, but who were not interviewed on camera, or consulted until the broadcast was virtually complete. In addition to his testimony about the program itself (which conflicted with it on almost every factual point), Carver testified, in one of the trial's few moments of historic interest, that "estimates" about the enemy's irregulars (the village defense units, the grandmothers and the children) were always so uncertain that he, on behalf of the C.I.A., had come to favor representing them not in numbers at all but in "prose narrative" form. As for a set of notes, entitled "An Interview with George Carver," which Crile took of their interview, Carver quietly but repeatedly characterized them as deceitful ("The rest is Mr. Crile's invention"); and he characterized Adams himself, and testified that he had so characterized him to Crile, as a man who "was often in error but seldom in doubt."

As it turned out (in one of the bizarre facts, like Halevy's maid at gunpoint, that often emerge upon discovery), from early 1968 until 1973, when he left the C.I.A., Adams, according to his deposition, had "purloined" documents from the C.I.A. files and buried them, in "a leaf bag," near his home, in Virginia. The leaf bag had "sprung a leak," with the result that many of the documents were destroyed. In 1973, just before quitting the C.I.A., he testified on behalf of Daniel Ellsberg in *United States* v. *Russo and Ellsberg.* His intention had been to say that since the "estimates" of enemy troop strength were anyway "faked," there could be no violation of national security in leaking them to the press. This position seemed reasonable enough. One difficulty, however, which emerged on Adams' cross-examination in *Westmoreland,* was that in the Ellsberg case he had also given such testimony as this:

> The questions arose in the intelligence community's mind as to whether to count a guy that stuck a pungi stick in the ground as part of the Order of Battle. That is among the problems which arose. *It is very difficult to decide who to count.*

And:

> The problem always was in Vietnam to sort out who was a soldier
> and who wasn't. A person that lays a grenade on a path with a trip
> wire . . . *Now, whether you consider this man a military man or a
> civilian, I couldn't say.*

And:

> Now, even in the guerrillas . . . you are not absolutely sure how
> many guerrillas to count. The same problem arises with the self-
> defense, secret self-defense and particularly the political cadre.
> . . . *It is very difficult to decide who to count.*

And, while all these answers were sound and reasonable enough,
they were absolutely in conflict with both the thesis of the broadcast and the defendants' theory of the case, in that both allowed
for no such difficulty, or honest difference of opinion, about "who
to count," and who was "a military man or a civilian." These
answers, in other words, were at almost perfect odds with the
whole notion of "conspiracy." Adams tried to explain away these
earlier expressions of allowance for honest, good-faith doubt by
saying he had to modify his real views, in the Ellsberg case, in
anticipation that Hawkins (who "despised that Ellsberg fellow")
was going to commit perjury, and say that the figures Ellsberg
leaked were honest. But, apart from the sheer confusion inherent
in an "explanation" of that kind (less than honest testimony was
required of Adams in anticipation of perjury from Hawkins on the
other side), the possibility became distinct that *both* Adams and
Hawkins were prepared to be less than honest, on the broadcast
and in court. And for a moment the whole case seemed to tilt, as
to which side was engaged in deception and conspiracy to deceive.

In 1975, after his article was published in *Harper's,* Adams
appeared before the Pike Committee, and his testimony there, too,
created difficulties for him on cross-examination in *Westmoreland.*
In answer to a question from a congressman, as to whether a
specific document he was testifying about was classified, Adams
had replied, for example, "A lot of this has not yet been made
public. This is taken from notes that I took." The difficulty was
that the document came not from "notes that I took" but from

the C.I.A. files he had "purloined" and buried in his leaf bag. In answer to another question, what was the basis for the figure in a statement in his *Harper's* article that as "many as 10,000 American soldiers had been killed in the Tet Offensive" (the actual figure was about a thousand), Adams had replied: "That number was too high. *I flipped out that one by mistake.*" He had also testified that military intelligence estimates of the rate of infiltration by North Vietnamese soldiers into South Vietnam, in the months preceding Tet, were "a bit low, but basically honest."

Early in Adams' cross-examination, he received from Judge Leval a relatively mild variant of the instruction given repeatedly to Crile:

> THE COURT: All right. . . . I would simply like to give one instruction to Mr. Adams. Mr. Adams, you have to answer the question that's put to you. It's been my observation that, on several instances, where you thought there was something to be said that countered the thrust of the question, you simply didn't answer the question, but went straight to what you would have regarded as the rebuttal.

There were nine paragraphs, not counting interpolated "O.K."s and "all right"s from the witness, of this particular instruction.

> My observation has been that, several times, you have simply left out the answer to the question that was put to you. . . . So please be aware of that. And also, as a general proposition . . . it's not a debate. . . . I would also suggest to you . . . a large part of what you're being examined about has to do with material that you were not personally familiar with. . . . You have a tendency frequently to assert things as facts . . . when you were not present and you know it only by virtue of having been told. . . . So try to avoid the form of asserting facts to be true when they are things that you know only by virtue of having been told, in the course of interviews, or having read them in books.

Adams was, in general, a more courteous witness than Crile, and more inclined to abide by the instructions from the judge. Yet there was about both witnesses an aura not only of the prerogatives of social class but of having condescended to participate as advocates and not as witnesses in the proceedings. For Adams, however, the remaining factual difficulties were basically two: that in all the years of his wandering, since 1967, like the Ancient Mariner, with his tale of suppressed estimates, he had always included, among the culpable, officials (military and civilian) higher in rank than Westmoreland; and that, in all his "lists," "chronologies" and other notes, until just before he began working on the broadcast, he had never once (and neither had anybody else) so much as mentioned the more than a hundred thousand North Vietnamese who, the program alleged, infiltrated South Vietnam in the five months before Tet.

The first problem was presented more acutely by another witness, Greg Rushford, for eight months an investigator for the Pike Committee, and a devout believer in Adams. On direct examination by Boies, Rushford seemed an effective witness on CBS's and Adams' behalf, telling what he had said, during the making of the broadcast, to Adams and to Crile. On cross-examination, however, by Dorsen (over heavy objections by Boies) and despite his denials that this person or that had acted in furtherance of the conspiracy, Rushford soon began alluding, with a kind of dark ebullience, to a "larger web" (a phrase reminiscent of the phrase "a wider conspiracy" that Judge Leval had used to characterize what the plaintiff was trying to prove Rushford believed). In the first bench conference, which Boies requested to state his objections to Dorsen's mild inquiries into Rushford's real beliefs, Judge Leval asked Dorsen (and Dorsen replied in the affirmative) whether he was "arguing that Adams and Crile, or somebody else at CBS, might have regarded Rushford as ' . . . far out. . . .' " A bit later, in response to further objections, the judge stated that Dorsen's line of questions was appropriate "to the extent that the examination is directed to what was told to Adams and to Crile, and not simply to exploring this witness's views to show that he's a kook." That was the first, or "larger web," problem: that Adams' conspiracy-to-suppress theory had always extended, before "The Uncounted Enemy: A Vietnam Deception," to officials higher than Westmoreland, including (in direct contradiction to the program's central thesis) President Johnson and the Joint Chiefs. West-moreland could hardly have conspired to deceive his military and civilian superiors in a deceit in which they were his co-conspirators.

But the second problem, the hundred thousand North Viet-namese infiltrators, whom nobody, *including Adams himself,* had ever detected before "The Uncounted Enemy: A Vietnam Decep-tion" alleged that Westmoreland suppressed them, proved insu-perable. Not surprisingly, Adams found it difficult to explain why, in the fifteen years between the alleged infiltration and the broad-cast, nobody had noticed or heard of these hundred thousand men. The broadcast was unequivocal:

> WALLACE: But CBS Reports has learned that during the five months preceding the Tet Offensive, Westmoreland's infiltration analysts had actually been reporting not seven or eight thousand, but more than 25,000 North Vietnamese coming down the Ho Chi Minh Trail each month, and that amounted to a near inva-sion. But those reports of a dramatically increased infiltration were systematically blocked.

In other words, *more* than a hundred thousand, in fact, more than a hundred and twenty-five thousand. Source X, the National Secu-rity Agency, which monitored troop movements electronically, had not reported them. (And, since Source X emanated from Washington, Westmoreland could not have suppressed *those* re-ports.) Adams, as a witness:

> Q. Is it your testimony that *the first time* all of this was made public was in January, 1982, by CBS Reports?
> A. That is among the reasons why I think that "The Uncounted Enemy" is an extraordinarily valuable piece of documentary work, *because it told this story,* as I understand it, *for the first time.*
> Q. All these people coming up with studies, all these 100,000 to 150,000 unreported infiltrators, as you say, *it took fifteen years* before this information came to light, Mr. Adams?
> A. That's the long and the short of it.

And with this preposterous testimony, on behalf of this preposterous "journalism," in these two preposterous (but also highly serious and embittered) lawsuits, something about the process that had brought everyone to court came, inadvertently and quietly ("That's the long and the short of it"), to light. Because at this point it became clear that, however absurd the rest of the program may have been, the infiltration part of the thesis was plain dishonest. It might well be true, for instance, that in all the years since 1967 Adams had sincerely believed that his "estimate" of six hundred thousand enemy troops was right, and that the irregulars (the sympathizers, the grandmothers and the children) should be included in the Order of Battle, the official category of soldiers, armed guerrillas and other military men—although to treat noncombatants or civilians as soldiers would be an outright violation of the Geneva Conventions, and inhumane. And it could also be believed that when his "estimate" was not accepted, by the American military or within the C.I.A., and when the irregulars were not included in the Order of Battle (though they were, at all times, listed in a category of their own), he sincerely believed that his "estimate" had been not in good faith rejected but dishonestly "suppressed." From a notion that "estimates" of irregulars were "suppressed," it was a short emotional jump to the idea that there had been a "conspiracy" to suppress them. In Adams' original, and sincere, version, the purpose (and the historical dimension) of the "conspiracy" to suppress his "estimates" was to conceal the fact that we *should not have been in* that war. That is, if the size and the composition of the enemy in Vietnam had been as Adams in his "extrapolations" analyzed them, then the war in Vietnam was not a war but an insurrection. And the United States did not belong in Vietnam. Now the "extrapolations" and the "insurrection" view turned out (by both American and North Vietnamese accounts, as well as by historical events themselves) to be mistaken: there were fewer than ninety thousand enemy fighters in the all-out effort at Tet. But the second part was a sound, ultimately almost unarguable proposition. The United States, it is generally acknowledged, underwent its own disaster in that war. The trouble was that there was no *link* between the proposition and Adams' "estimates." By 1980, when Crile enlisted Adams for the broadcast, there was another difficulty: even the proposition that the United States did not belong in Vietnam was too widely shared, and too dated, to be, by any stretch of the imagination, news. And Adams' view (and Crile's) had subtly but radically shifted: the link between the "estimates" and the "conspiracy" to suppress them was now formulated in terms not of purpose but of result. The effect of the "suppression" of Adams' "estimates" was no longer concealment of the fact that the United States *did not belong* in the war in Vietnam; *it was the explanation of why the war was lost.* This fitted in perfectly with television's invariable preference for the simple. Everything else fell, or was cut, or nudged, or elided, into place.

But Adams, the hero as "intelligence" analyst, totally alone, was not, even for television, a credible story. So McChristian was made to seem to have held similar views, and to have been fired for them (though McChristian had not held such views, and though documents showed he had left to take a command he wanted, while Westmoreland had requested him to stay). And Hawkins was made to seem to have held similar views, and to have joined in the suppression of them (though Hawkins had not held such views, either, and had "blocked" or forgotten almost the entire period, until Crile and Adams came along). And Allen, of the C.I.A., was made to seem to have held such views, and, when he failed to express anything like them, was re-rehearsed, and re-interviewed and implored. (Crile: "Come to the defense of your old protégé, Sam Adams." Allen: "No, I don't remember. Refresh me." Crile: "I'll refresh you. . . ." Allen: "Is it really kosher to go over this?" Crile: "Oh, this is what we do.") This is what we do. And Carver, Komer, McNamara, Bunker, Nitze, Wheeler, Bundy, Sharp and others in a position to have knowledge of the matter were ignored. Rostow was interviewed, and, when his interview too convincingly undermined the theory, the interview was discarded. Graham was interviewed, and cut to twenty-one seconds. And Davidson was consigned to his "deathbed," and left out. Several people (besides Allen) who more or less agreed, or who had heard rumors to the effect that official estimates of enemy troop strength were in some way inaccurate, were represented as more knowledgeable, and more highly placed, than in fact they had been (George Hamscher, for instance, a lower-echelon bureaucrat stationed in Honolulu, as "head of M.A.C.V.'s delegation," from Saigon); and even *their* views were cut, distorted and elided. (Cut: Meacham, "No numbers were faked"; five others, specifically denying "conspiracy." Elided: Hawkins, "These figures were crap," among countless other examples.)

The story seemed to require a villain. President Johnson, along with any number of others, was, again, not by any stretch of the imagination news. Westmoreland, then. He was interviewed, with technical questions he had not in fourteen years had occasion to consider, by Mike Wallace (with Crile's script) at his most adversarial. When Westmoreland, within days, sent a letter containing corrections, Crile told Wallace it was not "relevant," and ignored it. Then the story, as it worked out, was relatively simple, and it became essentially this: Sam Adams, lone intelligence analyst, had, on the basis of a "captured enemy documents," made the first accurate "estimates" of enemy troop strength; Westmoreland, briefed (and shocked), privately, with similar "estimates" by Hawkins and McChristian, fired McChristian, suppressed the "estimates" and led a "conspiracy" to deceive, among others, the President and the Joint Chiefs. As a result, the American military was unprepared for, and American soldiers suffered unnecessary slaughter and defeat at, Tet. Then Adams was vindicated. The C.I.A., having regained its courage, used Adams' honest "estimates" to brief the Wise Men and the President. But, in at least two ways, the vindication came too late. President Johnson chose not to run again, and the United States lost the war in Vietnam.

The story had its own utter and obvious absurdity, not least in making Westmoreland capable of suppressing information that was at all times available to so many people, including in particular the President, from so many sources and through so many different channels. But it was apparently not enough. There remained the matter of the hundred thousand to hundred and fifty thousand North Vietnamese soldiers, surreptitiously infiltrating South Vietnam in the five months preceding Tet. No source (American, North Vietnamese or other), including Sam Adams, had ever mentioned them before. And one might have thought that even a low-level "intelligence" analyst would have seen a difficulty even with the simpler story, as it stood. The highest estimate of enemy troops, regular and irregular, who engaged in the Tet offensive was eighty-five thousand. If Adams' initial "estimate" of six hundred thousand, regular and irregular (all of whom should have been included in the Order of Battle), was accurate, the question, posed almost inescapably, was: What were the remaining five hundred and fifteen thousand *doing* during Tet? Or if, as would be understandable, they were just being irregulars—children and grandmothers—aloof from the offensive, why *compound* the difficulty, with a hundred thousand to a hundred and fifty thousand regular North Vietnamese soldiers infiltrating South Vietnam, unseen by anyone (because their existence was concealed by Westmoreland), until CBS made its revelation, in 1982. That is, were these *regular soldiers,* or at least sixty-five thousand of them, idle during Tet as well? And the answer, "the long and the short of it," as Sam Adams put it in his testimony, was that, though the element of the mass phantom infiltrators made no conceivable sense, *it made a better story,* in that it seemed like a reporting coup. So that, from a sincerely held belief, that he was right about the irregulars and that the failure of others to agree reflected a conspiracy against the truth; from what was from one point of view the fifteen-year crusade of the self-important intelligence bureaucrat but, from another, an almost touching personalization of the war, Adams and Crile and finally (with all the exaggeration fierce advocacy and solemn testimony under oath can bring to bear) CBS (and of course Boies and Cravath) came to embrace what was only a device of plotting melodrama, and then engaged in major litigation on behalf of ninety minutes of factually false and intellectually trivial "documentary." They thought it must be true, because it would have been a scoop.

It is, of course, the press's business to go after scoops. Or part of the press's business. And certainly the press shares in the mortal right to make mistakes. There is, however, a fundamental incompatibility between the values embodied in the very concept of scoops and any sort of rigidity about them. The claims journalism normally, and rightly, makes appear to be quite modest—just daily inquiry, no time really to check, recourse to documents is the work of scholars, truth will emerge, history will decide. Duncan, *Time*'s chief of correspondents, actually said in his trial testimony, defending his decision not to correct what he insisted was the "misinterpretation" by every other publication, including *The*

New York Times, of the paragraph in *Time,* "I have an assumption, and it is normally true, that erroneous reports in the press . . . correct themselves in a rather short time. Particularly, I assumed that . . . readers everywhere around the world, that they would then know what the magazine had said, rather than the false reports [in all the other publications, based on *Time*], and that that would be corrected." What Duncan had done was to tell *The New York Times* reporter, in effect, that *"Time* stands by its story." After Westmoreland's press conference, after the article in *TV Guide,* after CBS's own praiseworthy investigation, which resulted in the Benjamin Report, the president of CBS News, Van Gordon Sauter, issued not the report itself but a press release that contained the statement "CBS News stands by the broadcast." Now, it is a long jump from the scoop (*"Time* has learned," "CBS has learned") to the reflex that each "stands by" its paragraph or its broadcast. It implies some *interim confirmation.* And in both cases this implication turned out to be almost perfectly misleading. *Time* felt that it had some legal or professional obligation not even to investigate. And the Benjamin Report revealed the unprofessional basis of almost every editorial decision in the making of the program. From there, however, it is a quantum jump not even to admit doubt or to consider a retraction but, on the contrary, to undertake what is in reality not a defense at all but a grand assault, with all the most costly and aggressive strategies of major litigation. The reporting coup, if that's what it was, has now gone from its initial formulation (*"Time* has learned," "CBS Reports has learned"), through its reiteration and defense (*"Time* stands by its story," "CBS News stands by the broadcast"), to an actual attempt legally to *enforce* it. The First Amendment is, in essence, a protection for diversity against the exercise of centralized, governmental or quasi-governmental power; it is not only trivialized, it cannot possibly be properly invoked, on behalf of the enforcement of a scoop.

It is notable that what "has learned," and who "stands by" were phrased in institutional terms: not Halevy or Adams (or Wallace or Crile) but a magazine and a network "learned." There is in the phrase an overtone not just of inside information but also of the vast authority of the entire institution, something more than even the dimension of trust already embodied in publishing or broadcasting, under his own byline, what a reporter writes or says. The inside-dopester overtone of this kind of journalism was manifested, in almost wonderful unconscious idiocy, when Halevy, at his deposition and then at trial, referred repeatedly to a Lebanese *press official,* "code name Max." Barr, with Halevy on the stand, seemed unfazed, even charmed, by this testimony:

A. The pending question is if I met Israelis.
Q. Yes.
A. Yes, I did.
Q. Who did you meet?
A. I met an Israeli official.
Q. More than that, you won't tell us?
A. Let's call him—I think I used an initial for him. I will say Mossad official Mr. L.
Q. When you say a Mossad official, was it a high, low official?
A. Deputy Mossad chief.
Q. A high Mossad official?
A. Yes.

A. So I asked a Phalangist official who served at the Phalangist unit—
Q. Press information?
A. Press-information unit—by the name of Max.
Q. Max?
A. It's a code name.
Q. That is what he is known as?
A. Yes.

As it turned out, neither "Mossad official Mr. L," nor "Phalangist official," "press-information unit," "code name Max" had told the witness anything of consequence. But the remarkable thing was that, when it suited the defense's purposes, the shield law was waived without a qualm, and a presumed source was identified with the highest specificity (there existed, after all, only one "deputy Mossad chief"), to establish the high level of the reporter's contacts. But a *flack,* in the journalists' and the attorneys' enchantment with mystification, is accorded the secrecy, and the romance, of a "code name."

It may be that the question "Max?" ranks beside the answer "That's the long and the short of it" among the great moments in recent judicial history. It may also be, however, that what emerged from both these cases about the profession of modern, mass-communications journalism is that readers and viewers need to be alert, from time to time, to what really is a kind of code. *"Time* has learned," as witness after witness testified, in *Sharon,* means that *Time* is not as certain as it is about information that is not introduced by such a phrase. The same is presumably true of "CBS has learned." But one does not need Mike Wallace's voice or intonation to sense that the phrase is also intended to introduce something momentous, in the nature of a major scoop; and the scoop itself is, likely as not, something a reporter heard somewhere, or thought he heard, and for which he claims a somewhat secret, and therefore valid, provenance. But the code may extend, particularly in television, to the minutest detail: just because the camera cuts, for instance, to someone nodding while someone else is speaking, the nodding person need not (as is implied, as seems authentically *recorded*) have agreed with what the speaking person is saying; he may not even have heard it; he may not even have been present; there was just some footage of somebody speaking and some footage of somebody nodding, and the producer wanted, in this way, to make a point. Or, just because there is a question followed by an answer, the person answering may never even have heard the question he appears (as he seems authentically recorded) to have answered; the question may never have been posed to him; or he may in fact have answered it an entirely other way; or there was some footage of him answering some quite other question, or no question at all. Something analogous, of course, is possible in print journalism. But the illusion of *authenticity,* the person bodily there, is not the same.

These were the specific "sources" (apart, that is, from prior publications, "many," "you name it" and "so many it's unbelievable") that *Time*'s correspondent claimed for the paragraph that contained the sentence about what *"Time* has learned," the sentence, in fact, that prompted Sharon to ask for a retraction and, when *Time* decided instead to reiterate and "stand by" it, brought on the entire suit: Source 1, referred to at the trial as General

No. 1, and (rather confusingly, since the sources were designated entirely differently at trial than at depositions) referred to in Halevy's, Kelly's and Duncan's depositions as Source B, who told Halevy that "crucial new notes exist" concerning Sharon's condolence call of September 15, 1982, on the Gemayels at Bikfaya. Source 3, referred to at the trial as Intelligence Person 3, and in the various depositions as Source A, who either (as Halevy repeatedly implied at his deposition; and as Kelly unequivocally stated, at both his deposition and the trial, Halevy had told him at the time) showed Halevy the "new notes, or minutes," or (as Halevy testified at trial) *"read"* them, or "pieces" of them, to Halevy over the telephone. This Source 3 (or A, or Intelligence Person 3) in any event told Halevy that the "new notes" revealed that Pierre Gemayel, father of Bashir and Amin, had said that the death of Bashir "must be avenged" and that Sharon had made "no response." On the other hand, Source 3 (or A, or Intelligence Person 3) also told Halevy that it was Sharon who "apologized" for having, in the course of a condolence call, "to talk business"; and the "business" in question, according to Halevy, was "revenge." So there was considerable ambiguity, according to Source 3 (or A, or Intelligence Person 3), whether Pierre Gemayel initiated the subject (and Sharon made "no response") or Sharon brought it up by starting to "talk business." Another thing Source 3 (or A, or Intelligence Person 3) told Halevy was that he (Source 3) had been called to testify before the Kahan Commission, and that the "notes," or "minutes," of Bikfaya (which he had either shown to Halevy or read him excerpts from) had been submitted to the commission in their entirety. Source 4, referred to at the trial as Government Official 4 (and in the depositions as Source C), who also "read" to Halevy from the notes, and added that "these notes will never be published," because they showed "greater involvement of the Gemayels and Sharon" in the massacres at Sabra and Shatila. All these were the "sources" of Halevy's Memo Item of December 6, 1982.

For anyone able or inclined to follow this somehow Biblical enumeration, there arises an immediate question: Where, in the whole account, is Source 2? Well, Source 2, who became known at the trial as General No. 2, as it were *sprang* into the case on Halevy's second day on the stand. He had never been mentioned in Halevy's deposition (or anybody else's); nor had the information that, it turned out, he (reading, like Intelligence Person 3 and Government Official 4, to Halevy from the "notes") provided for the Memo Item of December 6th. Source 2 (or General No. 2) had said (or "read") to Halevy, for instance, that Sharon said, at the Bikfaya meeting, that the assassination of Bashir Gemayel was a "Syrian-Palestinian conspiracy," for which there must be "retaliation." Quite apart from the fact that (according, at least, to the Kahan Report) Sharon knew at the time that the assassination was the work not of Palestinians at all but of a Lebanese group (which, on the night of September 14, 1982, had actually asked the Israelis for protection against the Phalangists), the Mourabitoun, the remarkable thing about Halevy's summoning up this new "confidential source," Israeli General No. 2, at trial, is that he had never mentioned either this "source" or his information to anyone before. Not at his deposition, where, he explained (as though he had not been questioned in the greatest detail about who or what all his "sources" might have been), "Nobody asked me"; also, "But, by the way, Mr. Gould, at that time I did not see the great significance you are finding in that statement." And not even to anyone at *Time*—to whom the news that Sharon actually advocated "retaliation" would presumably have been of greater interest, and even precision, than either Halevy's original formulation ("gave them the feeling, after the Gemayels' questioning, that he understood their need to take revenge . . . and assured them that the Israeli army would neither hinder them nor try to stop them"), or even the writer William Smith's final text ("discussed with the Gemayels the need for the Phalangists to take revenge"). And, if Sharon had so forthrightly proposed "retaliation," what was the need for either of these delicate circumlocutions—or for that other phrasing, by Halevy at his deposition, " 'Gave them the feeling' could be a body movement, could be silence, could be a non-outspoken rejection of their raising the issue, and could also be indifference to the fact"? (Also: "Could also be read as meaning a verbal communication . . . ? A verbal communication? No.") Halevy had, at trial, this explanation:

THE COURT: . . . Did you tell anyone at *Time* about General Number 2 and what he conveyed to you?

THE WITNESS: No, sir. Because if I would have conveyed it, the military censor would have taken it out.

With this answer, Halevy's presence (and his apparent readiness to say anything at all, as if factual matters were a thing of barter, or of haggling in a *souk*) were not so disorienting, *Time*'s whole position fell, perhaps not for the first time, to smithereens. Because, if the paragraph that purported to convey a state secret were true, the military censor would have taken it out as well. But Judge Sofaer, remembering that "the military censor" could scarcely have interposed himself between the witness and, for example, Kelly, who was right beside him at the office, went mildly on:

THE COURT: Mr. Kelly was with you in Jerusalem? He was your chief, your bureau chief?
THE WITNESS: Yes—no, at the time—
THE COURT: Did you tell him?
A. You mean at the time—
THE COURT: In December, when you wrote this story?
A. I think he was the bureau chief.
Q. Did you tell Mr. Kelly, who was the bureau chief at the time, what General Number 2 had told you?
A. I don't recall.

In any event, on February 10, 1983, when Kelly asked him to check whether the substance of his Memo Item was really in Appendix B, and Halevy used the phone in the adjoining office, Source 1 (or B, or Israeli General No. 1) was "unreachable." Source 2, or General No. 2 (who, since he was not mentioned at the depositions, had no alphabetic designation in the case), said, "It all started at Bikfaya. Go back to Bikfaya . . ."—words that struck Halevy not only as significant but as "Shakespearean." Source 3 (or A, or Intelligence Person 3) told Halevy about Appendix B precisely what was apparent from the published document (that Appendix B contained the names of agents, and other matters that, for reasons of defense and foreign policy, must remain secret). And Source 4 (or C, or Government Official 4) told him what was also plainly stated in the Kahan Report, as published: that Appendix B was "a reference book and index, a code book." Halevy said he asked him whether various notetakers at secret meetings were listed in the Appendix (as even a cursory reading of the report made clear they were); Source 4 (or C, or Government Official 4) said that they were, and also that Appendix B was "secret." On the basis of these conversations, Halevy told Kelly either in words ("It's in there") or in substance or body language ("thumbs up, a sort of all clear") that the information in his Memo Item of December 6th was accurate, and that he had confirmed that it was in fact contained in Appendix B. On the basis of this assurance, Kelly completed his telex; Smith wrote his paragraph; *Time* published; serious news publications worldwide took the story up. And with this paragraph, this testimony, this witness, *Time* litigated as though the entire First Amendment were at stake, and continued to "stand by its story," with what it called the "minor" exception of its location in Appendix B, till long after the jury verdicts were all in.

A. Revenge, and I again repeat myself, Mr. Gould, the word revenge . . . was mentioned by Pierre Gemayel at Bikfaya.

A. You got my answer three times. You want it again?
Q. Yes, I want it again.
A. With pleasure. I said before and I will say it again that the matter of retaliation was brought up by Sharon. Reprisal was brought up by Sharon.

A. This is, how do you call that? You . . . call that giving them the feeling. You call that . . . will neither hinder nor stop them. I don't like to talk about it. I hate the subject. I am telling you, sir, it's painful, but—
Q. I am sorry.
A. I am sorry. I haven't finished. This is a very clear type of giving the feeling. A very clear type.
Q. I want you to tell me what kind of gesture . . . body movement or gesture that conveys to the observer that the Israeli army would neither hinder them nor try to stop them.
MR. BARR: Your Honor, I don't think—
THE COURT: I will permit it. Why would there need to be a body movement if Source 2 had told you that [Sharon] had asked for a reprisal, in effect, as you say, and then Pierre had said he

wanted to avenge and he didn't say anything. Why would there have to be any body movement at all?

MR. BARR: Indeed, but who said there was?

THE COURT: You don't know anything about a body movement having occurred?

A. No, sir.

Q. Why did you say it then here?

MR. BARR: He didn't say it.

Q. I will read it again.

[Colloquy]

A. Sir, I refused to believe it then, I refuse to believe it now. I am an Israeli. I am an officer of the [Israel Defense Force] . . . I don't want to believe it 'til this moment.

THE COURT: All right, we will go to lunch.

Q. Green light means go ahead, doesn't it?

A. Green light normally means go ahead, yes, sir.

Q. And Green Light for Revenge means Go Ahead with Revenge?

A. Green Light for Revenge means Green Light for Revenge.

Q. It means Go Ahead for Revenge, does it not?

A. It means Green Light for Revenge.

MR. BARR: What is the point of this inquiry?

A. Nobody asked me.

THE COURT: I gather you are reiterating your answer that no one asked you about it, is that right?

A. Nobody asked me. . . . I sat there. Mr. Gilbert was very nice to me. He let me tell the whole story. It was going on for—

Q. General Number 2, Syrian-Palestinian conspiracy, reaction, retaliation. Did you say anything about that at your deposition?

A. During my deposition Mr. Gilbert walked me through the Worldwide Memo word by word. . . . He was not interested to get the whole story. . . . I answer whenever I am asked.

Q. The fact is, sir, that in your deposition you were asked repeatedly about your sources, isn't that right?

A. Correct, and in my deposition I also refused to say—

THE COURT: So your position is not that Mr. Gilbert didn't ask, but that you didn't answer, or what is your position?

A. Mr. Gilbert took me through the Memo Item word by word . . .

THE COURT: You did not understand him to be asking you about
your sources about General Sharon at that time?
A. General—
THE COURT: Yes.
A. Definitely not.

A. . . . I was never asked about it.
MR. BARR: Can we confer about this a moment.
THE COURT: I don't see any need for it . . .
[Bench conference. The sole bench conference of this trial.]

Q. I am simply pointing out to you that that is different from what
you said, is it not, at your deposition?
A. Sir, I will try—
Q. Is it or is it not?
A. Why don't you ask Mr. Gilbert? He asked me the question. He
got an answer.

Halevy, it developed almost incidentally in his trial testimony,
had filed a story, early in Israel's incursion into Lebanon, in which
he had described Sharon as "a true statesman"—a phrase and a
story that *Time* did not use. Duncan had written Halevy a letter,
after the commencement of the lawsuit, which included the words
"Lie low on Sharon. You will be rewarded." Kelly, for all the
information *Time*'s attorneys tried to show he possessed before
writing Take Nine, seemed to think there had been *two* meetings
between Sharon and the Gemayels during the condolence call at
Bikfaya; and Duncan, for all the information similarly imputed to
him, seemed to think Sharon had actually *attended* the funeral of
Bashir Gemayel and discussed revenge with the Phalangists there.
The development in the case that most probably triggered Israel's
reaction, in providing access to the relevant documents in the case,
however, occurred during Duncan's cross-examination, when defense attorneys were trying to resuscitate his credibility after the
debacle of the personnel files. In one of his last questions to
Duncan, on a low-key, wonderful direct, Goldstein had asked,
sensibly enough:

Q. Mr. Duncan, if Justice Kahan understood General Sharon's
statement [during his public testimony in October] to be that he

had had a discussion of revenge at the funeral . . . a public admission of that fact, there wouldn't have been any need to put that particular fact into a secret appendix, would there?

And Duncan had replied, in what had begun to appear a *Time*-like way:

A. Might depend on what information that discussion at the funeral was in conjunction with.

The remainder of Duncan's answers on direct were equally unself-consciously meaningless. And, within moments, Saunders, on cross-examination, turned Duncan's testimony into a provocation and an attack on Israel through the Kahan Commission itself. More than five times, Saunders put to Duncan the question whether he had noticed "inconsistencies between General Sharon's testimony before the Kahan Commission and what the Kahan Commission actually found." Again and again, in other words, Saunders suggested, or coached and invited the witness to suggest, that in its published findings the Kahan Commission ignored and suppressed evidence (in the form of Sharon's public testimony) which it already had:

Q. When did you first begin to perceive these inconsistencies that you have been testifying about?
A. I saw these items when I read the full report. I may have seen them earlier. I remembered some of them and I saw the rest of them when I read the full report this fall.

Soon the chief of correspondents was being led by counsel like a schoolboy through testimony that Justice Kahan, by not asking "follow-up questions" of Sharon, was concealing evidence of "inconsistencies."

Q. My question, sir, does the fact that Justice Kahan does not indicate in that passage that I just read to you—let me try this again. Does the fact that Justice Kahan in that passage that I just read to you did not follow up the question—

THE COURT: Or elsewhere.

Q. —or elsewhere, anywhere else in the public testimony in such a way as to indicate during that testimony that the Kahan Commission had in its possession information [the "among us" in Sharon's October public testimony] that it believed to be inconsistent with [its findings], does that fact indicate to you that the Kahan Commission had no such evidence?

A. No, it does not.

Q. Why not?

A. Because we know from the passages that have been presented here *that it did have such evidence.*

In other words, the case had become, at this juncture, no longer merely that Sharon lied but that Justice Yitzhak Kahan and the Kahan Commission lied as well.

On January 2, 1985, right after the Christmas and New Year's holiday (and thirteen days after the plaintiff had completed his presentation and Saunders had said, on behalf of the defendant, "Yes, your Honor. We will rest"), it began to seem clear that, in response to a letter drafted jointly, on Christmas Day, by Judge Sofaer and the attorneys for both parties, Israel was going to respond to the court's request for relevant documents and other information, in a form all parties could accept. The main questions were how soon Sharon's and *Time*'s Israeli attorneys, together with Justice Kahan himself, would be given access to the evidence (whether it would be in time, for instance, to reach the jury within a week), and, of course, what the evidence would show. Meanwhile, a last witness, Laurie Kuslansky, took the stand. A graduate of Queens College in 1976, and holder of a master's degree in linguistics from Columbia ("Q. Do you recall the topic of your thesis? A. Roughly, yes. I believe it was 'Vowel Lengthening in Tiberian Hebrew' "), Ms. Kuslansky was now a doctoral candidate at Columbia and had served as an interpreter for various agencies, private and governmental. She had also been, close to a hundred times, an official translator for the courts. Halevy had testified unequivocally at his deposition that the phrase "among us" (Hebrew *etslenu*) in Sharon's public testimony before the Kahan Commission on October 25, 1982 ("Revenge exists, without a doubt. Exists revenge. . . . The word 'revenge' also appeared, I would say, also in discussions among us"), could mean only "among Sharon and the Gemayels": "There is a sentence—I'm not sure I'm quoting it correctly, I don't want to mislead you— Mr. Sharon says, 'The matter of revenge was discussed among us.' There is a very clear reference, to the best of my understanding, that he's referring . . . to meetings with the Phalange or with Lebanese officials. This is one. This comes on top of everything." And that he, Halevy, had relied, above all ("This is one. This comes on top of everything"), on this public testimony of Sharon's, in writing what became the paragraph that said, "Sharon also reportedly discussed with the Gemayels the need for the Phalangists to take revenge." No other *Time* witness claimed, as did Halevy, to have read the words in Hebrew (or even to speak or understand Hebrew); but every other *Time* witness claimed, like Halevy, to have relied for the paragraph in question on this October public testimony of Sharon's.

Ms. Kuslansky, who seemed genuinely concerned with the exacting standards of her own profession, twice tried to correct what seemed to the court relatively minor errors in the entire text (she pointed out, for example, that even the official translation left out Sharon's second "also" in "The word 'revenge' also appeared, . . . also"). On cross-examination:

> Q. I am just focussing on the sentence at issue, Miss Kuslansky.
> THE COURT: I think you should make that clear to her because she is a professional translator and has very high standards, apparently.

But on what had become, improbably, one of the central issues of the trial she left no doubt:

> Q. Now, in your professional opinion can you tell his Honor and the jury who the speaker is referring to in that sentence, by the English phrase "by us," "in discussions by us"?

A. Yes, I can. . . . My interpretation is that the speaker was referring to Israeli colleagues or other Israelis.

Q. Would it be correct to read that as a reference to discussions with Arabs?

A. No, it would not. . . .

Q. In your professional opinion would anyone fluent in conversational Hebrew understand that to be referring to discussions with Lebanese or Arabs?

A. No.

And it turned out that the particular word *etslenu* connoted "among us" or "by us" in the sense of "*chez nous,*" or "among the brothers," or, as the witness put it, "domestic, national, family, or familial closeness, affiliation, or connection, one of exclusivity." Three of the jurors who would decide the case were white, two were black, one Hispanic; two were men, and four were women. There had always been a slight but undeniable undercurrent of racism in the conduct of the case. One of the jurors, a young black woman, seemed perceptibly to flinch when Gould, with a courtroom style perhaps adapted to another era and another urban ethnic composition, turned his back on witnesses, used New York inflections, and seemed sarcastically to nag instead of question. None of this was characteristic of his pleasant and extremely cultivated persona out of court. Saunders, on cross-examination, now asked the witness whether *etslenu* could refer only to "Israeli *Jews.*" After a pause, recorded even in the transcript, Ms. Kuslansky answered, "That would be my assumption, yes." Did it exclude Israeli *Arabs?* Not necessarily. Finally, with a sort of wistful indirection, Ms. Kuslansky put it this way:

> So long as things are the way they have been and still are, there is still no reason that would make me accept *etslenu* to mean "we," spoken by an Israeli, to mean we, Israelis and Arabs.

The defense put on no translator of its own. And the slight racial undercurrent turned out to play no role in the outcome of the case.

By January 9, 1985, the evidence had arrived from Israel; and Judge Sofaer decided that his agreement with the Israeli government obliged him to clear the courtroom temporarily and permit the attorneys to present some of that evidence to the jury under seal. Members of the press objected, and the objection led to an extraordinary interlude. The afternoon session had begun unremarkably. "We will have to have a conference," Judge Sofaer said in open court, jury not present. "A juror has taken ill, and is now in the nurse's office . . . and his blood pressure is a little low." Defense counsel pointed deadpan and accusingly at plaintiff's counsel, who said, also deadpan, "Mr. Barr points at me. I object to that."

"I don't know what caused the juror's reaction," Judge Sofaer said, in the same tone. "Maybe it was the imminent arrival of Floyd Abrams." The judge and Abrams, a well-known New York attorney, were friends. "Whatever caused [the juror's] reaction, there it is; and we have a problem that I think we can deal with in the robing room after we finish dealing with other members of the press. . . . Mr. Abrams, you wished to be heard?"

"Yes, your Honor," Abrams said. "Your Honor, I am here on behalf of the Washington Post Company, *New York Times,* Newsweek Company, Philadelphia News Company, CBS, and NBC, to ask your Honor, to move that your Honor reconsider the order that your Honor entered this morning, barring the press and public from a portion of the trial today. . . . The basis of the motion, your Honor, is the First Amendment."

This was the First Amendment's first, and only, overt appearance in either trial. Its net result was to delay for a few hours (while Barr and Gould went, side by side, to argue before the appellate bench that the case should be allowed to take its natural course) the presentation to the jury of a few minutes' testimony, in a cleared courtroom, and under seal. The testimony itself was made public, with the consent of the Israeli government, in the open courtroom a few days after that. The unwell juror, about whom the attorneys for both sides expressed intense concern, also recovered late that afternoon.

The Israeli government had granted attorneys for both sides, in the presence of Justice Kahan, access to these documents: Appendix B; all notes and all testimony relating to Sharon's meeting on September 15, 1982, with the Gemayels at Bikfaya; all notes and all testimony relating to an earlier meeting, on September 15, 1982, between Sharon and the leaders of the Lebanese forces, at Karantina; all documents relating to the meeting, on September 12, 1982, between Sharon and Bashir Gemayel; and all notes and all testimony relating to any other meetings between Sharon and the Phalangists between September 14th and September 16, 1982, when the massacres occurred. Justice Kahan, in the presence of attorneys for both sides, was to reply yes or no to each of three questions: "Does the document contain any evidence or suggestion that Minister Sharon had any discussion with the Phalangists in which either person mentioned the need for revenge?"; "Does the document contain any evidence or suggestion that Minister Sharon had a discussion with the Gemayel family or with any other Phalangist, at Bikfaya or elsewhere, in which Minister Sharon discussed the need to avenge the death of Bashir Gemayel?"; "Does the document contain any evidence or suggestion that Minister Sharon knew in advance that the Phalangists would massacre the civilians if they went into the camps unaccompanied by I.D.F. troops?" Gould had said in the robing room that if the answer to any of these questions with respect to any document or testimony before the Kahan Commission was yes, "this case disappears before my eyes," and that he would say as much in open court. The answer, to all three questions, for all the documents and testimony was, no. (*Time*'s Israeli attorney raised what was, in effect, a single "reservation": that there might have been relevant testimony presented to the Kahan Commission's investigators but not technically brought before the commission itself; there might also not have been such testimony; in any event, he had not seen it and therefore could not join in a reply about it, either way.)

After the summations and an exceedingly complex charge to the jury by Judge Sofaer (the intricacies of libel law since *Sullivan* are such that no one could understand the judge's charge when he read it aloud; but the Second Circuit has recently encouraged sending the charge, on tape or in manuscript, into the jury room; Judge Sofaer sent the manuscript), the jury received its Verdict Forms, which contained the following questions: Was the paragraph concerning Sharon defamatory, and if it was defamatory was the defamation aggravated by its attribution to Appendix B;

was the paragraph, by "clear and convincing evidence," false (because of conflicting case law, if the jury had not found it "clearly and convincingly" false Judge Sofaer would have sent the jury back to decide whether it was false "by a preponderance of the evidence"); was the paragraph published, clearly and convincingly, with "actual malice," that is, with "knowledge that it was false" or with "reckless disregard" as to whether it was false or not, or with "serious doubt" that it was true? If the answer to any of these questions (except the one about Appendix B) was no, there was no point in going on to the next question; the case was closed. That is, if it was not defamatory there was no point in deciding whether it was false. If it was not defamatory and false, there was no point in deciding if it was published with "actual malice." The trial was "bifurcated," with the consent of both parties, to clarify and simplify the decisions as the jury reached them. If all the verdicts were yes, there would be a second, "mini-trial" to determine the damages, if any.

No one is allowed to enter or to leave the courtroom while the judge is reading his charge; and, immediately after the charge, the jury was sequestered. The jury in *Sharon* was one of the most careful and conscientious in recent judicial memory. Almost immediately, it asked for a blackboard, cough medicine, three-ring binders, file folders, chalk, portions of transcript, "a quality dictionary," whether, over the weekend, the jury room would have heat. The jury had received the charge on January 14, 1985. By the morning of January 16th, the jurors had reached a verdict on defamatory meaning: Yes, the paragraph was defamatory, and yes, the defamation was aggravated by its attribution to Appendix B. The defense attorneys asked that the jurors be polled. They came out to be polled. They resumed deliberating. *Time* issued a press release to the effect that the jury was mistaken. There ensued what had to be the two full days of greatest tension in the trial. Because if the paragraph was defamatory and not false, then Sharon was far worse off than if he had never brought suit. On January 18th, the jury reached its second verdict. Again, the defense attorneys asked that the jury be polled:

THE COURT: Good afternoon, ladies and gentlemen. I understand you have reached a verdict.

THE CLERK: Mr. Foreman, would you read your verdict.

THE FOREMAN: The verdict on falsity, the question is: Has plaintiff proved by clear and convincing evidence the falsity of the facts in the paragraph that imply the defamatory statement or statements we found *Time* has made? We found yes, the plaintiff has so proved.

Now two things happened: the press, and particularly *Time,* seemed completely to lose its bearings; and the period between the first two verdicts proved not to be nearly the time of greatest tension in the trial. *Time* issued a press release stating that *"Time* stands by the substance of its story," with the "minor" and "irrelevant" misattribution to Appendix B. Ray Cave, *Time*'s managing editor (who had already testified, as had Duncan, that Halevy was one of *Time*'s three or four "finest" investigative reporters), held a press conference in the courthouse corridor to announce that *Time* had "reconfirmed" its story "as recently as a few days ago." The press corps, its solidarity broken in this unaccustomed way, was full of consternation and downright tactless in its questioning of Cave. "What did you do to check?" Herb Denton, of the *Washington Post,* asked, for example. "What did I do? Nothing. That's what you're trying to get me to say, isn't it," Cave replied. How had *Time* confirmed the story, then? Through its attorneys. The attorneys had got in touch with the "sources"? Yes. Directly? No. How? Through David Halevy. Had not the judge shown prejudice in insisting that the verdicts come out like this, in stages —a public-relations disaster? (In fact, the defense attorneys had suggested the process, to clarify the verdicts for an appellate court if *Time* found it necessary to appeal and, more urgently, to avoid a jury's getting from "defamation," through "falsity," to "actual malice" too easily and in one fell swoop.) *Time* was beginning to let sit any aspersions on the jury and on Judge Sofaer. Meanwhile, the jury seemed to have embarked upon an endless stage of its deliberations. A verdict, when it comes, can be somewhat like the birth of a colt (the anticipation, the awkwardness, the small miracle); and the falsity verdict had been a bit like that. Lord Weidenfeld, an extraordinary and seemingly ubiquitous person, a Viennese-born English publisher, who had recently formed an enterprise with Ann Getty, had blown in (like the mysterious "Mr.

Baldwin," who arrives at all the critical junctures in *Scoop*), all the way from London, at the precise moment the falsity verdict was announced. But now, with a short break on evenings when they were tired, and a longer break on January 20th, to watch the Super Bowl, the jury deliberated. A grandchild of one of the court's more intimidating-looking marshals had a starring role in a commercial that would run during the Super Bowl; the marshal had begun showing reporters pictures of this grandchild, and was relieved to be allowed to watch the game as well. The jury asked for more documents, deliberated. It took a long time for counsel to agree on which parts of which testimony were directly called for in each of the jury's voluminous requests. By January 22nd, all the attorneys were extremely amicable, alternately reminiscing about past cases and giving reporters benign instruction in the law. There was talk of the Allen, or "Dynamite," Charge, with which judges may admonish juries that seem to have reached an impasse. But there was, in this case, no indication of an impasse. From the jurors' handwritten notes, which they left on a table (and which were found and preserved, when the trial was over, by the clerk), it was clear that they were simply proceeding, in a systematic and orderly way, through every passage of the judge's long and complicated charge. The reporters, who had, of course, like all other spectators, been locked in during the reading of that charge, now pored over it. Some had brought newspapers and paperbacks; but it was impossible, through the hours, to pay attention to any written thing other than that charge. "They can stay in there for three months and say, 'We're not deadlocked; we're just deliberating,' " Saunders said late in the afternoon on January 23rd. "There would be nothing anyone can do." Gould said that when early English juries took too long deciding, sheriffs would stop sending food in. He also said that, in an earlier day in New York, plaintiff's attorney would have managed to send in, "in a juror's sandwich," a copy of *Time*'s press release—or even the pages of that week's issue, which regretted the misattribution to Appendix B, and then reiterated that the paragraph was substantially true.

At 9 a.m. on January 24th (the eleventh day of its deliberations), the jury sent the judge a note: "When we reach a verdict, are we legally permitted to make an amplifying statement of our findings beyond that outlined in the jury form? Of course we can and would send this statement to you first, along with the verdict sheet." This caused Judge Sofaer and the attorneys to deliberate. But there was nothing in the Federal Rules that prohibited such a statement. The judge and counsel agreed that the judge should instruct the jurors to be sure that their verdict was unanimous, and that their statement, if any, was consistent with it.

THE CLERK: Mr. Foreman, has the jury agreed upon a verdict?

THE FOREMAN: We have.

THE COURT: Mr. Foreman, I would like you to inform us of your verdict first, and thereafter I am permitting you to make the statement you wish to make in behalf of the jury. Does the jury unanimously agree to its statement as well as to its verdict? Go ahead.

THE FOREMAN: Actual malice. To the question "Has plaintiff proved by clear and convincing evidence that a person or persons at Time Incorporated responsible for either reporting, writing, editing, or publishing the paragraph at issue did so with actual malice in that he, she or they knew, at the time of publishing any statement we have found was false or defamatory, that the defamatory statement was false or had serious doubts as to its truth?" To that question we find the answer is no, plaintiff has not so proved by clear and convincing evidence. . . .

THE COURT: Would you read your statement, Mr. Foreman.

THE FOREMAN: The statement that amplifies what we found: "We found that certain *Time* employees, particularly correspondent David Halevy, acted negligently and carelessly in reporting and verifying the information which ultimately found its way into the published paragraph of interest in this case."

THE COURT: Does anyone want the jury polled?

MR. BARR: No, your Honor.

THE COURT: Is that your verdict, ladies and gentlemen? So say you all?

THE JURORS: Yes.

The jurors were an administrative secretary; a retired watch supervisor in an electric and steam plant; a secretary in public relations; a telephone-company marketing specialist; a psychologist; and the foreman, a computer programmer. At *Time*'s press conference immediately following the verdict, Barr said, "We won, flat-out and going away."

On February 19, 1985, the Tuesday after Washington's Birthday weekend, Room 318 of the federal courthouse was crowded. The rows set aside for the press specifically accredited for this trial, the rows set aside for relatives of the litigants, and the rows set aside for press with other accreditation had for months been occupied informally by anyone who wanted to sit there. This day, the atmosphere was, for some reason, festive. Over the weekend, Burt, tired, disinclined to entrust Dorsen with the summation to the jury (and just before he was scheduled to rehearse and videotape a summation of his own), had suddenly, without discussing it with any other attorneys in the case, called Westmoreland and told him that all his attorneys were agreed: it was time to sign a Joint Statement and discontinue the lawsuit. Westmoreland signed. Burt went to a dinner party of attorneys from Cravath, where Boies congratulated him on his conduct of the case. The first that Dorsen or any of Westmoreland's other attorneys heard of any of these developments was from the press. According to Jay Schulman, a trial consultant on Burt's small staff, Mrs. Westmoreland was at first very angry, believing that the lawsuit, once begun, should be pursued until the end; then she loyally made the best of it. Dorsen was preparing to resume the cross-examination of Hawkins when the first reporters called. Westmoreland did not know until the following day that none of his attorneys except Burt had recommended, or even known about, the possibility of a Joint Statement or a "discontinuance." It had come as a complete surprise as well to Judge Leval, who was working on several rulings and his own charge to the jury. But by this Tuesday morning the signing (minus Adams) lay two days in the past. Mrs. Westmoreland sat in her accustomed place, a few rows from the rear, near the aisle, on the left. Five young women, who turned out to be paralegals, were asked to move from one of the rows set aside for relatives of the litigants. They were replaced by several young members of the Westmoreland family. It might have been a wedding. It might have been anything. It could not possibly make sense to anyone who was not an American. It might not make sense to anyone at all.

"Hello," Mrs. Westmoreland said to someone who was about to pass her in the crowded aisle. "Oh, Mike, I'm so glad this is over." Mike Wallace stopped and leaned over, as though greeting an old friend, or a veteran from the same unit, in the same campaign. "Let's get together," he said to Mrs. Westmoreland. "Oh, let's," she said. "I mean it," Mike Wallace said. "Let's really get together and let our hair down." Mrs. Westmoreland assented to this as though it were the most ordinary thing in the world.

The short proceeding that closed the case seemed unsatisfactory. "I think it is safe to say," Judge Leval said, "that no verdict or judgment that either you or I would have been able to render in this case would have escaped widespread disagreement." Both attorneys praised the jury. Boies cheerfully admitted that he would have liked to give his summation. "It would have been an historic opportunity . . . for me to give my closing summation," he said. "Both of us will miss that. I may miss it more than you do." Burt thanked the jury "for your presence here, at an event that itself becomes a part of history." Then Judge Leval did an extraordinary thing. He said he was going to thank the jurors personally in the jury room. He invited them to come "back into the courtroom, and meet and talk to counsel, meet and talk to the parties in the case": "You are most welcome to do that. It is not an obligation. You are welcome to do it. There is no rule that forbids it. So you may come out and chat. I am sure that counsel and the parties are eager to shake your hands, and to talk to you about the events of the last five months in this courtroom." And suddenly all questions, of law and of journalism, in this in some ways wildly aberrational lawsuit seemed to evaporate, as litigants, press, family, witnesses, former soldiers, lawyers, jurors milled about, in something out of an American *8½*.

In early 1986, a full year after the trial in Room 110 on Foley Square, *Time* admitted, as part of a settlement before an Israeli court, that it had been wrong not just about Appendix B but about the entire discussion at Bikfaya, and that there had been between Sharon and the Phalangists no discussion of revenge. As part of the settlement, *Time* also agreed to pay some of Sharon's legal fees. Members of the *Time* hierarchy and of the defense team at Cravath still insist, however, that the original paragraph was true, and imply that they had no choice but to settle before what was after all an Israeli court. They also point out that Judge Sofaer, some months after the Sharon case, left the federal bench to accept the job of legal adviser to the State Department, a position in which, they add somewhat darkly, he deals with problems of terrorism and the Middle East. The suggestion of a coverup, including the whole State of Israel and an American judge, thus lingers at *Time* and at Cravath. David Halevy has been assigned to *Time*'s Washington bureau, where he recently had three bylines in a single issue of the magazine. George Crile has become a producer of CBS's *60 Minutes*.

As for Westmoreland, the lore persists that the two legendary witnesses brought him down, and has been augmented by the widespread notion not only that CBS resoundingly and literally won but that there was an actual jury verdict against Westmoreland and the war in Vietnam. Attorneys and other observers who know Dan Burt use words like "panicked" and "irrational" to describe what happened to Westmoreland's chief counsel in the case. Burt read the daily press accounts of what was happening in court, believed them and crossed over for reassurance to Boies, chief counsel for the other side, and, as he heard Boies' appraisals and advice (including the repeated suggestion that he fire the most experienced and effective member of his team), became perhaps more "estranged" from his own staff. On the other hand, in a way not shown by the trial transcript, Dorsen's courtroom style was somewhat nervous; and it was, of course, not yet clear what effect he was having or would have upon the jury. And Burt himself, with his scant young staff (none of whom, like Burt, had ever tried a jury case before), was exhausted to a point one of his closest associates and his client described as approaching breakdown. He had done far better than Boies in the pretrial battle of leaks to the press (and CBS hired an outside public-relations firm, with five full-time employees, for the duration of the trial). But even very early in the trial, Burt's confidence had begun to unravel. "By the second day," his close associate said, "he knew he was terrible." According to Burt himself, the greatest blow had been Judge

Leval's decision, in drafting his charge in the trial's last days, to use only the "clear and convincing" standard on falsity—without Judge Sofaer's fallback "preponderance of the evidence" standard. "Your Honor, if we lose this thing," Burt, evidently under extreme stress, actually said to Judge Leval in arguing for the "preponderance" standard, "it'll kill the old man." The "old man," however, was perfectly able to perceive the demoralization and near-collapse of his chief attorney. The client, even a general, could scarcely go forward in the case without a lawyer. So the talk of settlement began. Burt says he perceives the Joint Statement as a sort of victory. Asked, however, how he would have done if he had been, during the trial's last days, as fit as he was when the trial began, he says, with his pretrial confidence, "I would have killed them." Around Boies, who most recently took over for Texaco in the Pennzoil suit, there has grown up another kind of lore, which holds quite simply that he is, as a litigator, invincible.

If there was a moral to be drawn from both cases, however, it seemed rather this: that received ideas, as so often upon examination in detail, happened to be wrong. The received, the right-minded, the liberal position in both cases was that the press defendants were protecting some valued and fragile Constitutional right against the assaults of whatever ideology was personified by two former military men. The reality had to do, rather, with the fragility, under the combined assault of modern newsgathering and contemporary litigation, of the shared sense of historic fact. More than five years ago, an Israeli newspaper, *Davar,* ran an exposé of a "scandal" to the following effect: that Ariel Sharon had erected, and charged to the government, an enormously expensive fence, to protect the large farm that he owns in Israel. Sharon, insisting that there was no truth to the story, that there was in fact no fence, demanded a retraction. The newspaper stood behind its story. Sharon turned to the Israeli press council, asking that the council check to see that there was, around his property, no fence. The press council at first replied that, since Sharon (on account of certain events in his military history) did not come before it "with clean hands," the council would undertake no investigation. Sharon brought a formal case. In its decision, the council denounced Sharon as, in effect, a brute and not fit to appear before it. The last sentence of the verdict, however, was terse: "There is no fence." CBS and *Time,* as valuable institutions, may have engaged with their attorneys in this major litigation in all good faith. But the facts have a value and a fragility of their own. And there was no fence.

CODA

A nother illustration both of Cravath's tendency to over-litigate, to the very boundaries of legal ethics, and of the peculiar way in which corporate law firm and corporate media client worked together occurred in the Westmoreland case. It was a relatively minor instance, a sort of byway of the litigation, and it occurred in the case of former C.I.A. Director Richard Helms. Helms had filed an affidavit in support of General Westmoreland and was to appear as a reputation witness on Westmoreland's behalf. His deposition, at the Washington offices of Cravath, had been scheduled for February 22, 1984. The preceding week it came to the attention of Helms' lawyer, John G. Kester, of Williams & Connolly, that Cravath had been routinely videotaping depositions of Westmoreland's better-known witnesses—forming, as a by-product of the lawsuit, a priceless archive for CBS of video-tapes of famous people being interviewed, under oath, which CBS could subsequently put to any use it liked. "They were videotaping practically everybody," as Kester subsequently put it. "In victory, they would have these leading witnesses as a wonderful entertainment or news resource. And CBS could use, for instance, the Rusk deposition even if it lost."

Boies had requested Kester to send him, prior to the deposition, the documents Helms would be bringing pursuant to the subpoena by Cravath. Accordingly, Kester sent Boies, on February 21, 1984, by messenger, copies of the requested documents, along with a letter stating that while Helms would certainly comply with the subpoena and appear, as scheduled, for his deposition, he would not consent to being videotaped. When Kester arrived with Helms at the Cravath offices the following morning, Boies said (according to Kester), "We're going to videotape the deposition." Kester replied, "The hell you are." Kester wanted to put Helms' position on record with the court stenographer, but Boies (with Cravath as the "hostile" party paying for the deposition) refused to open the record.

Boies had what a lawyer in another litigating style would regard as no legal case whatever. Videotaping depositions, according to Rule 30(b)(4) of the Federal Rules of Civil Procedure, is authorized only by written consent of the parties or by order of the court. Boies had neither—although the following day, February 23, 1984, he obtained such written consent from Dan Burt.

Nonetheless, submitting a sworn affidavit to the effect that he had received on February 22, 1984, a letter from counsel for Mr. Helms "which announced that Mr. Helms would not appear to testify at a video-taped deposition" (the affidavit also stated as fact that Helms' "failure to appear . . . continues"), Boies moved immediately, on March 6, 1984, to have Helms held in contempt of court. Kester replied with a brief and a supporting affidavit, attaching a signed receipt, dated February 21, 1984, from Cravath for the letter and the documents, and further correcting the record by pointing out that Helms *had* in fact "appeared," as scheduled, on February 22, 1984, and remained ready to be deposed by normal stenographic means.

When Cravath lost, in the district court in Washington, its motion to have Helms held in contempt, and when that court issued an order explicitly "denying . . . permission to videotape the pretrial deposition of Richard M. Helms," Boies actually appealed. Kester also appealed, claiming Helms should be awarded costs for attorney's fees, including those incurred in defending against the motion to hold him in contempt.

By the time, on August 20, 1985, when the United States Court of Appeals for the District of Columbia issued its unanimous decision, the Westmoreland trial had been "discontinued," so the Cravath appeal had become moot. (There would have been no point in seeking to videotape a witness's deposition when the trial itself was over.) But the three-judge appellate court went to special lengths, in rendering its unanimous verdict, not only to grant Helms' appeal for costs but to impose "sanctions" on both CBS and Cravath. "This case illustrates the need for imposing judicial sanctions against groundless litigation," the court said. Citing Rule II of the Federal Rules of Civil Procedure, which requires that the court "shall impose" sanctions, against the attorneys, "when warranted by groundless or abusive practices," the court held "that sanctions should have been imposed against appellee [CBS] and/or its counsel" under Rule II, and that Cravath "had absolutely no reasonable basis in law or in fact" for its contempt petition. It left open for the lower court to decide only "whether this sanction should be imposed against appellee [CBS], its counsel, or both": "Even though it is the *attorney* whose signature violates the rule, it may be appropriate under the circumstances to impose a sanction on the client." "Rule II," the court went on, "is specifically designed to deter groundless litigation tactics and stem needless litigation costs to courts and counsel. . . . When groundless pleadings are permitted, the integrity of the judicial process is impaired." The court granted Helms attorney's fees both for defending against the motion and for the costs of the appeal, "in addition to any other sanction the district court may find appropriate, against appellee [CBS], its counsel, or both, supported by specific findings."

In other words, CBS and Cravath proceeded, with this entirely peripheral witness, in what the appellate court characterized as this "satellite litigation," with an aggressiveness so fierce, so persistent and (as the appellate court ultimately found) so groundless that it actually incurred sanctions, for itself and for its client, in litigating and then appealing over a single witness to Westmoreland's reputation—who, as it happened, never did appear in court. This was what counsel and its client regarded, and would proudly refer to, as "hardball." (The case was settled, between Helms and CBS, on November 8, 1985. The terms of the settlement were confidential, so Helms' lawyer, Kester, was unable to comment on either the amount or whether it was paid by CBS or Cravath.)

In my own case, and in this notion of "hardball," it ought

perhaps not to have been surprising that, in an extension of their methods in the broadcast and at trial, CBS and Cravath (and their public-relations firm) produced a document of more than fifty pages, with attachments and a covering letter six single-spaced pages long—whose main purpose was intimidation. The intimidation was directed at *The New Yorker* (where most of this book originally appeared, as two pieces, in June) and more particularly at Knopf, with a view to suppressing or at least delaying publication of the book.

The covering letter, signed by Van Gordon Sauter, President of CBS News, was addressed to William Shawn, Editor-in-Chief of *The New Yorker,* copies to Robert Gottlieb, Editor-in-Chief of Knopf, and to me. But no letter or memorandum was so much as sent to Mr. Shawn, or to Mr. Gottlieb or to me, until several days after the documents had been disseminated as widely as possible to the press. The first page of the covering letter described the pieces, rhetorically, as worse than "merely unfair, mean spirited, or misguided," but also as "plainly false, gross misrepresentations and distortions of the record." The accompanying pages purported to set forth factual errors in the text.

The documents themselves, in spite of a certain detailed mendacity, were dull enough. In a book of this length there are often a few errors of some sort. But two things about the CBS-Cravath material were remarkable. For all their length and characteristically intemperate tone, the memorandum and the covering letter did not, upon close examination, find any factual errors at all. And, as a legal matter, they put Knopf effectively on notice that if there *were* any factual errors in the book, CBS might sue Knopf for libel. This, again, was presumably what CBS and Cravath (and their public-relations firm) would call, and pride themselves on as, "hardball." As a result, all the manifold, intricate misrepresentations and falsifications in CBS-Cravath's own document had to be disentangled and rebutted before Knopf could go to press. This produced a document, by me, which is in itself extremely dull and need not be included here. But, for all the First Amendment implications of trying to pursue the tactics of the litigation to the point of trying to suppress and delay a book of reporting on the trials, the text is virtually identical to what appeared in *The New*

Yorker, and the CBS-Cravath harassment did not lead to (or require) a single change in the manuscript.

For the record, however, and after all the demonstrably false statements in CBS-Cravath's memorandum and covering letter were sorted out, the accusations in the document were basically (and repeated at great length) three: that I had not interviewed any of the defendants' witnesses; that I had ignored "numerous references" in Adams' "notes and book chapters" to the alleged, surreptitious and previously unreported one hundred thousand to one hundred fifty thousand North Vietnamese infiltrators into South Vietnam in the five months preceding Tet; and that I had ignored the testimony of the minor, low-level "military intelligence officers and C.I.A. officials" whom CBS put on the stand to bolster its own case. Specifically, the memorandum named: Ronald Smith, Richard D. Kovar, Douglas Parry, John Barrie Williams, Donald W. Blascak, George Hamscher, Michael Hankins, Bernard Gattozzi, Russell Cooley and (as it turned out, the trial's last witness) one Colonel (at the time Major) Norman House. I will turn to them in a moment. I was almost seriously tempted to use them. I left them out, however, not only because none of them had or could testify from any personal knowledge of the events at issue at the trial but because I wanted to avoid what Cravath would presumably pride itself on: overkill. More precisely, I did not want to make these altogether minor characters appear, by their own testimony, ridiculous.

To begin, however, with the first point. The book does not purport to contain interviews. It is based on attendance at and the study of transcripts of the depositions and the trials. It is not, of course, in the tradition of this genre of trial reporting to interview the participants; and, taking only the very recent past (Hannah Arendt, Sybille Bedford, Rebecca West), I cannot think of a single important writer about trials who has done so. The CBS participants had ample opportunity to make their position, their views and their motives known—first, of course, on the broadcast itself; then in innumerable press conferences before, during and after trial; and finally, most important, in their testimony, under oath, at trial. I cannot see what more complete, relevant or truthful account the participants would give in interviews than they had already given under oath. (And to see to what unfair and untruthful uses the interviewing process itself can be put, one has only to turn to "The Uncounted Enemy: A Vietnam Deception.")

As for the second point, Adams' notes were "updated" throughout and after the making of the broadcast. What was in them *before* is obviously the issue here. He made no mention of the alleged one hundred thousand to one hundred fifty thousand North Vietnamese infiltrators either in his original article in *Harper's,* or in his testimony in the Ellsberg case, or in his testimony before the Pike Committee, where (as is pointed out elsewhere in this book) he actually testified that M.A.C.V.'s estimates of North Vietnamese infiltration in the months preceding Tet were "a bit low but basically honest." Finally, as he confirmed in his deposition (and directly contrary to what was asserted in the CBS-Cravath memorandum), there was no mention whatever of the alleged one hundred thousand to one hundred fifty thousand infiltrators either in the completed sections of Adams' book or in the "précis" for the remaining chapters—at least as late as the time of his deposition, in September, 1984.

And the third point. Adams first heard the allegation about the one hundred thousand to one hundred fifty thousand North Vietnamese infiltrators (whose existence Westmoreland had for fifteen years allegedly suppressed) just before Crile's production of his Blue Sheet, from Bernard Gattozzi, a lieutenant whose work had to do with processing figures for enemy gains and losses and not at all with infiltration. Gattozzi, who, like Gains Hawkins, had had (until Crile and Adams made contact with him) a "total memory block," said that he had "overheard" the infiltration figure from another lieutenant, Michael B. Hankins. Hankins, one of several analysts who *were* working on infiltration (though not, as Cravath throughout its Motion for Summary Judgment described him, as "M.A.C.V.'s principal enemy infiltration analyst" in the years in question), testified, among other things, that he did not have access to all Source X information, that he believed M.A.C.V. intelligence acted in "good faith" and that, in any event, though his job had been analyzing "hard figures" on "documented infiltrators," he had been "playing around" with a "mathematical methodology" and with "projections," which he "could never fully validate." At his deposition Hankins could not recall what he had said about this to Adams. At his own deposition Adams could not recall it, either. And from Adams' notes of their conversation it is impossible to tell what Adams asked or Hankins said about infiltration, if in fact they discussed it at all.

Gattozzi, in any event, told what he thought he had overheard from Hankins to Major Russell Cooley, who did not have access to all Source X information either, and who spoke to Adams and to Crile during the making of the broadcast (indeed, Cooley actually appeared on "The Uncounted Enemy"), relaying as fact that there were "pressures" to lower figures from General Westmoreland, whom Cooley (like all the other minor witnesses whom the CBS-Cravath memorandum says I did not mention) had never met. As it happens, however, I do mention Russell Cooley in the body of the book. Cooley's superior, and Gattozzi's and Hankins', was Lieutenant Colonel Everette Parkins, who, according to rumors heard by Cooley (and according to the broadcast itself), was "fired" because he tried to report infiltration at twenty-five thousand a month. Five people were present at Parkins' so-called "firing." Three of them talked to Adams or to Crile before the broadcast. None confirmed Cooley's or the broadcast's account. Parkins himself denied it, as did his superior, Colonel Charlie Morris, who did the alleged "firing." Morris denied the thesis of the broadcast, in its entirety and in its details, and said so in a pre-broadcast interview (which, of course, was never used) to Crile. In his affidavit Parkins stated, among other things:

I am aware of the statements in the CBS documentary "The Uncounted Enemy: A Vietnam Deception" that I was "fired" from my assignment at C.I.C.V. because I had discovered massive enemy infiltration in the Fall of 1967, and that my superiors refused to send this information forward, and that I became so incensed over this matter that I shouted at one of my superiors. *These statements are not true.*

. . . I was not pressured to lower my estimates of enemy infiltration. I did not have reports with estimates of enemy infiltration sent

back to me with orders to use different numbers. I never stated to
anyone that such things had occurred. . . . I know that the *CBS*
broadcast inaccurately portrayed the events that related to myself.
. . . It is my belief that there was no conspiracy. . . .

Etc. And Parkins went on to say that he had told these things to
Adams and to Crile.

Douglas Parry, Donald Blascak and John Barrie Williams.
Douglas Parry, whom Cravath presented as a "specialist on
enemy irregular forces," was in fact, in 1967–1968, a young, minor
and inexperienced analyst for the C.I.A. "I was a beginner at the
time," he said at his deposition. "I was no super analyst." And he
acknowledged that he "learned" how to analyze captured documents from George Allen—and Sam Adams. It became clear at
trial that, far from being a source for Adams (or for Crile), Parry
relied on Adams as his source. Donald Blascak, another minor
official with no firsthand knowledge, was an Army major and an
employee of the C.I.A. He was a particularly ineffective witness,
and another "source" who received his ideas about the quality of
M.A.C.V. estimates from Sam Adams, rather than the other way
around. And John Barrie Williams was yet another Army major,
a desk officer at the Defense Intelligence Agency who had actually
advocated removal of the irregulars from the formal Order of
Battle, and who gave such testimony as "Unfortunately, there
may have been those of us within our own organizations, and I
speak of the defense establishment, who started to believe what we
were saying and thereby misled ourselves." In other words, his
testimony, such as it was, was speculation about self-deception
rather than evidence of conspiracy—which he was, anyway, too
far removed from M.A.C.V. and even the C.I.A. to have observed.

George Hamscher, a minor officer based in Honolulu who appeared on the broadcast, is also, as it happens, mentioned in the
body of the book. (He was the person misleadingly identified as
"head of the M.A.C.V. delegation" to a joint conference of military and civilian intelligence, when he was not only not the
"head," he was not even a member either of the delegation or even
of M.A.C.V.) Hamscher had spoken, on the broadcast, of a meeting in a small room of the Pentagon where six military men, under

the direction of Colonel Danny Graham, had met and "arbitrarily slashed" estimates of enemy troop strength. What I did not mention, among other things, was that four of the six Hamscher recalled as present at the meeting denied it, that several witnesses testified that Colonel Graham was in Saigon at the time the alleged "slashing" took place, that only John Barrie Williams gave any sort of support for Hamscher's account, and that there was no documentary or other evidence that any estimates were cut, let alone "slashed" at all. Another thing I did not mention was that in his second affidavit Hamscher virtually recanted what he had said on the broadcast, and in his first affidavit, and at his deposition (which was nonetheless read into the court record by Cravath), as the product of "bias":

> My saddest sense of realization is that Sam Adams' quest, taken as a crusade by so many of us who helped him, appears to have been a *reckless vendetta* that became a money-making scheme. In any event, I will no longer take any side. More importantly, I want to rid myself of bias.

(In a subsequent affidavit, executed for Cravath, he partially recanted part of his recantation. Not surprisingly, Cravath used only his deposition and did not put Hamscher personally on the stand.)

George Allen, Sam Adams' friend and George Carver's deputy at the C.I.A., was another person whom I did in fact mention in the body of the book. He was the one who was re-rehearsed and interviewed twice, the second time after having been shown videotapes of other interviews. What I did not mention was that at his deposition Allen admitted that he had made a pre-broadcast deal with Crile—namely, that he would consent to be interviewed on camera only if Crile promised that the broadcast would not say anything derogatory about the C.I.A. I did not mention, either, that at his deposition Allen also admitted that he had not been "candid," either before the Pike Committee or in his interview with CBS. He had even changed his affidavit in such a way that it would be more favorable to the defendants, discussing parts of it with a CBS lawyer who persuaded him that the changes were necessary. And Allen asked to have the oath reread to him on the second day of his deposition, to verify whether he had to tell "the whole truth." Quite apart from his comments on the outtakes ("I don't know what you want me to say, George"; "Is it really kosher to do this?" etc.), these admissions and colloquies at his deposition, and his testimony at the trial itself, made him a far from effective witness in the case.

But the three of these minor witnesses whom I was most tempted to use, and whom I left out because they seemed so thoroughly and almost comically discredited on the stand, were Ronald L. Smith, Richard D. Kovar and Norman House. Smith was head of the South Vietnam branch of the C.I.A.'s Office of Economic Research, and did not join the C.I.A. until 1968, when he finished his tour as technical sergeant in the Air Force. He had worked closely and admiringly with Sam Adams. His virtual disintegration on the stand occurred when Dorsen referred him to a post-Tet C.I.A. document, of March 31, 1968, wherein the C.I.A.'s "best estimate" of enemy troop strength pre-Tet differed from M.A.C.V.'s by only five thousand men. "Mr. Smith," Dorsen asked him, with his usual mildness, "*what happened to the one hundred thousand infiltrators?*"—who were nowhere mentioned in the document. Smith began to falter and to waffle, but continued to insist that there were "certainly" one hundred thousand to one hundred fifty thousand infiltrators that M.A.C.V. was not reporting. Dorsen again called his attention to the *C.I.A.'s own* March, 1968, report, drafted by Smith himself. "And you don't mention them in this document, do you, Mr. Smith?" he asked. A few questions later Smith became suddenly inspired: "I will tell you exactly what happened to those troops. Probably one hundred thousand of them were *killed* . . . "; "Are you saying, Mr. Smith," Dorsen inquired, "that M.A.C.V. underestimated [enemy] *casualties* by one hundred thousand?" In other words, it was not just the fact of the surreptitious infiltration of the one hundred thousand to one hundred fifty thousand which had been suppressed by General Westmoreland; it was the fact of their surreptitious *deaths* on the battlefield as well. With this, the disintegration of the witness became embarrassingly apparent: " . . . You are way out of line. Yes, M.A.C.V. probably did [suppress the killing of the one hundred thousand] . . . I don't have the figures in front of me." But the point was made, and Dorsen in his questioning repeatedly stressed it: "Mr. Smith, *is there one word of reference* [in the C.I.A. document about pre-Tet enemy troop strength] to alleged infiltration of one hundred thousand to one hundred fifty thousand for the period prior to the Tet offensive?" And the witness simply could not get around the fact that there was none.

Kovar, another employee of the C.I.A., fared in some ways worse. He had not been in Vietnam since 1958, for one thing, and had had no contact with military men from M.A.C.V., let alone with Westmoreland. He based his testimony largely on what he himself characterized as Washington "corridor talk" (and what Judge Leval called talk at "the water fountain"), mostly with George Allen—and Sam Adams. But the turning point for Kovar came when he testified, under oath, that he had seen all drafts of the important document issued by the joint conference of military and civilian intelligence, S.N.I.E. 14.3-67, and that it never mentioned the Vietcong irregulars, specifically what were called the Self Defense and the Secret Self Defense, at all. Again and again Kovar repeated this point: that there had been no mention of them. Then Dorsen read into the record paragraph after paragraph in the document in question which specifically addressed the problem of the irregulars, with particular attention to the Self Defense and the Secret Self Defense. An attorney from Cravath rose with an objection, that Dorsen was trying to use Kovar's testimony, in contrast with the document itself, to prove "recent fabrication." This elicited from the judge the following comment: "THE COURT: I understood Mr. Dorsen's examination to be directed to a different kind of point, to convey that [the witness] *did not know what he was talking about,* that he said both now and at his deposition that [the document] did not include any reference to the SD and the SSD, and Mr. Dorsen demonstrated by referring to the text that there were six paragraphs, or five paragraphs that discussed [them]." Earlier, at the close of the witness's examination on direct, Judge Leval had said, outside the presence of the jury, that Kovar's last answer "expressed opinions *beyond the witness' competence.* . . . The answer has been given to the jury. I don't suppose that can be undone"; and invited plaintiff's counsel to apply to have the answer stricken. Now, on cross-examination, the judge said again that Dorsen's questions were "designed to undermine the witness' competence, to show that he is a witness who *doesn't really know his subject matter* and who doesn't know what he's talking about." And yet a third time the judge referred to Dorsen's "direct undermining as to whether this witness, as a truth witness, *is somebody who knows what he's talking about.*" So much for the witness Kovar.

Norman House, the witness after Hawkins and the last witness in the case, was in a way my favorite witness. A lower-echelon officer at C.I.I.E.D. and then at C.I.C.V., Colonel House testified on direct that M.A.C.V. "had evidence, hard evidence" that, at Tet, "all the South Vietnamese civilians would rise up and throw the foreigners out"—which, of course and as it happened, they did not do. He also testified that "The infiltration—the official infiltration estimates that were provided [prior to Tet] were completely dishonest," and that "in my estimation, General Westmoreland must have orchestrated that party line." On cross-examination, however, Dorsen began with what seemed an innocuous and even irrelevant line of questioning concerning Westmoreland's deputy and second-in-command, General Creighton W. Abrams: was the witness's "experience with General Abrams . . . favorable?" "I would say it was outstandingly favorable," House replied happily. "If I could elaborate on that, I would like to say something about General Abrams." And House went on to say that Abrams had "a lot of insight, as to what the war . . . the Tet offensive, what it was all about. . . . Quite often General Abrams would *come to my shop and ask me personally* [for] intelligence conclusions and estimates that we were arriving at." What was the witness's "opinion" of Abrams' "integrity"? Objection. In the ensuing bench conference Dorsen brought out that "General Abrams was the Number Two person in the [M.A.C.V.] chain of command" (a fact of which the witness was apparently completely unaware), and would therefore have had to be "intimately involved" in "orchestrating" the alleged "conspiracy." The judge himself commented that Dorsen's questioning was directed toward eliciting "evidence of bias, since [the witness] didn't have a basis for distinguishing who was doing what that he wasn't privy to. . . . I think [Dorsen's] very point is that [the witness] didn't have pre-Tet experience with *any* of these people . . . in command circles." Objection overruled. So the witness answered, "I found Abrams to *have the highest*

integrity and it was an honor to work with him." Then Dorsen
elicited the devastating testimony that this witness "never knew
that Abrams was General Westmoreland's deputy in August, September, October, November and December of 1967—even [as late
as] when [the witness] spoke to Adams, while the broadcast was
being produced, in 1981."

Then came my favorite testimony. In answer to a question
why "the populace" [court transcript "populous"] *did not* rise
up," as had allegedly been predicted in the witness's documents:
"I felt *the enemy* had made a *strategic blunder,* because we had
good solid information which showed the deployment around
Saigon. . . . The mistake that I personally observed was that the
enemy, because they did not commit their reserves of North
Vietnamese regular forces that were around Saigon, *made a tactical mistake*—Thank God." In other words, these lower-
echelon intelligence bureaucrats, when their own estimates were
not borne out, never concluded that their estimates had in fact
been wrong. When the one hundred thousand to one hundred
fifty thousand North Vietnamese infiltrators did not materialize,
they concluded rather that something or somebody else was in
error. The answer to the question (raised earlier in this book),
What were these mass phantom infiltrators *doing* during Tet?,
was (according to Smith) that they were being "killed" and (according to House) that they were making "a tactical mistake."

The rest of the witness's testimony, while typical of these
lower-echelon members of the C.I.A. (who received their ideas
mostly from Sam Adams) and of the military (who simply did
not have access either to the M.A.C.V. command or to sensitive
Source X intelligence), was anti-climactic: "Q. Colonel House,
didn't you tell Mr. Adams that the enemy's *biggest mistake* was
in believing there would be a *popular uprising?* A. I may or may
not have, sir, said exactly those words, but in substance I would
have said that. Q. [Didn't you] tell Mr. Adams that C.I.C.V.'s
product [which House worked on] was *quite dated* and that
C.I.C.V. [which House worked for] was sort of a *historical file?*
A. I may or may not, sir, have used exactly those words. . . . I
may or may not in substance have said something like that, sir.
. . . Of course, you would have to *ask Mr. Adams* exactly what
he meant in his notes." And so forth. But the point was made,

in this last testimony of what became the last witness in the case, not only that the witness was not even privy to the fact (known to any reader of any newspaper even far from Saigon) that General Abrams, for whose "integrity" he had expressed such unqualified enthusiasm, was second in command (and became successor at M.A.C.V.) to General Westmoreland (who, the witness simultaneously believed, "orchestrated" the conspiracy) but that when the witness's own infiltration estimates were rejected, and proved at Tet unfounded, he attributed the rejection to a conspiracy on M.A.C.V.'s part and the actual events at Tet to the enemy's "mistake." (When Adams, on his cross-examination, was asked whether any of the five hundred thousand American soldiers then in Vietnam ran into the alleged one hundred thousand to one hundred fifty thousand North Vietnamese infiltrators, and would actually appear as witnesses at trial, he had actually said, "Yeah, I think we'll see a couple.") It was as though the absurdity of the defendants' case, in the testimony of these minor witnesses, became most intensely clear.

In the CBS-Cravath document, and even at the time of the trial, the question was raised, What *motive* could these lower-echelon people, now solid citizens more than fifteen years after the events in question, have for coming forward now with their testimony that estimates had been, in their view, dishonestly suppressed? Nearly all of them seemed, though not very well informed (and several levels away from where any personal knowledge of the alleged conspiracy could be acquired), sincere, even impassioned, and doubtless *were* sincere. In the case of the C.I.A. folk there seemed to be a genuine belief simply in what they had been told, over a period of years, by Sam Adams; and Adams was, by all accounts, a convinced, charming and persuasive advocate. There was something appealing about him even on the stand. As for the military folk, they had talked to Adams and they had heard rumors (what Judge Leval once referred to as "locker room scuttlebutt"); they also had bureaucratic rivalries and even scores to settle. House, for example, clearly detested Danny Graham; Allen was in rebellion against Carver; and so forth. Judge Leval (in perhaps the last of his few controversial decisions) admitted their testimony, in any event, not on the truth of the broadcast but on the state of mind of Crile and the other defendants: had these witnesses made their views, that is, known to the producers of "The Uncounted Enemy"?—a question which bore on the issue of actual malice, in its sense of "serious doubt."

But what should also not be underestimated as a motive is the momentum of the litigation itself, the fact that in terms of celebrity, limelight, playing for (as Adams, Crile, Wallace and, the no doubt not unpersuasive, Boies would have it) the "good" team, being a witness on behalf of CBS was by no means a bad, unattractive or unseductive role. The defendants, juggernaut though they may have been, presented themselves as underdogs and heroes, and, for even a minor witness, the part of hero is a sincerely desirable part. When there is a corporate press defendant, there is, moreover, no reward, in terms of press coverage, to being a witness on the plaintiff's side.

There were many things I wanted to mention in the body of the book but did not. To name just one example: in spite of McChristian's testimony that his cable, with the higher estimates, was blocked, and in addition to the documents and the testimony that his figures were in fact briefed within days to Westmoreland's superiors, including Admiral Sharp, there is a striking anomaly. The figures that McChristian's successor, Davidson, came up with, and that were subsequently adopted, were actually *higher* than those McChristian had advocated. Thus, his indignation cannot have had to do with the rejection of higher estimates in general. It must have had to do rather with the fact that they were not his *own* estimates, but higher estimates from another source. Another anomaly: in spite of Hawkins' testimony that he himself had ordered cuts, and that the figures he had presented at Langley were dishonest, there was no documentary or other evidence that there *had* been cuts; and the figures he briefed at Langley and the figures he briefed to (and thought had been rejected by) Westmoreland were substantially the same. The lifting (by Adams and by Crile) of what had been Hawkins' "total memory block" seems to have brought back "memories" of events that never in fact occurred. But the book seemed to me quite long and complicated enough as it was.

Another word about *New York Times* v. *Sullivan,* to which I feel I may have done an injustice by treating it so cursorily on my way to the material contained in the actual trials. *New York Times* v. *Sullivan* made a highly important contribution to the development of First Amendment law by holding, for the first time, that state libel laws are subject to Constitutional limitations. In the *Sullivan* case the defendants were *The New York Times* and four black clergymen, members of the Committee to Defend Martin Luther King, Jr.—relatively small, highly moral and dissenting voices within the solid, powerful, racist monolith that was Alabama, one of whose officials was the plaintiff in the case. (The alleged libel involved a few mistakes in an ad for the committee in *The New York Times.*) The great decision in the case addressed several complicated matters, but held essentially that criticism of public officials in the performance of their official function is for the most part (and in the absence of clear and convincing proof of "actual malice," in the new sense of "knowledge of falsity" or "reckless disregard") Constitutionally protected. The case favored, above all, dissent and diversity, in the context of the great moral movement that was civil rights, against oppression by monolithic power. It could not, however, have foreseen that in modern life it is the press itself that has, to a degree, become unitary, powerful and monolithic, suppressing the very diversity that it was the purpose of the First Amendment (and even of *Sullivan*) to protect.

Another unforeseeable result of *Sullivan:* since "actual malice" was redefined (by Justice Byron White speaking for the Court in *St. Amant* v. *Thompson*) to include "serious doubt," there have already been consequences of an entirely ironical and entirely unintended sort. Publications, in order not to be vulnerable, in any future lawsuit, to the charge that they had *in fact,* at any point in the writing or the publishing of a story, a "serious doubt," are beginning actively to discourage responsible inquiry, checking, editorial queries in the margin, all of which would constitute evidence (before courts that interpret *St. Amant* too simplistically and literally) that whoever asked, checked, made those queries in the margin did have that form of "actual malice" which is "serious doubt." It is obvious that this interpretation encourages almost everything that is undesirable and unprofessional in journalism— and that it is the opposite of what Justice White intended, in the entirety of his opinion for the Court in *St. Amant.* But many courts and (upon the advice of lawyers) many publications are beginning to apply just this literal, even perverse, interpretation. And the foreseeable practical results in journalism make it virtually certain that the formulation "serious doubt," for "actual malice," will not long remain the law. With the composition of the new Court, however, which was announced as this book was going to press, the likelihood is that any change in *Sullivan* would be only, and radically, for the worse.

To return, however, to the question of "hardball" and intimidation with which this rather diffuse coda began. There are normally only two reasons to videotape a deposition: the legitimate reason that the witness himself (through death, absence from the jurisdiction or some other eventuality) will not show up in court; and the less legitimate reason: intimidation. It is intimidating to be videotaped, testifying under oath, by the "hostile" party. It is daunting enough to be deposed even in the absence of videotape. Helms, as it happens, is an attractive, bright and apparently calm and socially-at-ease man (he was, after all, Ambassador to Iran); but he did not feel obliged to subject himself to that redoubled intimidation which consists in being personally and physically recorded for the benefit of the archive of what is, after all, an entertainment medium. As for intimidation and myself, I was at first taken aback by the sheer length and wide dissemination of the CBS-Cravath document—until I saw that, apart from the mindless aggressiveness which I had already described in my book, there was simply nothing in it. Then weeks after the CBS-Cravath document (which had itself appeared more than a month after the pieces in *The New Yorker* appeared), *Time* issued a memorandum of its own, relatively short but also apparently drafted by lawyers. Though it was no more impressive, convincing or factually sound than the CBS-Cravath memorandum, its tone, the manner and sequence of its distribution and its evident relative sincerity (*Time,* that is, actually to this moment, stands by its Bikfaya story) make me want to mention it no more than in passing here. And as for Knopf, they published. On that there is nothing more to say. There is still no fence.

A NOTE ON THE TYPE

The text of this book was set in a film version of a typeface called
Times Roman, designed by Stanley Morison (1889–1967) for *The
Times* (London) and first introduced by that newspaper in 1932.

Among typographers and designers of the twentieth century,
Stanley Morison was a strong forming influence as a typograph-
ical advisor to The Monotype Corporation, as a director of two
distinguished English publishing houses, and as a writer of sensi-
bility, erudition, and keen practical sense.

Composed, printed and bound by
The Haddon Craftsmen, Scranton, Pennsylvania

Typography and binding design
by Dorothy Schmiderer

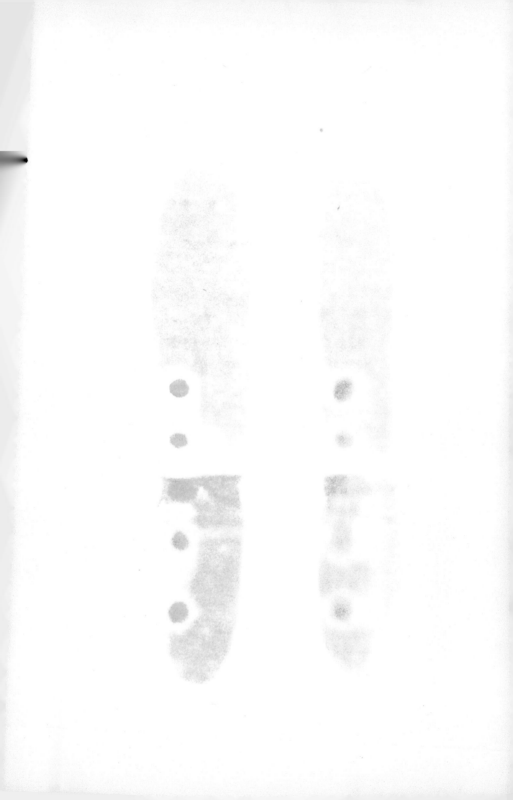